Mechanisms of Implicit Learning

Neural Network Modeling and Connectionism
Jeffrey L. Elman, Editor

Mechanisms of Implicit Learning

Connectionist Models of Sequence Processing

Axel Cleeremans

A Bradford Book
The MIT Press
Cambridge, Massachusetts
London, England

© 1993 Massachusetts Institute of Technology

This book was set in Palatino by The MIT Press and was printed and bound in the United States of America.

Library of Congress Cataloging-in-Publication Data

Cleeremans, Axel.
  Mechanisms of implicit learning : connectionist models of sequence processing /
  Axel Cleeremans.
    p. cm. — (Neural Network modeling and connectionism)
  "A Bradford book."
  Includes bibliographical references and index.
  ISBN 0-262-03205-8
  1. Neural networks (Computer science) 2. Implicit learning. 3. Connection machines.
I. Title. II. Series.
QA76.87.C54   1993
006.3'3—dc20   92-35739
                                                                                CIP

A l'enfant invisible

Contents

Series Foreword

The goal of this series, Neural Network Modeling and Connectionism, is to identify and bring to the public the best work in the exciting field of neural network and connectionist modeling. The series includes monographs based on dissertations, extended reports of work by leaders in the field, edited volumes and collections on topics of special interest, major reference works, and undergraduate and graduate-level texts. The field is highly interdisciplinary, and works published in the series will touch on a wide variety of topics ranging from low-level vision to the philosophical foundations of theories of representation.

Jeffrey L. Elman, Editor

Associate Editors:
James Anderson, Brown University
Andrew Barto, University of Massachusetts, Amherst
Gary Dell, University of Illinois
Jerome Feldman, University of California, Berkeley
Stephen Grossberg, Boston University
Stephen Hanson, Princeton University
Geoffrey Hinton, University of Toronto
Michael Jordan, MIT
James McClelland, Carnegie Mellon University
Domenico Parisi, Instituto di Psicologia del CNR
David Rumelhart, Stanford University
Terrence Sejnowski, The Salk Institute
Paul Smolensky, University of Colorado
Stephen P. Stich, Rutgers University
David Touretzky, Carnegie Mellon University
David Zipser, University of California, San Diego

Preface

I like to think of this book as a book about elementary learning processes, even though such a claim to generality is unquestionably overstated. Indeed, this book is really about a phenomenon called *implicit learning*—"the process by which knowledge about the rule-governed complexities of the stimulus environment are acquired independently of conscious attempts to do so" (Reber, 1989). But thinking of implicit learning as an elementary ability to extract and to process structure—rather than as some mysterious faculty for learning without even knowing it—has the merit of putting the emphasis on the nature of processing rather than on the nature of knowledge. This perspective forms the basic motivation for this book: to explore what kinds of mechanisms may be sufficient to account for implicit learning data, and to instantiate these mechanisms in the form of computational models of performance. This approach to the field is different from previous research in several ways. First, even though implicit learning research is rapidly gaining increased recognition, the field is still marred by numerous debates about the nature of knowledge acquired implicitly. Every so often, new studies appear that force us to reconsider the validity of previous methodologies to elicit explicit knowledge (e.g., Perruchet, Gallego, & Savy, 1991; Perruchet & Amorim, 1992), or that demonstrate that previously established results do not hold very well when learning or testing conditions are altered even slightly (Dulany, Carlson, & Dewey, 1984; Perruchet & Pacteau, 1990). Perhaps the most enduring debate has to do with resolving the following question: How much conscious access do we really have to knowledge that the experimenter claims we acquired implicitly? To date, this question has not been answered satisfactorily. I believe there is a very good reason for this: It is the wrong question to ask. Studies that reveal methodological shortcomings are important, but they fail to help formulate the right kind of research strategy. In short, I believe that this kind of approach is not very productive. It may just be impossible to disentangle the contributions of explicit and implicit learning to performance in a given task, simply because we cannot turn off consciousness in normal subjects. (New studies with amnesics and other brain-damaged patients show much promise in helping to resolve some of these issues, however.)

An approach that has been somewhat more successful in this respect has been to try to identify experimental conditions under which implicit learning processes are most likely to operate—for instance, by exploring paradigms in which one may obtain dissociations between performance and ability to verbalize under some conditions but not others (e.g., Berry & Broadbent, 1984, 1988). This has led to solid advances in our knowledge of which factors affect performance and which affect ability to verbalize; but of course, it is still possible to object that the dissociation results are a reflection more of the particular conditions used than of an actual cognitive distinction between two modes of learning and processing. In the meantime, we have made very little progress on the nature of implicit processing itself. What are the mechanisms involved? Can we propose a detailed computational model of at least some aspect of implicit learning performance that is able to learn as subjects do and that uses mechanisms so elementary that the complex machinery of consciousness does not appear to be necessary? In this book, I present and explore such a model, in the context of sequence-processing tasks. The model is by no means a complete architecture for implicit learning; indeed, it lacks many features that would make it general and is even demonstrably wrong in some instances. But it is a first step in the direction of identifying plausible mechanisms for implicit learning performance. I think that once we have a repertoire of such mechanisms, we will be in a much better position to start attacking the really hard questions, such as what the relationship is between implicit and explicit processing, how conscious we are of knowledge acquired under implicit conditions, or what exactly the nature of knowledge acquired implicitly may be.

Acknowledgments

This book grew out of my work as a graduate student at Carnegie Mellon University. I think it would never have materialized had I not been given the chance to study there. The unequaled quality of the collective output of Carnegie Mellon's Department of Psychology, as well as its informal and friendly atmosphere, have never ceased to impress me. I am deeply indebted to my close collaborators during these years, James McClelland and David Servan-Schreiber. To say that "none of this would have been possible without them" is almost an understatement. Both were instrumental in generating some of the most important ideas in this book, and both appeared as coauthors of the papers on which chapters 2 and 3 are based (respectively: Servan-Schreiber, Cleeremans, & McClelland, 1991; Cleeremans & McClelland, 1991). Jay provided unparalleled support during the three years that I was his student. It is with him that I learned to do research, and he has shaped my thinking in more ways than he could possibly suspect. David's energy and insights kept our project moving forward on many different occasions. He also helped me define the direction I wanted to give to the subsequent empirical research. I remember one frantic evening during which I felt that none of my data made sense. After a few hours of intense discussion, he finally showed me the correct way to analyze the thousands of reaction times that I had collected, thereby restoring my confidence in this research. (On further analysis, his explanation didn't make sense after all, but that's not the point!)

Many others deserve thanks as well. The members of Carnegie Mellon's PDP research group all helped me develop my ideas in one way or another. Jeff Elman proposed that I turn my work into a book and deserves all my gratitude for making it possible. Thanks also for discovering such an interesting connectionist network! Alain Content and Gary Dell contributed several useful suggestions and caught a good number of incomprehensible sentences in the manuscript. Arthur Reber and Pierre Perruchet both helped me refine my thinking in different ways through numerous (and, fortunately, ongoing) epistolary discussions. I enjoyed countless hours of entertainment and solid friendship in the company of Norm, Leigh, Rob, and Lael. The Servan-Schreiber family has made life in Pittsburgh a memorable experience rather than the smoky nightmare we were told it would be. Emile and David, in particular, are both dear friends and inspirational colleagues. Teri Mendelsohn and the Stantons at the MIT Press were incredibly patient and supportive throughout preparation of this book. Thanks for bearing with my outrageously optimistic deadline estimates!

The work reported in this book was supported by a variety of funding agencies. My work was supported by grants from the National Fund for Scientific Research (Belgium) and from the Department of Psychology at Carnegie Mellon. The Belgian American Educational Foundation supported my first year at Carnegie Mellon, and its very existence provided much of the original impetus for me and my family to work abroad. David Servan-Schreiber was supported by NIMH Individual Fellow Award MH-09696-01. James McClelland was supported by NIMH Research Scientist Career Development Award MH-00385. Support for some of the computational resources was provided by NSF (BNS-86-09729) and ONR (N00014-86-G-0146).

Last but not least, Nathalie—que serait ma vie sans toi?

Mechanisms of Implicit Learning

Chapter 1
Implicit Learning: Explorations in Basic Cognition

Introduction

One of the central characteristics of human cognition is our capacity to adapt dynamically to environmental and internal changes, or, to put it simply, to learn. As Reber (1989) points out, most theoretical efforts in cognitive psychology and artificial intelligence during the 1970s tended to ignore this fundamental dimension of information processing—presumably in an effort to part with behaviorism. Recently, however, the emergence of connectionism, as well as new developments in other fields, such as adaptive production systems like SOAR (Newell, 1990) and ACT* (Anderson, 1983), has again reasserted the need to integrate learning in our thinking about processing and representational features of the cognitive system. These recent theories of cognition also provide the field with numerous new conceptual tools through which learning processes can again be explored.

But what exactly do we mean by "learning"? The general definition of learning as "a relatively permanent change in response potentiality which occurs as a result of reinforced practice" (G. Kimble, cited in Reber, 1985, p. 395) does not come close to capturing the many qualitative differences that contrast various learning situations. What does a rat finding its way in a maze share with a college undergraduate attempting to solve the Tower of Hanoi? Does practice at the Seibel task (Seibel, 1963) tap the same general processes as language acquisition?

Such questions cut across conceptual boundaries between what we view as rather different phenomena. But the underlying theoretical issue is as follows: Is learning a unitary phenomenon, or do we have to assume different mechanisms for knowledge acquisition in different situations? The empirical and theoretical literature widely acknowledges the existence of distinct types of learning, which are sometimes rooted in central architectural distinctions. Thus, one popular view distinguishes between procedural learning—or skill acquisition—and declarative learning (Anderson, 1983). Connectionist models (Rumelhart & McClelland, 1986) make assumptions regarding learning that are sometimes radically different from those made by adaptive production systems (Langley & Simon, 1981; Newell, 1990), not to mention earlier frameworks such as statistical learning theory (Estes, 1957; see also Kintsch, 1970, and Rouanet, 1967; for reviews). Elsewhere, one also reads that "learning by doing" is not exactly the same thing as "learning by examples" (Anzai & Simon, 1979; Zhu & Simon, 1987) or that language acquisition is distinctly different from everything else (Chomsky, 1980). Langley and Simon (1981) go so far as to suggest that "if a system has many components, such as the human cognitive system has, there may be many ways in which it can be modified, each constituting a different form of learning" (p. 368). Although this last observation does not entail any claim about the diversity of the underlying mechanisms, it seems clear that current thinking endorses the idea that learning can take many forms, depending both on the material and on the specific elements of the cognitive system that are engaged in the task at hand.

One notion that still elicits widespread skepticism, however, is the idea that learning can proceed without awareness, that is, that performance changes can occur without corresponding changes in verbalizable knowledge or without awareness that one is actually learning something (and a fortiori, without intention to learn). In a way, this is surprising given the long history of the idea that information processing can occur outside consciousness (see James, 1890; Bartlett, 1932; Neisser, 1967). Reber (1965, 1967) has dubbed the kind of learning that takes place under these conditions *implicit learning*. To quote Reber (1989) again: ". . . implicit learning is characterized by two critical features: (a) it is an unconscious process and (b) it yields abstract knowledge. Implicit knowledge results from the induction of an abstract representation of the structure that the stimulus environment displays, and this knowledge is acquired in the absence of conscious, reflective strategies to learn" (p. 219). It is important to note that both these claims are the object of a continuing controversy (see Dulany, Carlson, & Dewey, 1984, 1985; Reber, Allen, & Regan, 1985). Indeed, for some authors (e.g., Dulany et al., 1984; Perruchet & Pacteau, 1990; Perruchet & Amorim, 1992), implicit learning is not really unconscious, whereas for others (e.g., Vokey & Brooks, 1992), it may well be so but then the resulting knowledge need not be cast as abstract. Intermediate positions also exist. For instance, one may dispute the fact that learning itself is unconscious, but agree with the notion that using the acquired knowledge does not necessarily entail awareness of that knowledge (Servan-Schreiber & Anderson, 1990). Because of these diverging views, the expression *implicit learning* may be used descriptively, to refer to a specific class of empirical phenomena, or as a particular hypothesis about the underlying processes. In this book, I will use the expression *implicit learning* in an essentially phenomenological way, without strong commitment to any particular theoretical position about either of Reber's claims. This perspective may seem surprisingly cautious given that this is a book aimed at contributing to knowledge about implicit learning, but I propose to take a more basic approach to the problem. Indeed, despite the variety of theoretical positions about the status of knowledge acquired implicitly, the fact remains that in many situations, learning does not proceed in the explicit and systematic way characteristic of traditional models of cognition (Newell & Simon, 1972). Rather, it appears that a substantial amount of our knowledge and skills is acquired in an incidental or unintentional manner. The evidence supporting this claim is overwhelming. For instance, Reber (1989) provides a detailed analysis of about 40 detailed empirical studies that document the existence of implicit learning. But despite this wealth of evidence, few models of the mechanisms involved have been proposed. Thus, Reber (1989) never comes to grips with the question of knowing what kinds of mechanisms might account for implicit learning performance. In that sense, his characterization of the field is distinctly atheoretical. This lack of formalization can doubtless be attributed to the difficulty of assessing subjects' knowledge when it does not lend itself easily to verbalization. In other words, whereas concept formation or traditional induction studies can benefit from experimental procedures that reveal the organization of subjects' knowledge and the strategies they use, such procedures often appear to disrupt or alter the very processes they are supposed to investigate in implicit learning situations (see Dulany et al., 1984, 1985; Reber et al., 1985, for a discussion of this point). Further, tools and methods developed during the past decade, such as protocol analysis (Newell & Simon, 1972; Ericsson & Simon, 1980), have also contributed to the impression that the analysis of implicit behavior is just short of impossible, if not unsound (but see Nisbett & Wilson, 1977). As Broadbent (1977) puts it: "The use of words and other symbols in decision making has encouraged the idea that such decisions are taken merely by familiar logical processes, or, if they are not, then they should be" (p. 192).

Nevertheless, an understanding of such learning processes seems to be an essential step toward developing insights into central questions such as the relationship between task performance and verbalizable knowledge, the role that attention plays in learning, or the complex interactions between conscious thought and the many other functions of the cognitive system. Developing such an understanding of what mechanisms may account for implicit learning performance is the purpose of this book. In other words, I propose to explore implicit learning from an information-processing perspective. As the book unfolds, it will become clear that this approach leaves many important questions unanswered, but I think that the shift of focus that it entails is well worth the effort. Naturally, to start to demonstrate how modeling may help advance our knowledge of the processes involved in implicit learning, we need a specific computational theory and a specific experimental paradigm. For reasons that I will motivate in detail later in the book, I chose to focus on sequence-learning as the experimental paradigm and on connectionist architectures as the modeling framework. Thus, the book is essentially a report on my attempts at modeling human sequence-learning performance within the connectionist framework. But I hope to show how this work helps not only to resolve issues specific to sequence-learning, but also to deepen our understanding of implicit learning in general. A further aim is to demonstrate how modeling work may be specifically useful in helping to frame larger issues in productive ways.

The book is divided into seven chapters. In this chapter, I first provide a brief overview of the few paradigms through which implicit learning has been studied. Next, I specify a general information-processing framework for thinking about implicit learning and detail several instantiations of that general framework by reviewing specific models that have been proposed to account for performance in specific experimental situations (no model can claim generality yet, although some come quite close). In chapter 2, I introduce and discuss the computational properties of a connectionist model of sequence processing (the simple recurrent network, or SRN model) that forms the basis for most of the modeling work described later. The contents of that chapter are largely based on work conducted in collaboration with David Servan-Schreiber and James McClelland (e.g., Cleeremans, Servan-Schreiber, & McClelland, 1989; Servan-Schreiber, Cleeremans, & McClelland, 1991). Chapter 3 is dedicated to work on sequence acquisition conducted in collaboration with James McClelland (Cleeremans &

McClelland, 1991). I report on two experiments and on simulation work. The purpose of the first two experiments was to document the existence of implicit learning in a situation that is considerably more complex than the typical tasks used in this paradigm, and that was designed to provide the means of assessing performance in greater detail than before. Next, I show how the SRN model may be applied to model the experimental data and discuss in depth how well it is able to do so. In chapter 4, I present several extensions of the model and show how it yields new insights into the effects of certain variables affecting sequence-learning performance, such as attention or the availability of explicit knowledge about the structure of the material. I also report on preliminary work with an amnesic patient who demonstrates implicit learning despite dramatic memory deficits on explicit memory tasks. In chapter 5, I introduce two other general classes of models of sequence processing (one of which is instantiated by two different architectures) and describe a situation designed to test specific predictions of each of the four models. Next, I report on a third experiment implementing this situation and discuss the results. In chapter 6, I explore a sequence-learning situation that is different from the choice reaction situations described elsewhere in the book in that it requires subjects to make overt responses (see Kushner, Cleeremans, & Reber, 1991). The accompanying simulation illustrates the limits of the SRN model. I also discuss issues related to knowledge representation and transfer. Finally, chapter 7 contains a general discussion of the issues raised in the book (as well as of some issues not raised in the book!) and proposals for further work.

Empirical Studies of Implicit Learning

The classic result in implicit learning situations is that "subjects are able to acquire specific procedural knowledge (i.e., processing rules) not only without being able to articulate what they have learned, but even without being aware that they had learned anything" (Lewicki, Czyzewska, & Hoffman, 1987, p. 523). Further, the resulting body of knowledge can often be shown to be quite a bit more complex than what would be expected from a cursory assessment of the conditions under which learning took place. Three different implicit learning paradigms have yielded consistent and robust results: artificial grammar learning (see Reber, 1989, for a complete review), process control (Berry & Broadbent, 1984, 1987, 1988; Cleeremans, 1986, 1988; Hayes & Broadbent,

1988), and sequential pattern acquisition (Cleeremans & McClelland, 1991; Hebb, 1961; Nissen & Bullemer, 1987; Lewicki et al., 1987; Lewicki, Hill, & Bizot, 1988; Pew, 1974). In the following section, I review each of these paradigms in turn. This short review is by no means intended to be complete or even to give a fair coverage of the many contentious issues that this and subsequent research has attempted to resolve (see Berry, in press, and Reber, 1989, for extensive reviews). Instead, I simply want to give a feel for the kind of tasks that have been used to explore implicit learning phenomena, and to highlight some of the most basic results obtained in each situation. Doing so will set the stage both for an attempt to specify a general framework for thinking about implicit learning tasks and for the more detailed exploration of sequence-learning situations contained in chapter 3. I will, however, discuss more recent studies when useful, and I will return to the contentious issues at several points in discussion sections throughout the book.

Grammar Learning
The artificial-grammar-learning task that Reber first explored in 1965 (Reber, 1965, 1969) has, over more than 30 years, gradually become the most prominent paradigm for the exploration of implicit learning, particularly in its relationships with awareness and conscious thought. The material used by Reber consists of strings of letters generated from a finite-state grammar, such as the one illustrated in Figure 1.1. In a finite-state grammar, strings of symbols may be generated by recording the label of an arc chosen among the possible arcs emanating from a particular node and by repeating this process with the node pointed

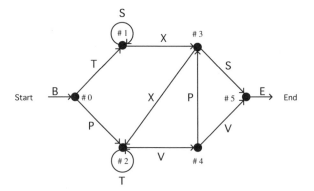

Figure 1.1
A small finite-state grammar similar to the kind used by Reber and his associates (Reber, 1989) in artificial-grammar-learning experiments.

to by the selected arc, until the end node is reached. Thus for instance, the string 'BTSSXXTVVE' is one that could have been generated by the finite-state grammar represented in Figure 1.1. Miller (1958) had already shown that subjects were better able to memorize structured strings of this kind than random ones, even when kept unaware of the difference between them. Reber augmented this basic design by adding a discrimination task. The core of his task thus consists of two phases. During the first phase, subjects are asked to process (e.g., memorize, observe) a set of strings generated from a finite-state grammar. As in Miller's design, subjects are kept unaware of the structured nature of the material. The second—and unexpected—phase of the task consists of asking subjects to discriminate among "grammatical" and "nongrammatical" strings. This new material typically embodies old strings, new grammatical strings, and new nongrammatical strings.

In his first series of experiments, Reber (1967) asked his subjects to memorize a set of strings presented in sequence until a learning criterion was attained. In the subsequent discrimination task, subjects could judge the grammaticality of new strings that were or were not consistent with the structure of the grammar, despite the fact that they were unable to motivate their classification judgments. This basic effect is very robust. It was often replicated, under different conditions, and by several different authors (Brooks, 1978; Dulany et al., 1984; Mathews, Buss, Stanley, Blanchard-Fields, Cho, & Druhan, 1989; Morgan & Newport, 1981; Servan-Schreiber & Anderson, 1990). Obviously, during the memorization task, subjects must have acquired knowledge that could subsequently be put to use in the second part of the experiment. This knowledge was acquired in an incidental and unintentional way, since subjects had been told neither that the material was structured nor that anything else beyond memorizing it was required.

Later experiments by Reber and others considerably refined this basic result, notably by exploring the effects of explicit strategies on learning and discrimination performance. For instance, Reber (1976) has shown that encouraging subjects to "look for rules" during the memorization task results in a deterioration of performance on the grammaticality test, thereby suggesting that lack of awareness of the nature of the material actually entails a learning advantage in this situation. However, Reber, Kassin, Lewis, and Cantor (1980) found that the interference caused by explicit strategies disappeared when the structural properties of the material were made more salient by manipulating the display arrangement of the strings. In other words, conscious attempts to identify regularities in the material work best when the regularities are obvious; they are disruptive when the regularities are masked by the complexity of the material.

More recent studies indicate clearly, however, that subjects do have access to a significant portion of the knowledge acquired during the first phase of the task. Reber and Lewis (1977) already showed that subjects trained to solve anagrams based on a finite-state grammar increased their ability to verbalize their knowledge as training progressed, albeit not as fast as their ability to solve the puzzles. Dulany et al. (1984) asked subjects to indicate which portions of the test strings they thought were crucial in helping them to decide on the grammaticality of the strings, and found that these detailed, explicit reports could account for most of the classification performance. A study by Perruchet and Pacteau (1990) demonstrated that subjects could rate the grammaticality of isolated bigrams, a result that was extended by Dienes, Broadbent, and Berry (1991). The latter authors showed that classification performance correlated significantly with performance on a stem continuation test, in which subjects were asked to choose among several possible successors to fragments of grammatical strings. Further, they also showed that intentional versus incidental learning instructions failed to reveal differences in classification performance (in a dual-task design), thus suggesting that there may in fact be very little difference between implicit and explicit learning strategies. Of course, it may always be argued that the tests used to elicit explicit knowledge or to induce explicit learning strategies are not appropriate or place new demands on subjects. For instance, Dienes et al. (in press) rightly point out that classification is typically considered as a test of implicit knowledge in artificial-grammar-learning tasks, but as a test of explicit knowledge in some sequence-learning tasks (Willingham, Nissen, & Bullemer, 1989). This confusion only indicates that finding out exactly what subjects are aware of in implicit learning situations is a very hard problem. Nevertheless, these and other studies suggest that subjects have access to a larger part of their implicit knowledge than previously thought—a consideration to which I will return at various points in this book.

Finally, another interesting issue that is becoming increasingly important in implicit learning research is transfer. Subjects demonstrate a remarkable ability to transfer knowledge acquired implicitly from one setting to another. For instance, Reber (1969) asked subjects to memorize strings from a finite-state grammar and subsequently presented them with the task of memorizing new strings that were generated either from the same grammar or from a different one and that used either the same set of letters or a different one. He found that recall performance on the second set of strings was better than on the first when the second set had been generated from the same grammar, even when the actual letters that made up the strings were different! Mathews, Buss, et al. (1989) reported essentially similar results. These data appear to provide strong support for Reber's contention that implicit learning is abstract, in the sense that subjects end up developing knowledge that accurately reflects the rules of the grammar independently of their instantiation in the form of relationships between specific letters. However, as Brooks and Vokey (1991) point out, this need not necessarily be the case. They suggest that the savings Reber and Mathews, Buss, et al. observed may be accounted for by assuming that subjects draw abstract analogies to individual memorized strings, rather than by assuming that they base their performance on knowledge of the grammar as abstracted over many training items. Independently of which theoretical interpretation turns out to best explain behavior, these results are a real challenge insofar as modeling is concerned. Chapter 6 contains a more detailed discussion of this problem.

Process Control
Elaborating on earlier results obtained by Broadbent and Aston (1978), Berry and Broadbent (1984) directly addressed the question of assessing the relationship between performance and verbalizable knowledge. In their tasks, subjects control the output of a simulated system (e.g., a sugar production plant or a mass transportation system) by determining the value of one or several input variables on each trial. After having received some practice at this task, they are asked written questions about the effects of different input values on the output of the system. Berry and Broadbent (1984) found that performance on the "system control task" was dissociated from performance on the questionnaire. In other words, subjects were unable to use explicitly the knowledge that nevertheless led to successful control during the task itself. Furthermore, the dissociation was not limited to the observation of good performance accompanied by poor verbalization. Indeed, Broadbent, FitzGerald, and Broadbent (1986) showed that adequate capacity to answer questions about the workings of a simulated economic system can go along with inability to control the same system. Thus, in this case, subjects seem to understand the relations between the variables

they control (the input variables) and those upon which the former have an effect (the output variables), but are nevertheless unable to implement this knowledge when given the task of reaching certain target values for the output variables by controlling the input. Other results (Hayes & Broadbent, 1988; Cleeremans, 1986, 1988) indicated—in agreement with Reber et al. (1980)—that inducing subjects to adopt explicit control strategies resulted in decreased task performance. Interestingly, an interaction between type of strategy (implicit vs. explicit) and type of system (salient relationship between input and output, or nonsalient relationship) was also found (e.g., Berry & Broadbent, 1988), again suggesting that conscious attempts to find structure in the material will only work if the structure is easy to find. More recently, Marescaux, Luc, and Karnas (1989) refined these results by showing that performance on the questionnaire is strongly dependent on the type of questions that it contains. When the questions are about situations that subjects actually encountered during the task, question-answering performance is much better than when subjects are asked about new situations. Thus, it would appear that questionnaire performance is based on memory for specific instances of successful interaction with the system. Marescaux (1991; see also Marescaux & Karnas, 1991) replicated this result, but also showed that there appear to be cases of associations between verbalizable knowledge and task or questionnaire performance. They analyzed verbal protocols from subjects who had performed the control task, and showed that subjects who volunteered the most general and useful rules were also those who were most successful at controlling the system. Subjects who failed to formulate any rule about the workings of the system were also worst at the task, but were nevertheless able to answer questions about it, as long as the questions used situations that they had previously encountered. Thus, successful control task performance appears to depend both on memory for specific instances and on the use of more general explicit heuristics. Whatever the form of the acquired knowledge is, it is clearly hard to verbalize. For instance, Stanley, Mathews, Buss, and Kotler-Cope (1989) showed that subjects could attain good levels of performance on a system control task well before they were able to communicate their knowledge to other subjects, even in conditions where they were free to describe their knowledge in whatever form they thought was best.

Sequential Pattern Acquisition
Even though the study of sequential effects in choice reaction time situations generated considerable interest in the 1960s, it is only fairly

recently that sequence-learning tasks have been recognized as a useful paradigm with which to explore implicit learning. Since most of this book is dedicated to sequence-learning, I will provide only a brief overview of the field in this section. The rationale underlying the basic paradigm is that responses reflect a rich sensitivity to the sequential structure present in the material. In most cases, this sensitivity to the temporal context is implicit, in that subjects fail to report noticing the relevant sequential contingencies. (As discussed later in this section, this issue is also becoming increasingly controversial, however.) Sequence-learning tasks come in three different varieties: probability-learning tasks, prediction tasks, and choice reaction time tasks.

During a typical trial in a choice reaction time task, subjects are presented with one of a number of different possible stimuli and are asked to respond by pressing a corresponding key. The dependent measure of interest is reaction time. Unknown to subjects, the sequence of successive trials typically contains regularities, such that the uncertainty associated with each trial may be reduced if previous trials (and, possibly, their order) have been encoded. Thus, a decrease in reaction time over training (greater, of course, than that observed when the material contains no sequential structure) is taken as an indication of learning. A well-known study by Lewicki et al. (1988) exploited this basic design. Subjects were asked to react to stimuli that could appear in one of four quadrants on a computer screen. Some of the trials could be predicted based on their predecessors; others were random. Over training, an advantage for the predictable trials progressively emerged, despite the fact that subjects appeared to remain unable to specify what the generation rules were or whether a pattern was present in the sequence. In another study, by Lewicki et al. (1987), subjects were asked to find a target digit in a complex matrix. Again, the location of the target was predictable on some trials but not on others. Further, in a later part of the experiment, the rules that defined where successive stimuli might appear were reversed. The results showed a sudden increase in reaction time when the change occurred, suggesting that subjects had acquired knowledge specific to the sequential contingencies present in the material. Other studies (e.g., Nissen and Bullemer, 1987; Cohen, Ivry, & Keele, 1990), including those reported in this book, elaborated on this basic paradigm in various ways; I will return to them in detail in chapters 3 and 4.

Prediction tasks use essentially the same design, but instead of being asked to react to the current stimulus, subjects are required to try to predict what the next stimulus will be (or where it will appear). Here, the usual dependent measure is the percentage of correct predictions achieved during training. Again, the typical result is that subjects' ability to predict the location of the next trial improves with practice, but they remain unable to specify what the relevant contingencies are. Only a few studies have exploited this design so far; chapter 6 contains a detailed account of one of them (see also Kushner et al., 1991). Interestingly, a similar kind of task is sometimes used as an explicit test of knowledge acquired in choice reaction time situations. Subjects are asked to generate the possible successors of an unfolding sequence, and their ability to do so is taken as an indication of their explicit knowledge of the sequence. An important difference between the two tasks, however, is that in the first case, subjects are asked to observe a series of events before predicting the successor, whereas in typical "generation tasks," feedback is given on every trial. As Perruchet and Amorim (1992) point out, the presence of feedback on every trial may place high demands on subjects and thus result in worse performance. I return to this point in chapter 6.

Probability-learning studies differ somewhat in that subjects are asked to observe a series of events and then to try to reproduce it. For instance, Millward and Reber (1968, 1972) presented subjects with a sequence of several hundred two-choice trials that contained increasingly remote contingencies, such that the occurrence of particular events was made to depend on progressively earlier trials. Subjects learned to encode these contingencies, as evidenced by an increasing propensity to produce the contingent event on trials on which it was supposed to occur. Yet their performance was at chance when they were asked to recall the crucial remote trials, suggesting that they had little explicit knowledge of the relevant regularities. This paradigm has not enjoyed the same popularity as the other two, so that little or no evidence based on it has appeared in recent years.

To summarize, it would appear that subjects acquire much of their knowledge without awareness in all three paradigms described above. It is worth pointing out, however, that these results are again not as clear-cut as they may first appear. Recent studies by Perruchet and his collaborators (Perruchet, Gallego, & Savy, 1990; Perruchet & Amorim, 1992), in particular, call for some reinterpretation of these data. But since this book is dedicated to sequence-learning in choice reaction time situations, I will expand further on these and other studies in later sections.

Other Related Empirical Studies
Performance improvements unaccompanied by correlated improvements in verbalizable knowledge have also been obtained in other situations involving the acquisition of structured or nonstructured material. Miller (1958) reported higher levels of free recall performance for structured strings over random strings. Hebb (1961) reported a similar result for repeated strings over nonrepeated strings, even though subjects were not aware of the repetitive nature of the material. Pew (1974) found that tracking performance was better for a target that followed a consistent trajectory than for a random target. Again, subjects were unaware of the manipulation and failed to report noticing any pattern. It is also interesting to note that the very large empirical literature about implicit memory (see Schacter, 1987, for a review), to which I will return briefly in chapter 4, similarly documents the fact that performance improvements (e.g., priming) can be obtained without conscious recollection of the material.

Finally, it appears that some animal studies may be relevant to implicit learning work. For instance, Capaldi (e.g., Capaldi, 1985; Capaldi & Miller, 1988; Capaldi & Frantz, in press) showed that rats trained to run from a start box to a goal box where food may or may not be present come to learn about the sequential structure of successive trials: The rats tend to run faster when they anticipate a reward, even in situations where the only information that allows them to do so is contained in the nature and in the order of previous trials. Thus, the rats possess an ability to encode the sequential structure of successive trials. This is not surprising. On the contrary, the surprising result would be to observe that sensitivity to sequential structure depends on cognitive resources possessed only by human beings. Indeed, in the light of evolutionary arguments of the kind recently put forward by Reber (1990, in press), it is only natural that implicit learning processes are shared by nonhuman species. That implicit learning processes are elementary and evolutionarily ancient also appears to be supported both by studies with psychiatric and neurologically impaired patients and by studies with children. For instance, Roter (1985) showed that children as young as 4 years of age performed as well as adults on a variant of the grammar-learning task. Abrams and Reber (1989) presented brain-damaged psychiatric patients with a short-term memory task and a grammar-learning task and showed that even though the patients failed to perform as well as normal controls on the memory task, their performance on the grammar-learning task was about as good as that of the controls. More recently, Knowlton, Ramus, and Squire (1992) extended these results by showing that amnesics perform as well as normal controls on the standard grammar-learning task, despite exhibiting significant deficits on a recognition test of strings generated from a similar grammar. Finally, the patients also performed more poorly than controls when prompted to base classification performance on an explicit comparison with the training strings—a result that is congruent with the idea that explicit memory of the training strings is not necessary for successful performance.

Discussion
If many robust results have emerged from the impressive array of experimental situations reviewed above, several of them are still somewhat contentious. Perhaps the simplest way to gain an overview of the main points is to consider another of Reber's definitions of implicit learning (see Reber, 1989). He endows implicit learning with three main characteristics: "(a) Implicit learning produces a tacit knowledge base that is abstract and representative of the structure of the environment; (b) such knowledge is optimally acquired independently of conscious effort to learn; and (c) it can be used implicitly to solve problems and make accurate decisions about novel stimulus circumstances" (p. 219).

To reword this definition, implicit learning is thought of as an essentially unintentional process by which a system acquires information about the structure of the stimulus environment in such a way that the resulting knowledge is general enough to be used with new instances, but is also hard to express. As noted above, the idea that learning can proceed in an implicit way has been under attack since its inception, however. In particular, the notions that implicit learning produces knowledge that is abstract and unavailable to consciousness are both the object of ongoing controversies. A number of experiments now appear to have demonstrated (1) that some knowledge acquired implicitly is in fact available to consciousness when elicited properly, and (2) that knowledge acquired implicitly need not necessarily be abstract. But many problems of interpretation remain. Which criteria should be used to decide how conscious or how abstract a particular bit of knowledge is? Addressing complex issues such as these in a purely empirical way is likely not to be very productive, for essentially three different reasons.

First, concepts such as "unconscious" or "abstract" are notoriously hard to define (see Berry, in press) and may in fact be just points on a continuum rather than one of the two branches of a binary alternative. That consciousness has degrees is confirmed by day-to-day introspections. Similarly, abstractness also appears to be a matter of degree, in that there are many ways to represent structure that fall between storage of unanalyzed instances and rule-like general descriptions. This diversity is reflected in the variety of theoretical positions now represented in the implicit learning literature. For instance, Brooks and Vokey (see Brooks, 1978; Brooks & Vokey, 1991; Vokey & Brooks, 1992) have argued that implicit learning performance is essentially based on memory for specific instances. By contrast, Reber (see for instance Reber, 1989) has always contended that implicit knowledge is best characterized as abstract, rule-like knowledge. As discussed in the introduction to this chapter, other researchers have adopted intermediate positions. For instance, both Dulany et al. (1984, 1985) and Perruchet and Pacteau (1990) stress the role that knowledge of short groups of elements plays in artificial grammar learning. Servan-Schreiber and Anderson (1990) pushed the latter idea a little further by proposing an information-processing model of implicit learning performance built around the notion that chunking is an efficient way of extracting structure from the environment. I return to these various approaches later in this chapter.

Second, systems based on abstraction and systems based on memory for instances may often be functionally equivalent. Dienes (1992) showed that both instance-based models (e.g., Hintzman, 1986) and simple delta-rule connectionist networks were able to learn the strings used in Dienes et al., 1991, although the latter models fared better overall in accounting for detailed aspects of the data. Cleeremans, Servan-Schreiber, and McClelland (in press) showed that connectionist networks (described at length in chapter 2) trained to predict successive elements generated from a finite-state grammar could develop internal representations that vary widely in terms of their degree of generality, yet remain undistinguishable based only on performance. Dienes and Fahey (1992) compared performance of instance and strength models (instantiated respectively by the model of Logan, 1988, and by a connectionist lookup table) and found that they accounted for system control performance equally well. Naturally, carefully designed transfer tests should be useful in contrasting the performance of instance-based models and of models that encode more general information, but the point is that there appears to be a large functional overlap between models that make sometimes very different assumptions about knowledge representation.

Third, even if the concepts of "abstraction" and of "consciousness" were binary, it might be very hard to design discriminating experiments that allow us to distinguish between the effects of explicit knowledge and strategies, on the one hand, and the effects of implicit knowledge, on the other hand. The basic empirical problem is that performance in any given task almost certainly involves both explicit, code-breaking strategies and the more passive learning and observation processes referred to as "implicit learning." This simple fact makes it very hard to develop decisive arguments in favor of either posistion. For instance, if one recognizes that subjects engaged in an implicit learning task are nevertheless aware of what they are doing, then it is not surprising to find that they end up knowing something about the task and the material. It is not surprising either to find that this knowledge some-times correlates very well with performance. Should this be taken as evidence that knowledge acquired implicitly is in fact conscious? The answer depends on what theoretical stance one prefers, but the issue seems quite hard to settle in a purely empirical way.

This discussion suggests that many of the tasks considered in the review may in fact involve both explicit and implicit learning mecha-nisms. Further, these mechanisms may themselves involve knowledge and processes that vary in their availability to consciousness or in their degree of generality. What are the factors likely to influence which mixture of learning processes will tend to operate in a particular task?

Two relevant dimensions may be *regularity salience* and *task demands*. "Regularity salience" is itself a multidimensional construct. Following Billman (1983; cited in Holland, Holyoak, Nisbett, & Thagard, 1986), one may view the concept of regularity salience as composed of some mixture of three elements:[1]

- *The number of cues and features present in the environment.* In implicit learning experiments, the number of features and cues typically far exceeds the system's ability to attend to them.
- *The amount of external feedback about the specific relevance of features and cues.* External feedback is usually minimal in implicit learning paradigms.
- *The validity of cues.* Again, typical implicit learning situations present subjects with noisy environments in which the cues are only partially valid and in which regularities are marred with excep-tions.

Another way to think about about regularity salience is in terms of stimulus associability, that is, the extent to which stimuli can be combined and related to each other in meaningful ways. From this analysis, it should be clear that the higher the regularity salience, the more likely subjects will engage in explicit problem-solving or regularity detection behavior. As a result, tasks with low regularity salience are more likely to elicit "pure" implicit learning strategies than those in which regularity salience is higher. Naturally, regularity salience can be manipulated experimentally, and a good number of studies, particularly by Reber and his associates (Reber, 1967, 1976; Reber & Allen, 1978; Reber et al., 1980), have been dedicated to doing just that. Taken as a whole (see Reber, 1989, for a review), the results clearly indicate that the lower the regularity salience, the less likely subjects are to engage in fruitless explicit regularity detection behavior. In contrast, these strategies are very efficient when regularity salience is high, because the regularities are there to be found and elaborated upon.

The impact of regularity salience interacts with task demands, however. This second dimension refers to how much the system needs to encode the stimulus and the context in which it is presented to perform according to task instructions. The higher the demands, the more likely subjects are to attempt using explicit learning strategies—with the well-documented drawbacks that they entail when regularity salience is low. The Broadbent tasks are an example of high-demand tasks because even partial success at controlling the system *requires* the relevant information to be encoded (of course, random control decisions will often result in partial success, but this is not a strategy that subjects tend to use systematically). By contrast, typical sequence-learning situations are characterized by low task demands because satisfactory performance levels (e.g., sizable reductions in reaction time) can be achieved even when the structure present in the material is not encoded at all. Task demands can also be increased directly, for instance by giving subjects specific instructions to look for structure. This basically has the same effect of making it mandatory (i.e., as a part of the instruction set) to encode the regularities present in the material.

Table 1.1 illustrates where different representative learning paradigms are located on these two dimensions (the list is by no means exhaustive). Naturally, this table is a necessarily arbitrary partition of more or less continuous underlying dimensions. The upper left cell contains paradigms (e.g., sequence-learning) that are characterized by low salience and low task demands and for which implicit learning strategies are the most likely to lead to successful performance. By contrast, the lower right cell contains tasks characterized by both high

Table 1.1
A classification of learning paradigms based on two dimensions.

Regularity salience	Task demands		
	Low	Medium	High
Low	*Complex sequence learning* Cleeremans & McClelland, 1991 Lewicki, Czyzewska, & Hoffman, 1987	*Grammar learning* Reber, 1967, 1976 Reber & Allen, 1978	*Process Control* Berry & Broadbent, 1984
Medium	*Simple sequence learning* Lewicki, Hill, & Bizot, 1988 Cohen, Ivry, & Keele, 1990	*Grammar learning* Reber, Kassin, Lewis, & Cantor, 1980	*Process Control* Cleeremans, 1988 Berry & Broadbent, 1988 *Grammar learning* Reber, Kassin, Lewis, & Cantor, 1980, Exp. 2
High	*Elementary tasks* Seibel, 1963	*Grammar learning* Reber, Kassin, Lewis, & Cantor, 1980 Servan-Schreiber & Anderson, 1990	*Problem solving and related tasks* Newell and Simon, 1972

salience and high task demands (e.g., problem solving), for which explicit strategies are most likely to yield success. The other cells all entail some combination of implicit and explicit learning strategies. High-salience and low-demand tasks are perhaps somewhat less interesting than many others because they are so elementary in nature. The worst paradigms—insofar as studying implicit learning in itself is concerned—are those with low salience and high task demands. Indeed, subjects exposed to these situations are most likely to attempt using explicit strategies and are also the most likely to fail in doing so because regularity salience is low.

In the introduction to this chapter, I argued that implicit learning research should focus on elaborating information-processing models of the learning mechanisms that operate in implicit learning situations. From this perspective, the above discussion suggests two research strategies: (1) identify and explore experimental situations in which implicit learning can manifest itself with as little intervention as possible from explicit strategies (i.e., focus on situations characterized by low salience and low task demands), and (2) explore what kind of mechanisms may be plausible candidates as processes of implicit learning. The next section is dedicated to this second point. I will return to the first point at length in chapter 3, but it should already be clear from the above analysis that sequence-learning situations appear to offer the

best chance of investigating implicit learning with as little contamina-
tion as possible from explicit strategies.

Models and Mechanisms

As noted earlier, few detailed models of the empirical results presented
above have been proposed so far. At a very general level, however, most
authors (Reber, 1989; Hayes, 1986, 1987, Hayes & Broadbent, 1988;
Brooks, 1978, Lewicki et al., 1988) agree that the detection of complex
covariations is the central process underlying implicit learning phenomena. In the artificial-grammar-learning situation explored by Reber,
covariations take the form of small groups of letters that compose the
strings. In the Broadbent process control tasks, the output of the system
covaries in a complex but consistent way with other variables. Similarly, in the paradigm explored by Lewicki et al. (1987, 1988), successive
events in the sequence covary in predictable ways, with specific stimuli
occurring only in the context of others. However, detecting covariations
must underlie many, if not all, learning processes, be they implicit or
not. Even problem solving can, in some cases (e.g., induction), be
characterized as involving the detection and processing of complex
contingencies between events. Bradshaw, Langley, and Simon's (1983)
analysis of scientific discovery pointed out that a good deal of structure
can be extracted from the data—provided one has the right selection
of data. The hallmark of implicit learning processes, as the evidence
reviewed in the previous section indicates, is that they proceed in an
unintentional way. An important implication of this is that any structure that emerges as the result of processing must be almost entirely
stimulus-driven, since the impact of conscious attempts to find structure is kept at a minimum by the nature of the instructions.[2]

Plausible mechanisms for implicit learning should therefore:

- Allow for the detection of covariations in some elementary and
unselective way,
- Yield a knowledge base that reflects the organization of relevant
covariations and is capable of influencing task performance,
- Be independent of conscious control and leave little or no directly
verbalizable knowledge.[3]

Various mechanisms compatible with the above descriptive constraints have been proposed as plausible implicit learning processes:
exemplar-based regularity detection mechanisms, chunking, classifier

systems, and, in a very general sense, connectionist systems. These mechanisms have typically been instantiated as particular components of models of performance in specific experimental situations, but they all share a number of basic assumptions about process and structure that are worth delineating here. In the next section, I attempt to go one step beyond mere phenomenology by proposing a set of information-processing principles that I contend must underlie any implicit learning mechanism. Sketching such a general framework for thinking about implicit learning processes will provide a useful context in which to discuss specific models in greater detail.

A General Framework for Studying Implicit Learning Processes
This section delineates a general information-processing framework for implicit learning, in the form of several principles about process and structure. The formulation is very general and may appear to be too underconstrained to be of any use, but the goal is to highlight what I believe are the necessary features of successful models of implicit learning. As discussed in some detail below, it is important to keep in mind that specific models have to provide some kind of operational instantiation of each principle, thereby giving them substance. One important point related to implementation issues that keeps appearing in the discussion of each principle is the distinction between rule-based and association-based systems (such as production systems and connectionist models respectively). I have attempted to phrase each principle in such a way as to be applicable to both kinds of models, but there are some important differences that cannot be adequately captured in this framework. In particular, learning has a very different flavor when it is association-based rather than rule-based, because in the latter case the system has to make additional and necessary assumptions regarding when and how new knowledge is created. I will return to this rather thorny point in the discussion.

Principle 1: Distributed Knowledge
Knowledge is distributed among many units that encode local information.

This principle is central to all models of implicit learning and is well supported by the empirical evidence. Many studies (e.g., Cleeremans & McClelland, 1991; Dulany et al., 1985; Reber & Lewis, 1977; Perruchet & Pacteau, 1990; Servan-Schreiber & Anderson, 1990) indeed suggest that knowledge acquired implicitly is fragmented, consisting of many local "microrules" that specify the relationship between elements of the stimulus display, the appropriate response to be made given that such information is present in the stimulus, and so on.[4] For instance, Servan-Schreiber and Anderson (1990) have shown that classification performance in the Reber task can be accounted for by assuming that subjects' knowledge consists of "chunks" that encode information about local covariations between letters of the training strings. Similar, if not identical, notions have been proposed by Reber and Lewis (1977) and by Dulany et al. (1985). In the absence of any unbiased term to designate such fragments of knowledge, I will call them *knowledge units*. Naturally, specific implementations make sometimes radically different assumptions about what constitutes a "knowledge unit." This is an issue that depends both on implementation choices and on the empirical data. At this level of discussion, whether a "knowledge unit" is an association, a recursive chunk, a production rule, the pattern of activity over the set of hidden units in a connectionist system, or some other kind of representation (such as stored exemplars, which may be viewed as microrules in and of themselves) is irrelevant and may be undecidable formally. This does not entail that the notion of "knowledge unit" is void of content, however, because each specific implementation has to give it some kind of operational definition. Note also that "knowledge fragmentation" need not be actually implemented in the knowledge structures themselves. Indeed, there may be instances where the fragmentation is purely functional, that is, at the level of the mechanisms that operate on the representations.

Principle 2: Graded Constraint Satisfaction
Knowledge units exert a graded influence on processing: Processing is constraint satisfaction, based on all the information available to the system.

Principle 2 is self-explanatory. Knowledge fragmentation does not necessarily entail that processing is also fragmented (in the sense that specific actions result only from the operation of specific knowledge units). Rather, it appears that implicit learning performance is often sensitive to the constraints set by the entire distribution of knowledge units (including the stimulus) and that this sensitivity is gradual. For instance, in the Reber task, knowledge may consist of many chunks that encode local constraints between parts of strings, but discrimination performance appears to be based on the constraints resulting from the whole set of chunks acquired during the memorization phase. In sequence-learning situations, response times appear to be proportional to the conditional probability of the stimulus computed over the entire training set. Again, design issues dictate how Principle 2 is actually implemented. A typical construct, found in all models based on production systems, is strength: Each knowledge unit has a strength associated with it that defines how big an influence it may have on processing. Other implementations are possible. For instance, one may have binary knowledge units that apply probabilistically, but this is clearly just a notational variant. Connectionist systems do not incorporate any explicit representation of strength (as associated with knowledge units), but it is obvious that the pattern of connectivity among processing units defines associations between possible stimuli and responses that vary in their intensity. Given this kind of representational system, it is only natural that processing be based on some form of constraint satisfaction, in which multiple sources of information are allowed to interact and to compete to produce a graded response. Architectures based on production system architectures, such as classifier systems, typically implement this by allowing knowledge units to enter into competition during a conflict resolution cycle, the specifics of which depend on the particular system. Connectionist networks, on the other hand, implement competition as a natural by-product effect of processing.

Principle 3: Knowledge Tuning
Learning consists of the gradual strengthening of knowledge units to satisfy task demands.

This principle really has two components. The first specifies that knowledge acquisition proceeds gradually, by strengthening specific knowledge units at the expense of others. To some extent, this notion taps into the classic distinction between procedural and declarative learning (Anderson, 1983). In some cases, I learn facts, either incidentally (for instance by watching the news and learning that *Challenger* has exploded) or by committing them to memory through active study; in other cases, I develop skills through extensive practice (I will not report on how long it took me to learn to drive a car!). Implicit learning is clearly of the latter type, in that what is learned is "working knowledge" about the stimulus environment, and not facts about it. Again, different architectures may make very different assumptions about how the principle is actually implemented. Association-based systems can implement Principle 3 *as is*, with little need for additional processing assumptions. In a connectionist network, for instance, some internal representations representing associations relevant to the task will come to prevail at the expense of others through adjustments to the weights of the connections to and from the relevant processing units. New situations are dealt with by using the knowledge corresponding to old similar situations. By contrast, rule-based systems must incorporate specific mechanisms for dealing with the question of knowing what to do when simple strengthening is not applicable. Specific rule-based systems tend to make very different assumptions regarding this point. A variety of algorithms that create new knowledge have been proposed, from procedural chunking in SOAR to genetic algorithms in classifier systems. Clearly, this a departure from Principle 3. It is my contention that implicit learning processes operating in quasi isolation rely almost exclusively on strengthening as the means to tune the knowledge base, but the empirical evidence to back this claim is rather spotty. Metatheoretically, systems based on strengthening are often more parsimonious in their assumptions. Further, there is no evidence so far that systems based solely on strengthening are *incapable* of accounting for the empirical data; it is just that few have been proposed. Further exploration of the power of association-based systems is needed to assess their potential as models of implicit learning. This is precisely the kind of research strategy that I think is also the most likely to result in advancing our understanding of the empirical phenomena.

Another design issue that is common to both approaches is to decide when to learn. Some systems assume that learning is failure-driven (i.e., error correcting), others that it is success-driven or unsupervised (i.e., driven by some internal measure of success). Among models that have been proposed for implicit learning mechanisms, failure-driven and unsupervised algorithms prevail, which accords well with the other principles outlined here.

The second part of Principle 3 indicates that which knowledge units are strengthened depends on how much they contribute to performance optimization (or, perhaps, satisfycing). Much in the spirit of rational analysis (Anderson, 1990) or Reber's own functionalism (Reber & Allen, 1978; Allen & Reber, 1980), both the learning processes and the knowledge base that they generate are assumed to be strongly constrained by the immediate requirements imposed by the task and by the cognitive system's own limitations in carrying out that task. There is substantial empirical support for this claim. For instance, Servan-

Schreiber and Anderson (1990) demonstrated that learning in the Reber task appears to be strongly determined by the chunking strategies used by subjects to memorize the strings. The work reported in this book (see chapters 3 through 6) shows that sequence-learning in choice reaction situations is well accounted for by prediction-based mechanisms that are optimal in decreasing response time. As discussed earlier, implicit learning paradigms may differ sharply in the nature of the task constraints they impose on processing and therefore lead to significant differences in the structure of the resulting knowledge.

Principle 4: Context Sensitivity
Processing is unselective: Events are processed in context.

Obviously, to become sensitive to covariations in the stimulus material in the absence of any knowledge about the relevance of specific elements with respect to the task, one must encode context information along with the *manifest stimulus*. This observation has led Hayes and Broadbent (1988) to develop the notion of *unselective processing*, or *u-mode processing* which they oppose to *selective* or *s-mode processing*. In this framework, the central feature of explicit learning strategies is that specific dimensions of the stimulus are attended to and processed, resulting in fast learning if the right dimensions were selected. By contrast, implicit learning strategies allow the system to remain sensitive to all dimensions of the stimulus and of the context it is presented in, at the cost of slow and gradual learning. It is interesting to note that this difference is also what distinguishes traditional symbolic approaches to information processing from association-based frameworks such as connectionist models. The latter typically start learning in a context-sensitive way and will only tend to develop more general representations under specific training conditions (see chapter 2 for a detailed example). By contrast, typical rule-based systems tend to learn by elaborating initially abstract representations with context information over training.

A problem common to both approaches, however, is to decide on what constitutes "the manifest stimulus" and what constitutes "the context." This is far from being easy to specify, except in some clear-cut experimental situations such as sequential choice reaction situations (where the manifest stimulus is the information presented at a given time, and the context is provided by the previous stimuli). In the Broadbent tasks, there is even no "stimulus" as such, since the subjects initiate each trial by giving a response. As discussed above, different implicit learning paradigms differ sharply in (1) the location of the minimal information that the system needs to make a response that realizes task instructions, and (2) how much the relevant dimensions of the stimulus array are emphasized by task instructions and other situational variables. In any case, one has to assume that context information is automatically encoded along with the manifest stimulus, even if only minimally so, in order to understand how implicit learning mechanisms operate. An important issue here is to identify limits on subjects' ability to encode relevant information present in the context. This is likely to depend, at least in part, on working memory limits (Baddeley, 1987), but the issue appears to be more complicated than that. In chapter 5, I return to this point in the context of the sequence-learning paradigm of Cleeremans and McClelland (1991).

Specific Instantiations: Variations on a Theme
Implicit learning mechanisms have generally not been proposed in the general and abstract form that I have used above. Rather, they are typically embodied in specific simulation models that attempt to capture performance in specific experimental situations. This is a desirable trait, of course, because it means that the proposed mechanisms have been elaborated and specified to the point that they can be implemented as computer programs. However, this state of affairs also makes it very hard to engage in detailed comparisons between the models. Richman and Simon (1989) were faced with a similar problem when comparing how well EPAM (Feigenbaum & Simon, 1962, 1984) and the interactive activation model (McClelland & Rumelhart, 1981; Rumelhart & McClelland, 1982) could account for word recognition performance. They discussed several difficulties associated with "theory testing." First, it is not clear how to map the parameters of one model onto the parameters of another one. Even worse, it is often not obvious which parameters or which components of a model are crucial to the underlying theory, and which are not. Further, processing principles may differ radically from one model to the next. For instance, localization is not very important in distributed connectionist networks, but it may be crucial in other kinds of models. Another type of problem arises from the fact that not all models have been elaborated to the same point. Overcoming this difficulty for the purpose of comparison would require reimplementation and adaptation of each model—a very complex enterprise that falls well beyond the scope of the work reported in this book.

In the case of implicit learning, the above difficulties are further compounded by the fact that models have generally been proposed in the context of different tasks, which may or may not involve the same combination of mechanisms. Thus, each model has to make a number of assumptions that may just be ancillary with respect to the main theoretical issues, but that are nevertheless essential to make comparisons with experimental data possible. The degree to which these auxiliary assumptions are embedded in the model itself often makes it hard to separate them from the essential features.

For all these reasons, the following review is of a rather general nature and falls short of providing the means of deciding which framework is best suited to model the empirical phenomena reviewed above. What I hope the review achieves, though, is to show that most of the models share a number of basic assumptions and that all in one way or another instantiate the general principles discussed above.

Exemplar-Based Regularity Detection Mechanisms   Brooks (1978) proposed that subjects presented with a concept formation task proceed by drawing analogies between stored exemplars (Hintzman, 1986) and new stimuli when asked to discriminate among instances and noninstances of the concept. However, this process of calculating the similarity of the current item to the stored ones is assumed to be entirely *nonanalytical*. In other words, the elements of the stimuli are not processed according to their validity in predicting category membership (since subjects are unaware of the existence of categories). Rather, similarity is evaluated by counting the number of features shared by the two stimuli being compared. The holistic character of this extremely simple mechanism naturally accounts for the fact that subjects are unable to specify the basis of their discrimination judgments, short of mentioning a similar old item. This basic mechanism was extended and incorporated in a model of the Broadbent control task by Cleeremans (1986) and by Karnas and Cleeremans (1987). We argued that an efficient strategy for dealing with unstructured and complex tasks is to build up a matrix associating stored previous situations with correct responses. In any new situation encountered by the subject, response selection is based on the similarity between the current and the stored situations. The comparison is nonanalytical; that is, it is assumed to be based on the number of common features rather than on a weighted computing of the similarities. This scheme thus implements an elementary form of competition among many knowledge units instantiated by simple associations between particular contexts and specific responses.

The model was used to capture control performance with Berry and Broadbent's sugar factory system. In this situation, subjects have to control the sugar output of the plant by entering the value of a single input variable (the number of workers) on each trial. The relationship between the number of workers and the output was such that the output depended on both the previous output and the new input. Subjects' task consisted of attaining a particular output value. The model was designed to account for the strong practice effect observed in this task and for the negative impact of selective, explicit strategies on performance. The aim of the simulation work was to identify the minimum processing resources necessary to perform the task.

The model consists of two procedures. On each trial, either of them computes the response. The general idea is to build a matrix associating the appropriate response (the work force needed to attain the target) to each of the 12 possible situations (the 12 production levels). On each trial, the response is thus selected by comparing the current situation (the previous production) to the stored situations. The matrix is of course empty at the start of the simulation. A new link is created each time the model attains the target by associating the previous response to the previous production. The model is thus entirely success-driven.

The second procedure is called whenever the first fails to select a response, that is, when the model finds itself in a new situation for which no information is recorded in the matrix. In one version of the model, responses selected by this procedure were random. This is an unrealistic assumption, since subjects enter the task with conscious hypotheses about the workings of the plant, but it allows for assessing the efficiency of a pure instance-based mechanism. Five hundred simulations using this version of the model were run. The results indicated that the performance of the simulation improves with practice and that the absolute levels of performance, as well as the rate of improvement, are very close to the corresponding human data.

In another version of the simulation, responses computed by the second procedure were generated either at random, or based on a simple heuristic. This heuristic computed the response based on the last change in production. If the last production was lower than the target and higher than the penultimate production, the system selected its previous response and increased it a bit, thus implementing subjects' erroneous assumptions that sugar output is monotonically related to the work force. A similar but inverted rule applied when the two previous production levels were both higher than the target. In all the other cases, response selection was random (i.e., the model guessed as a last resort). The results of this simulation showed that the model was now performing less efficiently than in the first case, much like subjects induced to adopt explicit control strategies (Cleeremans, 1986). The explanation of the performance deterioration resides in the fact that computing the response based on the simple monotonic rules described above tends to repeatedly expose the model to the same situations. As a result, it experiences fewer new situations, which in turn results in the matrix's being filled more slowly than in the first simulation.

To conclude, this model proved to be surprisingly successful at accounting for the experimental data, despite the elementary character of its core mechanism. Naturally, the model has many limitations as such. In particular, (1) it would require increasingly large amounts of storage when the situation becomes more complex, and (2) the model assumes that some features of the environment are selected. The first point can be dealt with by switching to another kind of representational scheme, such as distributed representations in connectionist systems, but the second one is clearly incompatible with Principle 4. Therefore, Hayes (1987) proposed another mechanism based on feature frequency processing. Feature frequency processing (Hasher & Zacks, 1984), the process by which subjects record the frequencies of observed events, has been shown to be a plausible explanation for many concept attainment situations. It is generally assumed to be automatic, or at least to require few attentional resources (Kellog & Dowdy, 1986). Hayes (1987) proposed that subjects in the Broadbent tasks automatically record the frequency of contingencies occurring between inputs and outputs of the system. Using a simulation inspired by Cleeremans (1986), Hayes could also build a fairly successful model of subjects' performance at the process control task. The model assumes the same set of explicit heuristics to guide performance when no information is present in the matrix. This time, however, the matrix contains frequency information about the covariations between all the variables in the environment. Hayes showed that by recording frequency information about these covariations after each trial (successful or not), the system progressively came to represent the relevant ones (as frequency peaks). Unlike Cleeremans's (1986) model, this mechanism therefore results in a system that starts with no particular bias, but that becomes gradually sensitive to the relevant covariations. Further, Hayes's set of simulations also confirmed that frequency processing was more efficient when the relationship defining the system is a complex one (i.e., of low salience), for which the explicit heuristics are usually inadequate. Again, the insight is that a surprising amount of structure can be extracted based on extremely simple mechanisms.

Finally, memory array models such as Estes's exemplar model (Estes, 1986; Medin & Schaffer, 1978) or Hintzman's multiple trace model (Hintzman, 1986) may be viewed as elaborations on the general idea that, as exemplars are processed, information about their features is stored and may be subsequently retrieved in the course of further processing. To date, these models have not been systematically applied to implicit learning data, even though there is some empirical support for the idea that performance in grammar-learning situations is based on memory of exemplars (see for instance McAndrews & Moscovitch, 1985, in which grammaticality and similarity were manipulated independently and shown to account equally well for classification performance). However, Dienes (1992) conducted a useful comparison between the performance of several different variants of these models on the artificial-grammar-learning task first introduced by Reber. The basic notion underlying processing in exemplar models is that similarity is computed based on the entire set of stored exemplars. The different models examined differ in exactly how this is done. For instance, Estes's (1986) feature probability model assumes that similarity is a function of the product of the perceived frequencies of features of the exemplar to be classified with respect to the stored items. In Estes's (1986) exemplar model, classification decisions are a function of a sum (across stored exemplars) of the products of similarity between test and stored items, computed on each feature. Hintzman's MINERVA 2 model (Hintzman, 1986) is somewhat more complex, but exploits essentially the same principles as the models described above.

In brief, it appears that if these models sometimes make distinct predictions about classification performance in artificial grammar situations, none of them could outperform often analytically equivalent connectionist systems, which I review in the following section.

Connectionist Models   Parallel distributed processing, models (PDP models; Rumelhart & McClelland, 1986) constitute a class of powerful, yet simple, learning mechanisms. The association-driven learning mechanisms found in connectionist models are based on detecting and elaborating task-relevant representations of covariations in the stimulus material. Learning consists of strengthening relevant knowledge units (here, connections) as a function of task constraints. This process is often error-driven, such as in back-propagation, but need not necessarily be so. Other, unsupervised learning procedures exist, by which processing units compete to respond to input patterns without external feedback; see for instance the competitive learning algorithm developed by Rumelhart and Zipser (1986). The internal representations developed by connectionist models are typically opaque: Because all the knowledge of the system is stored in its connections, this knowledge may only be expressed through performance—a central characteristic of implicit learning. Further, the internal representations themselves are often distributed and therefore have a very rich and possibly time-varying structure, in which the features critical to the task are not represented explicitly.

These characteristics—as well as others to which I will return throughout this book—make connectionist models very good candidates for mechanisms of implicit learning. Only a few connectionist models of implicit learning phenomena have been proposed so far. This book contains a detailed exploration of one of them, as well as discussions of other related models (e.g., Jennings & Keele, 1990). To the best of my knowledge, the only other example of a connectionist model applied to implicit learning data is provided by the work of Dienes (1992). Dienes has explored how a variety of connectionist and memory array models (e.g., Estes, 1986; Hintzman, 1986; see above) may account for performance in a version of the Reber task. He considered two classes of elementary connectionist models: auto-associators using either the Hebb rule or the delta rule for learning (see for instance McClelland & Rumelhart, 1985). The task of the models was to reproduce the input string as their output. How well they are able to do so is an indication of how well the presented string conforms to the constraints characterizing the set of strings that the network has been trained on. Dienes also examined how the coding of letter features (single letters vs. single letters and digrams) and their mode of presentation (successive vs. simultaneous) influenced performance. Each variant of each model was presented with 20 training strings from Dienes et al., 1991 and then tested on 25 new strings. In short, the results indicated that simultaneous auto-associators using the delta rule provided the best fits with the empirical data, both in terms of overall performance measures (e.g., percentage correct classifications) and in terms of the difficulty of grammatical and nongrammatical individual strings. These results held even under more realistic assumptions about string coding, such as the fact that it is likely that not all letters of each string are encoded perfectly during memorization. Dienes characterizes the knowledge acquired by the auto-associator as incorporating incomplete but representative rules of the grammar, but fails to discuss why the delta rule models are more successful than the others. Nevertheless, the model clearly embodies the principles discussed above: Knowledge is fragmented and distributed, processing is context-sensitive, and learning is gradual.

Chunking Since Miller (1956) first proposed chunking as a possible mechanism for overcoming short-term memory limitations, the concept has enjoyed widespread interest as well as a few semantic metamorphoses. Indeed, whereas Miller thought of chunking as a conscious recoding strategy, recent conceptions have tended to view it as a ubiquitous process that applies in an automatic way during processing. Procedural chunking—the process by which new productions that subsume the steps taken in a problem-solving episode are created—is indeed the core learning mechanism of the SOAR production system (Laird, Rosenbloom, & Newell, 1985; Newell, 1990). In SOAR, chunking is viewed as an automatic process, not as a strategy over which the architecture has control. In this form, chunking has been successfully applied to several phenomena revolving around the effects of practice in combinatorial environments, of which the Seibel task is a prime example. Recently, chunking has been proposed as the central mechanism for implicit learning (Servan-Schreiber & Anderson, 1990). The authors analyzed the Reber task by pointing out that memorizing strings of meaningless letters requires some form of recoding—or chunking—of the material. The interesting aspect of their analysis is the observation that the resulting knowledge is complex enough to be used to perform the rather different task of deciding whether other strings have been generated according to the same rules as the first ones. Thus, an extremely simple mechanism (chunking) ultimately leads to a body of knowledge that is far more complex and structured than what might be expected from a cursory examination of the memorization task.

The above ideas were embodied in a framework called *competitive chunking*. The model has been applied successfully to the data of Servan-Schreiber and Anderson (1990) and of Miller (1958). Competitive chunking models Reber's memorization task by elaborating hierarchical representations of each string. This is achieved by parsing each stimulus into chunks, through a process during which overlapping chunks compete to enter the final representation. The probability of entering and winning the competition is a function of chunk strength, itself a function of how frequently and recently chunks have been used. This parsing process is repeated until no more chunks can apply to the stimulus. In this manner, the model is able to exploit the redundancy inherent in any structured material and to build representations that can transfer to the learning of new material.

The discrimination task is modeled by assuming that decisions are taken probabilistically based on the number of chunks that the parsing of a string generates. Indeed, a parse that terminates with a high number of chunks is an indication that few or none of the high-level chunks that were built during the memorization part of the task could apply and thus that the string is not a familiar one. On the contrary, a new string that shares many structural similarities with the set of old strings will elicit a more successful parse and is thus more likely to be accepted as a grammatical string. Based on this model, Servan-Schreiber and Anderson (1990) could predict human performance levels on various types of strings, at both the memorization and the discrimination tasks.

Naturally, the above analysis builds on earlier work by Miller (1958) and by Reber and Lewis (1977). It had not escaped these authors that encoding small subsequences of the strings is a central process in this task. Reber and Lewis (1977), for instance, suggest that implicit learning builds on both a "differentiation-like process" and a "gestalt-like, global apprehension process." Competitive chunking, as applied to the Reber task, embodies both the processes envisioned by Reber and Lewis (1977). Indeed, the model makes the point that, if memorizing the material requires small subsequences to be differentiated and processed according to their encoding power, the discrimination decisions are assumed to be based on the overall familiarity of the current string.

Classifier Systems   Druhan and Mathews (1989) introduced a model of performance in situations based on the Reber task. Their THYIOS model is an instance of the classifier systems first explored by Holland et al. (1986). Classifier systems are siblings of production systems, in which rules are represented as strings of equal length composed of a condition part and an action part. Elements of the strings consist of symbols representing the presence or the absence of a particular feature, and of a wild card symbol matching either case (i.e., a "don't care" marker). Processing consists of encoding the input and evaluating how well it matches the constraints expressed in the set of available classifiers. Response selection is based on the outcome of a multiple-stage parallel conflict resolution process during which classifiers that match the input are allowed to compete against each other. Mathews, Druhan, and Roussel (1989) explored three different learning algorithms in the context of THYIOS: a genetic algorithm, an "exception" algorithm, and a "forgetting" algorithm. All three learning algorithms are error-driven (i.e., they apply when the system has made an erroneous response). The genetic algorithm randomly recombines (by "crossover") parts of classifiers that were successful in matching the input but failed to recommend the correct response. The algorithm also creates new rules by randomly altering some elements of old rules ("mutation"). The other two algorithms (the "exception" algorithm and the "forgetting" algorithm) aim to create new rules based on either the failure or the successes of particular old rules in determining the correct response. Features of the old rules (or of the input) are selected probabilistically and incorporated into new rules that specify whether to ignore or attend to these features. When compared with the empirical data, the forgetting algorithm is the most successful. Mathews, Druhan, and Roussel (1989) contend that this algorithm is the most plausible since it is the only one that does not require an initial set of rules to function, and since it uses the fewest processing resources. The system is clearly distributed and competition-based, and although learning does not proceed by pure strengthening, the stochastic rule recombination procedures ensure that useful knowledge units will come to exert a progressively greater influence on processing.

Discussion
It should be clear that most of the mechanisms proposed so far to account for implicit learning phenomena share many similarities in their general principles. For instance, all models produce knowledge that is fragmented, or distributed among many knowledge units that encode only local information. In most models, response selection is based on the influence of all available knowledge units and on the constraints set by the current stimulus. Learning typically proceeds through some form of strengthening of the most task-relevant representations that have developed through exposure to the material. Insofar as implementation issues are concerned, however, the different mechanisms fall into two distinct categories: rule-based systems and association-based systems. Association-based systems appear to be better candidates as models of implicit learning, at least on metatheoretical

grounds, because they typically implement more elementary mechanisms and require fewer additional assumptions than rule-based systems. However, most successful models of implicit learning that have been proposed so far are rule-based. Presumably, this reflects the fact that powerful association-based computational mechanisms have only recently been introduced. Even so, there appears to be little reason to assume that rule-based systems and association-based systems differ drastically either in their performance or in the basic assumptions that they instantiate. Moreover, as Anderson (1990) argues, it may simply be an intractable problem to decide which kind of representational system is better, or even which is the one that is actually used by the mind, should they be proven to be computationally equivalent. How, then, are we to decide which class of model is better? As I argued in the introduction to this chapter, I think that in the specific case of the field of implicit learning research, a better question is: "What kinds of mechanisms are successful both in accounting for the data and in instantiating general principles of implicit learning?" If this question does not help very much to constrain the range of possible mechanisms, it has the merit of *generating* new possible mechanistic accounts of the processes underlying implicit learning—which is exactly what I would contend this field is most in need of. Ultimately, which kind of model is best will be decided based on how general it is and on how successful it is at accounting for experimental data. But deciding among potentially equivalent models is premature at this point. The existing models are just not developed enough, and the experimental work itself is undergoing constant reinterpretation. Therefore, I think it is best to proceed with a wide exploration of what each model can do at this point.

   In the next five chapters, I report on work that partially implements this strategy. Chapter 2 introduces a parallel distributed model of sequence-learning that is successful both in modeling human performance and in instantiating the general principles outlined above. In chapters 3 through 6, I explore how this architecture may be applied to model experimental data from various sequence-learning situations.

Chapter 2
The SRN Model: Computational Aspects of Sequence Processing

I begin this chapter by describing a connectionist architecture capable of processing sequential material first introduced by Elman (1988), and which Servan-Schreiber, McClelland, and I called the *simple recurrent network*, or *SRN*. Next, I present several simulations in which the network is asked to predict the next element of sequences generated from finite-state grammars similar to the kind used by Reber (e.g., Reber, 1969) and provide a detailed analysis of the principles that govern processing, representation, and learning in this architecture. The orientation of this chapter is distinctly computational; that is, I made few attempts to relate its contents to the psychological issues that this book otherwise addresses. But because the material that follows has provided much of the theoretical foundation and motivation for the experimental work described later, I think it is useful to describe the computational aspects of the theory in detail before demonstrating how it may be used as a psychological theory. Further, this detailed exploration is important because several of the processing and representational characteristics of this model are rather different from more familiar ones. In this way, I hope to provide a more thorough understanding of the model than would be possible by simply describing it

The material from this chapter is largely based on work conducted in collaboration with David Servan-Schreiber and James L. McClelland (Cleeremans, Servan-Schreiber, & McClelland, 1989; Servan-Schreiber, Cleeremans, & McClelland, 1991). To reflect the fact that the original work was collaborative, the use of pronouns has not been changed in the text.

We gratefully acknowledge the constructive comments of David Rumelhart, Jordan Pollack, and an anonymous reviewer on an earlier version of the paper on which this chapter is based (Servan-Schreiber, Cleeremans, & McClelland, 1991). David Servan-Schreiber was supported by NIMH Individual Fellow Award MH-09696-01. Axel Cleeremans was supported by a grant from the National Fund for Scientific Research (Belgium). James L. McClelland was supported by NIMH Research Scientist Career Development Award MH-00385. Support for computational resources was provided by NSF (BNS-86-09729) and ONR (N00014-86-G-0146). Copyright 1991 by Kluwer Academic Publishers. Adapted by permission of the publisher.

and comparing its performance with the relevant data. This is particularly relevant in the light of recent concerns about the usefulness of theory building through the use of simulation models of performance, such as those expressed by McCloskey (1991).

A key aspect of sequence processing in general is the ability to maintain information about the context in which successive events take place. For instance, language abundantly illustrates that the meaning of individual events in a stream—such as words in a sentence—is often determined by preceding events in the sequence. The word *ball* is interpreted differently in *The countess threw the ball* and *The pitcher threw the ball*. Similarly, goal-directed behavior and planning are characterized by coordination of behaviors over long sequences of input-output pairings, during which goals and plans act as a context for the interpretation and generation of individual events.

The similarity-based style of processing in connectionist models provides natural primitives to implement the role of context in the selection of meaning and actions. However, until recently, most connectionist models of sequence processing have used a spatial metaphor to represent time. In these early models, all cues of a sequence are presented in parallel, and there is often an assumption that the sequence of relevant elements is of a fixed length (e.g., Cottrell, 1985; Fanty, 1985; Sejnowski & Rosenberg, 1987; Hanson & Kegl, 1987). Typically, these models used a pool of input units for the event presented at Time *t*, another pool for the event presented at Time *t+1*, and so on, in what is often called a *moving window* paradigm. As Elman (1990) points out, such implementations are not psychologically satisfying, and they are also computationally wasteful since some unused pools of units must be kept available for the rare occasions when the longest sequences are presented.

Recent work by a number of researchers, however, has specifically addressed the problems of learning and of representing the information contained in sequences in more powerful and elegant ways, and there is now a wide variety of algorithms in which past input or output history is allowed to modulate processing of current events by means of modifications to the learning rule or by the use of delay lines (see Williams and Zipser, in press, for a review). Our purpose in initiating the research described in this chapter was to explore the computational characteristics of the simplest models of this type. One such model was described by Jordan (1986). In this network, the output associated with each state was fed back and blended with the input representing the next state over a set of *state units* (Figure 2.1).

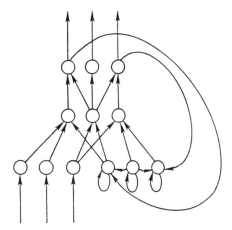

Figure 2.1
Jordan's (1986) Sequential Network.

After several steps of processing, the pattern present on the input units is characteristic of the particular sequence of states that the network has traversed. With sequences of increasing length, the network has more difficulty discriminating on the basis of the first cues presented, but the architecture does not rigidly constrain the length of input sequences. However, although such a network learns *how to use* the representation of successive states, it does not discover a representation for the sequence.

In 1988, Elman (1988, 1990) introduced an architecture—which we call the *simple recurrent network (SRN)*—that has the potential to master an infinite corpus of sequences with the limited means of a learning procedure that is *completely local in time* (Figure 2.2). In the SRN, the hidden unit layer is allowed to feed back on itself, so that the intermediate results of processing at Time $t - 1$ can influence the intermediate results of processing at Time t. In practice, the SRN is implemented by copying the pattern of activation on the hidden units onto a set of *context units*, which feed into the hidden layer along with the input units. These context units are comparable to Jordan's state units.

In Elman's SRNs, the set of context units provides the system with memory in the form of a trace of processing at the previous time slice. As Rumelhart, Hinton, and Williams (1986) have pointed out, the pattern of activation on the hidden units corresponds to an "encoding" or "internal representation" of the input pattern. By the nature of back-propagation, such representations correspond to the input pattern partially processed into features relevant to the task (e.g., Hinton, McClelland, & Rumelhart, 1986). In recurrent networks, internal representations encode not only the prior event but also relevant aspects of the representation that was constructed in predicting the prior event from its predecessor. When fed back as input, these representations could provide information that allows the network to maintain prediction-relevant features of an entire sequence. It can easily be induced from the architecture of the SRN (Figure 2.2) that it has the potential of doing so.

Consider first the class of computational objects called finite-state automata. Simply put, finite-state automata are capable of maintaining information about sequences of previous inputs. They do so by using a different state for each sequence of previous inputs and by producing a different response for each of these states. The following equations (adapted from Minsky, 1967) subsume these mechanisms, and constitute the definition of a finite-state automaton:

$$H(t + 1) = G(H(t), S(t)) \tag{1}$$

$$R(t + 1) = F(H(t + 1)) \tag{2}$$

Equation 1 says that the state H of the machine at Time $t + 1$ is a function G of its state at Time t and of the input S at Time t. Equation 2 says that the response R of the machine at Time $t + 1$ is a function F of its state at Time $t + 1$. Could SRNs mimic the behavior of such machines? Consider again the network illustrated in Figure 2.2. The activation pattern of the hidden units at any particular time (i.e., the

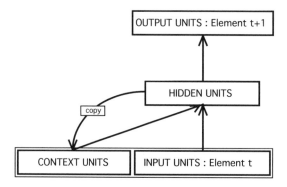

Figure 2.2
The simple recurrent network. Each box represents a pool of units, and each forward arrow represents a complete set of trainable connections from each sending unit to each receiving unit in the next pool. The backward arrow from the hidden layer to the context layer denotes a copy operation.

internal state of the network) is a function of the previous pattern of activation (now represented on the context units) and of the current input. In turn, the activation pattern of the output units on the same time slice—that is, the response of the network—is a function of the new activation pattern now prevailing on the hidden units. In other words, the SRN architecture seems to provide, prima facie, the means of implementing a finite-state automaton. Indeed, one could manually set the weights in the network to provide the appropriate transfer functions between each two pools of units so as to have the SRN mimic any particular finite-state automaton. Mozer and Bachrach (in press), for instance, show how it is possible to hard-wire a simple linear network to behave like an update graph—another way of representing a finite-state automaton. The problem we were most interested in when initiating this research was to determine whether SRNs could *learn* to behave like specific finite-state automata. In the following, we show that the SRN can indeed learn to closely mimic a finite-state automaton, both in its behavior and in its state representations. In addition, we show that SRNs can learn to process an *infinite* corpus of strings based on experience with a *finite* set of training exemplars. We then explore the capacity of this architecture to recognize and use nonlocal contingencies between elements of a sequence that cannot be represented easily in a traditional finite-state automaton. We show that the SRN encodes such long-distance dependencies by *shading* internal representations that are responsible for processing common embeddings in otherwise different sequences. This ability to represent simultaneously similarities and differences between sequences in the same state of activation relies on the graded nature of representations used by the network, which contrast with the discrete states on which traditional automata rely. For this reason, we suggest that the SRN and other similar architectures may be exemplars of a new class of automata, one that we may call *graded state machines*.

Learning a Finite-State Grammar

Material and Task
As in all of the following explorations, the network is assigned the task of *predicting* successive elements of a sequence. The stimulus set should exhibit various interesting features with regard to the potentialities of the architecture (i.e., the sequences must be of different lengths, their elements should be more or less predictable in different contexts, loops

and subloops should be allowed, etc.). In our first experiment, we asked whether the network could learn the contingencies implied by a small finite-state grammar. Reber (1976) used a small finite-state grammar in an artificial-grammar-learning experiment that is well suited to our purposes (Figure 2.3). Finite-state grammars consist of nodes connected by labeled arcs. A grammatical string is generated by entering the network through the "start" node and by moving from node to node until the "end" node is reached. Each transition from one node to another produces the letter corresponding to the label of the arc linking these two nodes. Examples of strings that can be generated by the grammar shown in Figure 2.3 are 'TXS', 'PTVV', 'TSXXTVPS'.

This task is interesting because it allows us to examine precisely how the network extracts information about whole sequences without actually seeing more than two elements at a time. In addition, it is possible to manipulate precisely the nature of these sequences by constructing different training and testing sets of strings that require integration of more or less temporal information.

The difficulty in mastering the prediction task when letters of a string are presented individually is that two instances of the same letter may lead to different nodes and therefore entail different predictions about its successors. For instance, an 'S' at Node #1 may be followed by itself or by an 'X', whereas an 'S' at Node #3 may only be followed by 'E', the end symbol. Thus, to perform the task adequately, it is necessary for the network to encode more than just the identity of the current letter. This task should still be relatively simple, however, since no more than two letters of context are ever needed to achieve perfect predictions (strictly speaking, all the network needs to do to perform this first

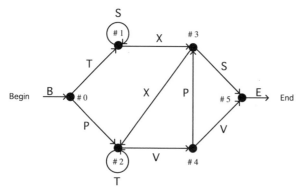

Figure 2.3
The finite-state grammar used by Reber (1976).

task accurately is to develop six different internal representations, one for each node of the grammar).

Network Architecture
As illustrated in Figure 2.4, the network has a three-layer architecture. The input layer consists of two pools of units. The first pool is called the *context pool*, and its units are used to represent the temporal context by holding a copy of the hidden units' activation level at the previous time slice. Note that the ensemble of connections to and from the context pool is strictly equivalent to a fully connected feedback loop on the hidden layer. The second pool of input units represents the current element of the string. On each trial, the network is presented with an element of the string and is trained to produce the next element on the output layer. In both the input and the output layers, letters are represented by the activation of a single unit. Five units therefore code for the five different possible letters in each of these two layers. In addition, two units code for *begin* and *end* symbols. These two symbols are needed so that the network can be trained to predict the first element and the end of a string (although only one *transition* symbol is strictly necessary).

In this first experiment, the number of hidden units was set to three. Assuming that hidden units take on binary values, this should be just enough resources for the network to develop the minimal representations needed to perform the prediction task accurately. Indeed, three units taking on binary activations could represent eight different states, two more than are actually needed to represent the states of the grammar, which contain all the information necessary to achieve op-

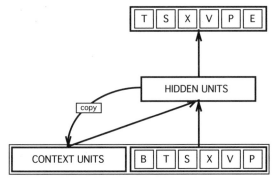

Figure 2.4
General architecture of the network.

timal predictions about the identity of the next element. Other values for the number of hidden units will be reported as appropriate.

Coding of the Strings

A string of n letters is coded as a series of $n + 1$ training patterns. Each pattern consists of two input vectors and one target vector. The target vector is a seven-bit vector representing element $t + 1$ of the string. The two input vectors are

- a three-bit vector representing the activation of the hidden units at Time $t - 1$, and
- a seven-bit vector representing element t of the string.

Training

On each of 60,000 string presentations, a string was generated from the grammar, starting with the 'B'. Successive arcs were then selected randomly from the two possible continuations, with a probability of 0.5. Each letter was then presented sequentially to the network. The activations of the context units were reset to 0 at the beginning of each string. After each letter, the error between the network's prediction and the *actual successor* specified by the string was computed and back-propagated. The 60,000 randomly generated strings ranged from 3 to 30 letters ($M = 7$, $SD = 3.3$)[1].

Performance

Figure 2.5a shows the state of activation of all the units in the network, after training, when the start symbol is presented (here the letter 'B'— for *begin*). Activation of the output units indicate that the network is predicting two possible successors, the letters 'P' and 'T'. Note that the best possible prediction always activates two letters on the output layer except when the end of the string is predicted. Since during training 'P' and 'T' followed the start symbol equally often, each is activated partially in order to minimize error[2]. Figure 2.5b shows the state of the network at the next time step in the string 'BTXXVV'. The pattern of activation on the context units is now a copy of the pattern generated previously on the hidden layer. The two successors predicted are 'X' and 'S'.

The next two figures illustrate how the network is able to generate different predictions when presented with two instances of the same letter on the input layer in different contexts. In Figure 2.6a, when the

String	**B** t x x v v						
	B	T	S	P	X	V	E
Output	00	53	00	38	01	02	00
Hidden			01	00	10		
Context			00	00	00		
	B	T	S	P	X	V	E
Input	100	00	00	00	00	00	00

(a)

String	b **T** x x v v						
	B	T	S	P	X	V	E
Output	00	01	39	00	56	00	00
Hidden			84	00	28		
Context			01	00	10		
	B	T	S	P	X	V	E
Input	00	100	00	00	00	00	00

(b)

Figure 2.5
(a) State of the network after presentation of the start symbol 'B' (following training). Activation values are internally in the range from 0.0 to 1.0 and are displayed on a scale from 0 to 100. The capitalized bold letter indicates which letter is currently being presented on the input layer. (b) State of the network after presentation of an initial 'T'. Note that the activation pattern on the context layer is identical with the activation pattern on the hidden layer at the previous time step.

letter 'X' immediately follows 'T', the network again appropriately predicts 'S' and 'X'. However, as Figure 2.6b shows, when a second 'X' follows, the prediction changes radically, as the network now expects 'T' or 'V'. Note that if the network were not provided with a copy of the previous pattern of activation on the hidden layer, it would activate the four possible successors of the letter 'X' in both cases.

To find out whether the network would generate similarly good predictions after every letter of any grammatical string, we tested its behavior on 20,000 strings derived randomly from the grammar. A prediction was considered accurate if, for every letter in a given string,

```
String          b t X x v v
```

	B	T	S	P	X	V	E
Output	00	04	44	00	37	07	00
Hidden			74	00	93		
Context			84	00	28		
	B	T	S	P	X	V	E
Input	00	00	00	00	100	00	00

(a)

```
String          b t x X v v
```

	B	T	S	P	X	V	E
Output	00	50	01	01	00	55	00
Hidden			06	09	99		
Context			74	00	93		
	B	T	S	P	X	V	E
Input	00	00	00	00	100	00	00

(b)

Figure 2.6
(a) State of the network after presentation of the first 'X'. (b) State of the network after presentation of the second 'X'.

activation of its successor was above 0.3. If this criterion was not met, presentation of the string was stopped and the string was considered "rejected." With this criterion, the network correctly "accepted" all of the 20,000 strings presented.

We also verified that the network did not accept ungrammatical strings. We presented the network with 130,000 strings generated from the same pool of letters but in a random manner—that is, mostly "nongrammatical." During this test, the network is first presented with the 'B', and one of the five letters or 'E' is then selected at random as a successor. If that letter is predicted by the network as a legal successor (i.e., activation is above 0.3 for the corresponding unit), it is then presented to the input layer on the next time step, and another letter is drawn at random as its successor. This procedure is repeated as long as each letter is predicted as a legal successor, until 'E' is selected as the next letter. The procedure is interrupted as soon as the actual successor generated by the random procedure is *not* predicted by the network, and the string of letters is then considered "rejected." As in the previous test, the string is considered "accepted" if all its letters have been predicted as possible continuations up to 'E'. Of the 130,000 strings, 0.2% (260) happened to be grammatical, and 99.8% were nongrammatical. The network performed flawlessly, accepting all the grammatical strings and rejecting all the others. In other words, for all nongrammatical strings, when the first nongrammatical letter was presented to the network, its activation on the output layer at the previous step was less than 0.3 (i.e., it was *not* predicted as a successor of the previous—grammatically acceptable—letter).

Finally, we presented the network with several extremely long strings such as:

'BTSSSSSSSSSSSSSSSSSSSSSSSSXXVPXVPXVPXVPXVPXVPXVPXVP XVPXVPXTTTTTTTTTTTTTTTTTTTTTTTTTTTTTTTTTTTTVPXVPXVPX VPXVPXVPXVPS'

and observed that, at every step, the network correctly predicted both legal successors and no others.

Note that it is possible for a network with more hidden units to reach this performance criterion with much less training. For example, a network with 15 hidden units reached criterion after 20,000 strings were presented. However, activation values on the output layer are not as clearly contrasted when training is less extensive. Also, the selection of a threshold of 0.3 is not completely arbitrary. The activation of output units is related to the frequency with which a particular letter appears as the successor of a given sequence. In the training set used here, this probability is 0.5. As discussed earlier, the activation of a legal successor would then be expected to be 0.5. However, because of the use of a momentum term in the back-propagation learning procedure, the activation of correct output units following training was occasionally below 0.5—sometimes as low as 0.3.

Analysis of Internal Representations
Obviously, to perform accurately, the network takes advantage of the representations that have developed on the hidden units, which are copied back onto the context layer. At any point in the sequence, these patterns must somehow encode the position of the current input in the

grammar on which the network was trained. One approach to understanding how the network uses these patterns of activation is to perform a cluster analysis. We recorded the patterns of activation on the hidden units following the presentation of each letter in a small random set of grammatical strings. The matrix of Euclidean distances between each pair of vectors of activation served as input to a cluster analysis program[3]. The graphical result of this analysis is presented in Figure 2.7. Each leaf in the tree corresponds to a particular string, and the capitalized letter in that string indicates which letter has just been presented. For example, if the leaf is identified as 'pvPs', 'P' is the current letter and its predecessors were 'P' and 'V' (the correct prediction would thus be 'X' or 'S').

From the figure, it is clear that activation patterns are grouped according to the different nodes in the finite-state grammar: All the patterns that produce a similar prediction are grouped together, independently of the current letter. For example, the bottom cluster groups patterns that result in the activation of the "End" unit (i.e., following the last 'V' or last 'S' in a string). Therefore, when one of the hidden layer patterns is copied back onto the context layer, the network is provided with information about the *current node*. That information is combined with input representing the *current letter* to produce a pattern on the hidden layer that is a representation of the *next node* (see the finite-state automaton equations). To a degree of approximation, the SRN behaves exactly like the finite-state automaton defined by the grammar. It does not use a stack or registers to provide contextual information but relies instead on simple state transitions, just like a finite-state machine. Indeed, the network's perfect performance on randomly generated grammatical and nongrammatical strings shows that it can be used as a finite-state recognizer.

However, a closer look at the cluster analysis reveals that within a cluster corresponding to a particular node, patterns are further divided according to the path traversed before that node. For example, looking again at the bottom cluster, patterns produced by a 'VV', 'PS', and 'SXS' ending of the string are grouped separately by the analysis: They are more similar to each other than to the abstract prototypical pattern that would characterize the corresponding "node."[4] We can illustrate the behavior of the network with a specific example. When the first letter of the string 'BTX' is presented, the initial pattern on the context units corresponds to Node #0. This pattern together with the letter 'T' generates a hidden layer pattern corresponding to Node #1. When that

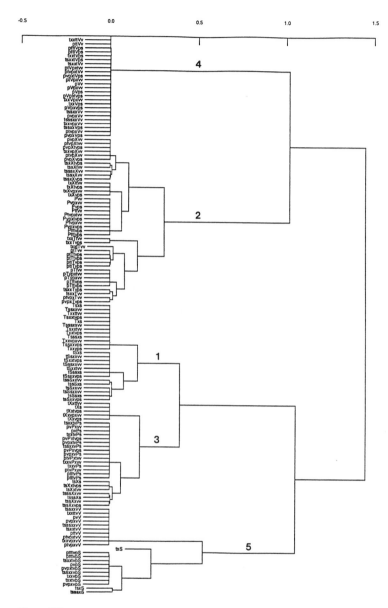

Figure 2.7
Hierarchical cluster analysis of the hidden unit activation patterns after 60,000 presentations of strings generated at random from the Reber grammar (three hidden units). A
small set of strings was used to test the network. The single uppercase letter in each
string shown in the figure corresponds to the letter actually presented to the network on
that trial.

pattern is copied onto the context layer and the letter 'X' is presented, a new pattern corresponding to Node #3 is produced on the hidden layer, and this pattern is in turn copied on the context units. If the network behaved *exactly* like a finite-state automaton, exactly the same patterns would be used during processing of the other strings 'BTSX' and 'BTSSX'. That behavior would be adequately captured by the transition network shown in Figure 2.8a. However, since the cluster analysis shows that slightly different patterns are produced by the substrings 'BT', 'BTS', and 'BTSS', Figure 2.8a is a more accurate description of the network's state transitions. As states 1, 1', and 1" on the one hand and 3, 3', and 3" on the other are nevertheless very similar to each other, the finite-state machine that the network implements can be said to approximate the idealization of a finite-state automaton corresponding exactly to the grammar underlying the exemplars on which it has been trained. With more training, the approximation would tend to become even better.

However, we should point out that the close correspondence between representations and function obtained for the recurrent network with three hidden units is the exception rather than the rule. With only three hidden units, representational resources are so scarce that back-propagation forces the network to develop representations that yield a

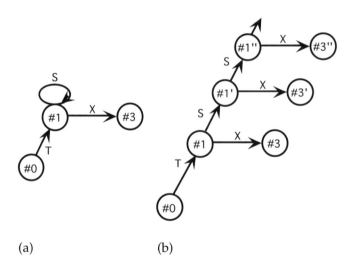

(a)   (b)

Figure 2.8
(a) A transition network corresponding to the upper-left part of Reber's finite-state grammar. (b) A transition network illustrating the network's true behavior.

prediction on the basis of the current node alone, ignoring contributions from the path. This situation precludes the development of different—redundant—representations for a particular node that typically occurs with larger numbers of hidden units. When redundant representations do develop, the network's behavior still converges to the theoretical finite-state automaton—in the sense that it can still be used as a perfect finite-state recognizer for strings generated from the corresponding grammar—but internal representations do not correspond to that idealization. Figure 2.9 shows the cluster analysis obtained from a network with 15 hidden units after training on the same task. Only Nodes #4 and #5 of the grammar seem to be represented by a unique "prototype" on the hidden layer. Clusters corresponding to Nodes #1, #2, and #3 are divided according to the preceding arc. Information about arcs is not relevant to the prediction task, and the different clusters corresponding to a single node play a redundant role.

Finally, preventing the development of redundant representations may also produce adverse effects. For example, in the Reber grammar, predictions following Nodes #1 and #3 are identical ('X' or 'S'). With some random sets of weights and training sequences, networks with only three hidden units occasionally develop almost identical representations for Nodes #1 and #3 and are therefore unable to differentiate the first from the second 'X' in a string.

In the next section, we examine a different type of training environment, one in which information about the path traversed becomes relevant to the prediction task.

Discovering and Using Path Information

The previous section has shown that SRNs can learn to encode the nodes of the grammar used to generate strings in the training set. However, this training material does not require information about arcs or sequences of arcs—the "path"—to be maintained. How does the network's performance adjust as the training material involves more complex and subtle temporal contingencies? We examine this question in this section, using a training set that places many additional constraints on the prediction task.

Material

The set of strings that can be generated from the grammar is finite for a given length. For lengths 3 to 8, this amounts to 43 grammatical

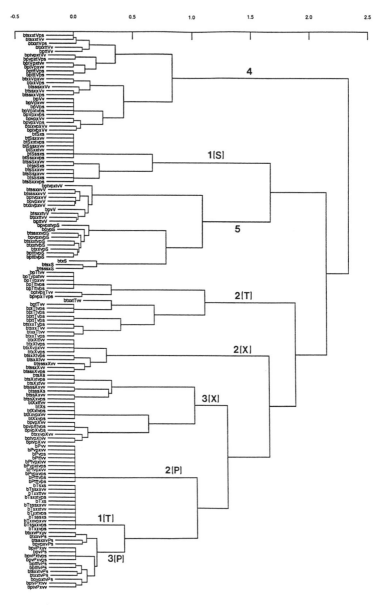

Figure 2.9
Hierarchical cluster analysis of the hidden unit activation patterns after 60,000 presentations of strings generated at random from the Reber grammar (15 hidden units).

strings. The 21 strings shown in Figure 2.10 were selected and served as training set. The remaining 22 strings can be used to test generalization. The selected set of strings has a number of interesting properties with regard to exploring the network's performance on subtle temporal contingencies:

- As in the previous task, identical letters occur at different points in each string and lead to different predictions about the identity of the successor. No stable prediction is therefore associated with any particular letter, and it is thus necessary to encode the position, or the node of the grammar.
- In this limited training set, length places additional constraints on the encoding because the possible predictions associated with a particular node in the grammar depend on the length of the sequence. The set of possible letters that follow a particular node depends on how many letters have already been presented. For example, following the sequence 'TXX', both 'T' and 'V' are legal successors. However, following the sequence 'TXXVPX', 'X' is the sixth letter and only 'V' would be a legal successor. This information must therefore also be somehow represented during processing.
- Subpatterns occurring in the strings are not all associated with their possible successors equally often. Accurate predictions therefore require that information about the identity of the letters that have already been presented be maintained in the system; that is, the system must be sensitive to the frequency distribution of subpatterns in the training set. This amounts to encoding the full path that has been traversed in the grammar.

These features of the limited training set obviously make the prediction task much more complex than in the previous simulation. One way to measure this additional complexity consists of rewriting the finite-state grammar augmented by the length constraints into a distinct but

TSXS	TXS	TSSSXS
TSSXXVV	TSSSXXVV	TXXVPXVV
TXXTTVV	TSXXTVV	TSSXXVPS
TSXXTVPS	TXXTVPS	TXXVPS
PVV	PTTVV	PTVPXVV
PVPXVV	PTVPXTVV	PVPXVPS
PTVPS	PVPXTVPS	PTTTVPS

Figure 2.10
The 21 grammatical strings of length 3 to 8.

equivalent grammar in which additional states are used to represent the length constraints. This analysis revealed that this equivalent grammar contains 64 different states—considerably more than the original 6. This problem is therefore obviously much more difficult than the first one.

Network Architecture
The same general network architecture was used for this set of simulations. The number of hidden units was arbitrarily set to 15. Note that this is more than is actually required to encode the 64 states of the length-constrained grammar (6 hidden units with binary encoding would suffice).

Performance
The network was trained on the 21 different sequences (a total of 130 patterns) until the total sum squared error (*tss*) reached a plateau with no further improvements. This point was reached after 2,000 epochs and *tss* was 50. Note that *tss* cannot be driven much below this value, since most partial sequences of letters are compatible with two different successors. At this point, the network correctly predicts the possible successors of each letter and distinguishes between different occurrences of the same letter—as it did in the simulation described previously. However, the network's performance makes it obvious that many additional constraints specific to the limited training set have been encoded. Figure 2.11a shows that the network expects a 'T' or a 'V' after a first presentation of the second 'X' in the grammar.

Contrast these predictions with those illustrated in Figure 2.11b, which shows the state of the network after a *second* presentation of the second 'X': Although the same node in the grammar has been reached, and 'T' and 'V' are again possible alternatives, the network now predicts only 'V'.

Thus, the network has successfully learned that an 'X' occurring late in the sequence is never followed by a 'T'—a fact that derives directly from the maximum length constraint of eight letters.

It could be argued that the network simply learned that when 'X' is preceded by 'P', it cannot be followed by 'T', and thus relies only on the preceding letter to make that distinction. However, the story is more complicated than this.

In the following two cases, the network is presented with the first occurrence of the letter 'V'. In the first case, 'V' is preceded by the

```
String     b  t  x  X  v  p  x  v  v

           B    T    S    P    X    V    E
Output     00   49   00   00   00   50   00
Hidden     27   89   02   16   99   43   01   06   04   18   99   81   95   18   01
Context    01   18   00   41   95   01   60   59   05   06   84   99   19   05   00
           B    T    S    P    X    V    E
Input      00   00   00   00   100  00   00
```

(a)


```
String     b  t  x  x  v  p  X  v  v

           B    T    S    P    X    V    E
Output     00   03   00   00   00   95   00
Hidden     00   85   03   85   31   00   72   19   31   03   93   99   61   05   00
Context    01   07   05   90   93   04   00   10   71   40   99   16   90   05   82
           B    T    S    P    X    V    E
Input      00   00   00   00   100  00   00
```

(b)

Figure 2.11
(a) State of the network after a first presentation of the second 'X'. (b) State of the network after a second presentation of the second 'X'.

sequence 'tssxx', while in the second case, it is preceded by 'tsssxx'. The difference of a single 'S' in the sequence—which occurred five presentations earlier—results in markedly different predictions when 'V' is presented (Figures 2.12a and b). The difference in predictions can be traced again to the length constraint imposed on the strings in the limited training set. In the second case, the string spans a total of seven letters when 'V' is presented, and the only alternative compatible with the length constraint is a second 'V' and the end of the string. This is not true in the first case, in which both 'VV' and 'VPS' are possible endings.

Thus, it seems that the representation developed on the context units encodes more than the immediate context—the pattern of activation could include a full representation of the path traversed so far. Alternatively, it could be hypothesized that the context units encode only the preceding letter and a counter of how many letters have been presented.

```
String    b t s s x x V v
```

	B	T	S	P	X	V	E							
Output	00	00	00	54	00	48	00							
Hidden	44	98	30	84	99	82	00	47	00	09	41	98	13	02	00
Context	89	90	01	01	99	70	01	03	02	10	99	95	85	21	00
	B	T	S	P	X	V	E							
Input	00	00	00	00	00	100	00							

(a)

```
String    b t s s s x x V v
```

	B	T	S	P	X	V	E							
Output	00	00	00	02	00	97	00							
Hidden	56	99	48	93	99	85	00	22	00	10	77	97	30	03	00
Context	54	67	01	04	99	59	07	09	01	06	98	97	72	16	00
	B	T	S	P	X	V	E							
Input	00	00	00	00	00	100	00							

(b)

Figure 2.12
Two presentations of the first 'V', with slightly different paths.

In order to understand better the kind of representations that encode sequential context, we performed a cluster analysis on all the hidden unit patterns evoked by each letter in each sequence. The resulting analysis is shown in Figure 2.13. We labeled the arcs according to the letter being presented (the *current letter*) and its position in the Reber grammar. Thus, 'V_1' refers to the first 'V' in the grammar and 'V_2' to the second 'V', which immediately precedes the end of the string. *Early* and *late* refer to whether the letter occurred early or late in the sequence (for example in 'PT . . .' 'T_2' occurs early; in 'PVPXT . . .' it occurs late). Finally, in the left margin we indicated what predictions the corresponding patterns yield on the output layer (e.g., the hidden unit pattern generated by 'B' predicts 'T' or 'P').

From the figure, it can be seen that the patterns are grouped according to three distinct principles: (1) according to similar predictions, (2) according to similar letters presented on the input units, and (3) according to similar paths. These factors do not necessarily overlap since the occurrence of the same letter several times in a sequence usually implies

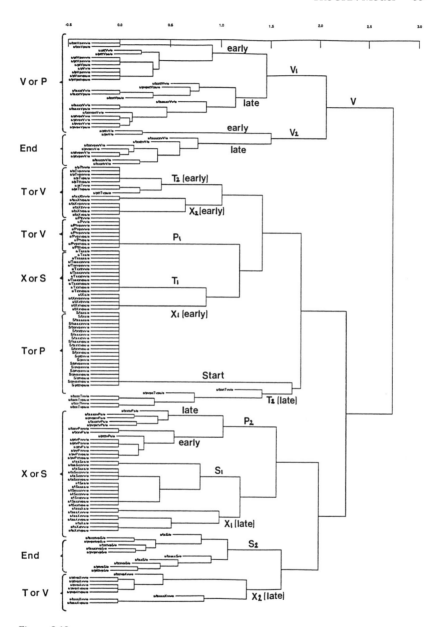

Figure 2.13
Hierarchical cluster analysis of the hidden unit activation patterns after 2,000 epochs of training on the set of 21 strings (15 hidden units).

different predictions and since similar paths also lead to different predictions depending on the current letter.

For example, the top cluster in the figure corresponds to all occurrences of the letter 'V' and is further divided between 'V_1' and 'V_2'. The 'V_1' cluster is itself further divided between groups where 'V_1' occurs early in the sequence (e.g., 'pV . . .') and groups where it occurs later (e.g., 'tssxxV . . .' and 'pvpxV . . .'). Note that the division according to the path does not necessarily correspond to different predictions. For example, 'V_2' always predicts 'End' and always with maximum certainty. Nevertheless, sequences up to 'V_2' are divided according to the path traversed.

Without going into the details of the organization of the remaining clusters, it can be seen that they are predominantly grouped according to the predictions associated with the corresponding portion of the sequence and then further divided according to the path traversed up to that point. For example, 'T_2', 'X_2', and 'P_1' all predict 'T' or 'V', 'T_1' and 'X_1' both predict 'X' or 'S', and so on.

Overall, the hidden unit patterns developed by the network reflect two influences: a "top-down" pressure to produce the correct output, and a "bottom-up" pressure from the successive letters in the path, which modifies the activation pattern independently of the output to be generated.

The top-down force derives directly from the back-propagation learning rule. Similar patterns on the output units tend to be associated with similar patterns on the hidden units. Thus, when two different letters yield the same prediction (e.g., 'T_1' and 'X_1'), they tend to produce similar hidden layer patterns. The bottom-up force comes from the fact that, nevertheless, each letter presented with a particular context can produce a characteristic mark or *shading* on the hidden unit pattern (see Pollack, 1989, for further discussion of error-driven and recurrence-driven influences on the development of hidden unit patterns in recurrent networks). The hidden unit patterns are not truly an "encoding" of the input, as is often suggested, but rather an encoding of the *association* between a particular input and the relevant prediction. It really reflects an influence from both sides.

Finally, it is worth noting that the very specific internal representations acquired by the network are nonetheless sufficiently abstract to ensure good generalization. We tested the network on the remaining untrained 22 strings of length 3 to 8 that can be generated by the grammar. Over the 165 predictions of successors in these strings, the network made an incorrect prediction (activation of an incorrect successor > 0.05) in only 10 cases, and it failed to predict one of two continuations consistent with the grammar and length constraints in 10 other cases.

Finite-State Automata and Graded State Machines
In previous sections, we have examined how the SRN encodes and uses information about meaningful subsequences of events, giving it the capacity to yield different outputs according to some specific traversed path or to the length of strings. However, the network does not use a separate and explicit representation for nonlocal properties of the strings such as length. It only learns to associate different predictions with a subset of states: those that are associated with a more restricted choice of successors. Again there are no stacks or registers, and each different prediction is associated with a specific state on the context units. In that sense, the recurrent network that has learned to master this task still behaves like a finite-state machine, although the training set involves nonlocal constraints that could only be encoded in a very cumbersome way in a finite-state *grammar*.

Finite-state automata are usually not thought of as capable of encoding nonlocal information such as length of a sequence. Yet finite-state machines have in principle the same computational power as a Turing machine with a finite tape, and they can be designed to respond adequately to nonlocal constraints. Recursive or augmented transition networks and other Turing-equivalent automata are preferable to finite-state machines because they spare memory and are modular—and therefore easier to design and modify. However, the finite-state machines that the recurrent network seems to implement have properties that set them apart from their traditional counterparts:

- At least in the simple cases we have examined so far, and for tasks with an appropriate structure, recurrent networks develop their own state transition diagram, sparing the designer this burden.
- The large amount of memory required to develop different representations for every state needed is provided by the representational power of hidden layer patterns. For example, 15 hidden units with four possible values—e.g., 0, .25, .75, 1—can support more than one billion different patterns (4^{15} = 1,073,741,824).
- The network implementation remains capable of performing similarity-based processing, making it somewhat noise-tolerant

(the machine does not "jam" if it encounters an undefined state transition and it can recover as the sequence of inputs continues), and it remains able to generalize to sequences that were not part of the training set.

Because of its inherent ability to use *graded* rather than discrete states, the SRN is definitely not a finite-state machine of the usual kind. As we mentioned above, we have come to consider it as an exemplar of a new class of automata that we call *graded state machines*. In the next section, we examine how the SRN comes to develop appropriate internal representations of the temporal context.

Learning

We have seen that the SRN develops and learns to use compact and effective representations of the sequences presented. These representations are sufficient to disambiguate identical cues in the presence of context, to code for length constraints, and to react appropriately to atypical cases[5]. How are these representations discovered?

As we noted earlier, in an SRN, the hidden layer is presented with information about the current letter, but also—on the context layer—with an encoding of the relevant features of the previous letter. Thus, a given hidden layer pattern can come to encode information about the relevant features of two consecutive letters. When this pattern is fed back on the context layer, the new pattern of activation over the hidden units can come to encode information about three consecutive letters, and so on. In this manner, the context layer patterns can allow the network to maintain prediction-relevant features of an entire sequence.

As discussed elsewhere in more detail (Servan-Schreiber, Cleeremans, & McClelland, 1988, 1989), learning progresses through three qualitatively different phases. During a first phase, the network tends to ignore the context information. This is a direct consequence of the fact that the patterns of activation on the hidden layer—and hence the context layer—are continuously changing from one epoch to the next as the weights from the input units (the letters) to the hidden layer are modified. Consequently, adjustments made to the weights from the context layer to the hidden layer are inconsistent from epoch to epoch and cancel each other. In contrast, the network is able to pick up the stable association between each *letter* and all its possible successors. For example, after only 100 epochs of training, the response pattern generated by 'S_1' and the corresponding output are almost identical with the pattern generated by 'S$_2$', as Figures 2.14a and 2.14b demonstrate. At the end of this phase, the network thus predicts all the successors of each letter in the grammar, independently of the *arc* to which each letter corresponds.

In a second phase, patterns copied on the context layer are now represented by a unique code designating which letter preceded the current letter, and the network can exploit this stability of the context information to start distinguishing between different occurrences of the same letter—different arcs in the grammar. Thus, to continue with the above example, the response elicited by the presentation of an 'S$_1$' would progressively become different from that elicited by an 'S$_2$'.

Finally, in a third phase, small differences in the context information that reflect the occurrence of previous elements can be used to differentiate position-dependent predictions resulting from length constraints.

```
Epoch    100
String   b S s x x v p s

          B    T    S    P    X    V    E
Output   00   00   36   00   33   16   17
Hidden   45   24   47   26   36   23   55   22   22   26   22   23   30   30   33
Context  44   22   56   21   36   22   64   16   13   23   20   16   25   21   40
          B    T    S    P    X    V    E
Input    00   00  100   00   00   00   00
```

(a)

```
Epoch    100
String   b s s x x v p S

          B    T    S    P    X    V    E
Output   00   00   37   00   33   16   17
Hidden   45   24   47   25   36   23   56   22   21   25   21   22   29   30   32
Context  42   29   53   24   32   27   61   25   16   33   25   23   28   27   41
          B    T    S    P    X    V    E
Input    00   00  100   00   00   00   00
```

(b)

Figure 2.14
(a) State of the network after presentation of the first 'S' in a sequence, after 100 epochs of training. (b) State of the network after presentation of the second 'S' in a sequence, after 100 epochs of training.

For example, the network learns to differentiate between 'tssxxV', which predicts either 'P' or 'V', and 'tsssxxV', which predicts only 'V', although both occurrences of 'V' correspond to the same arc in the grammar. In order to make this distinction, the pattern of activation on the context layer must be a representation of the entire path rather than simply an encoding of the previous letter.

Naturally, these three phases do not reflect sharp changes in the network's behavior over training. Rather, they are simply particular points in what is essentially a continuous process, during which the network progressively encodes increasing amounts of temporal context information to refine its predictions. It is possible to analyze this smooth progression toward better predictions by noting that these predictions converge toward the optimal conditional probabilities of observing a particular successor to the sequence presented up to that point. Ultimately, given sufficient training, the SRN's responses *would become* these optimal conditional probabilities (that is, the minima in the error function are located at those points in weight space where the activations equal the optimal conditional probabilities). This observation provides a tool for analyzing how the predictions change over time. Indeed, the conditional probability of observing a particular letter at any point in a sequence of inputs varies according to the number of preceding elements that have been encoded. For instance, since all letters occur twice in the grammar, a system basing its predictions on only the current element of the sequence will predict all the successors of the current letter, independently of the arc to which that element corresponds. If two elements of the sequence are encoded, the uncertainty about the next event is much reduced, since in many cases, subsequences of two letters are unique and thus provide an unambiguous cue to its possible successors. In some other cases, subtle dependencies such as those resulting from length constraints require as many as six elements of temporal context to be optimally predictable.

Thus, by generating a large number of strings that have exactly the same statistical properties as those used during training, it is possible to estimate the conditional probabilities of observing each letter as the successor to each possible path of a given length. The *average* conditional probability (ACP) of observing a particular letter at every node of the grammar, after a given amount of temporal context (i.e., over all paths of a given length) can then be easily obtained by weighting each individual term by its frequency. This analysis can be conducted for paths of any length, thus yielding a set of ACPs for each order considered[6]. Each set of ACPs can then be used as the predictor variable in a regression analysis against the network's responses, averaged in a similar way. We would expect the ACPs based on short paths to be better predictors of the SRN's behavior early in training, and the ACPs based on longer paths to be better predictors of the SRN's behavior late in training, thus revealing the fact that, during training, the network learns to base its predictions on increasingly larger amounts of temporal context.

An SRN with 15 hidden units was trained on the 43 strings of length 3 to 8 from the Reber grammar, in exactly the same conditions as described earlier. The network was trained for 1,000 epochs, and its performance was tested once before training, and every 50 epochs thereafter, for a total of 21 tests. Each test consisted of (1) freezing the connections, (2) presenting the network with the entire set of strings (a total of 329 patterns) once, and (3) recording its response to each individual input pattern. Next, the average activation of each response unit (i.e., each letter in the grammar) given six elements of temporal context was computed (i.e., after all paths of length 6 that are followed by that letter).

In a separate analysis, seven sets of ACPs (from order 0 to order 6) were estimated in the manner described above. Each of these seven sets of ACPs was then used as the predictor variable in a regression analysis on each set of average activations produced by the network. These data are represented in Figure 2.15. Each point represents the percentage of variance explained in the network's behavior on a particular test by the ACPs of a particular order. Points corresponding to the same set of ACPs are linked together, for a total of seven curves, each corresponding to the ACPs of a particular order.

What the figure reveals is that the network's responses are approximating the conditional probabilities of increasingly higher orders. Thus, before training, the performance of the network is best explained by the 0th-order ACPs (i.e., the frequency of each letter in the training set). This is because before training, the activations of the response units tend to be almost uniform, as do the 0th order ACPs. In the next two tests (i.e., at Epoch 50 and Epoch 100), the network's performance is best explained by the first-order ACPs. In other words, the network's predictions during these two tests were essentially based on paths of length 1. This point in training corresponds to the first phase of learning identified earlier, during which the network's responses do not distinguish between different occurrences of the same letter.

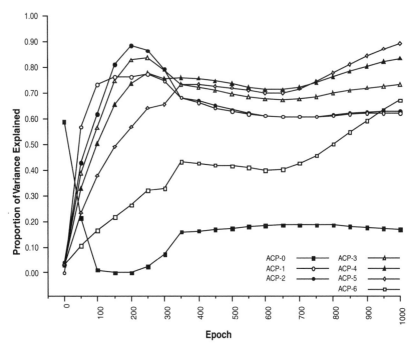

Figure 2.15
A graphic representation of the percentage of variance in the network's performance
explained by average conditional probabilities of increasing order (from 0 to 6). Each
point represents the r^2 of a regression analysis using a particular set of average
conditional probabilities as the predictor variable, and average activations produced by
the network at a particular point in training as the dependent variable.

Soon, however, the network's performance comes to be better explained by ACPs of higher orders. One can see the curves corresponding to the ACPs of order 2 and order 3 progressively take over, thus
indicating that the network is essentially basing its predictions on paths
of length 2, then of length 3. At this point, the network has entered the
second phase of learning, during which it now distinguishes between
different occurrences of the same letter. Later in training, the network's
behavior can be seen to be better captured by ACPs based on even
longer paths, first of length 4, and finally of length 5. Note that the
network remains at that stage for a much longer time than for shorter
ACPs. This reflects the fact that encoding longer paths is more difficult.
At this point, the network has started to become sensitive to subtler
dependencies such as length constraints, which require an encoding of
the full path traversed so far. Finally, the curve corresponding to the

ACPs of order 6 can be seen to rise steadily toward increasingly better fits, only to be achieved considerably later in training.

It is worth noting that there is a large amount of overlap between the percentages of variance explained by the different sets of ACPs. This is not surprising, since most of the sets of ACPs are partially correlated with each other. Even so, we see the successive correspondence to longer and longer temporal contingencies with more and more training.

In all the learning problems examined so far, contingencies between elements of the sequence were relevant at each processing step. In the next section, we propose a detailed analysis of the constraints guiding the learning of more complex contingencies, for which information about distant elements of the sequence has to be maintained for several processing steps before it becomes useful.

Encoding Nonlocal Context

Processing Loops
Consider the general problem of learning two arbitrary sequences of the same length and ending by two different letters. Under what conditions will the network be able to make a correct prediction about the nature of the last letter when presented with the penultimate letter? Obviously, the *necessary and sufficient condition* is that the internal representations associated with the penultimate letter are different (indeed, the hidden units patterns *must* be different if different outputs are to be generated). Let us consider several different prototypical cases and verify whether this condition holds:

PABC X   and   PABC V   (1)

PABC X   and   TDEF V   (2)

Clearly, Problem 1 is impossible: since the two sequences are identical up to the last letter, there is simply no way for the network to make a different prediction when presented with the penultimate letter ('C' in Problem 1). The internal representations induced by the successive elements of the sequences will be strictly identical in both cases. Problem 2, on the other hand, is trivial, since the last letter is contingent on the penultimate letter ('X' is contingent on 'C'; 'V' on 'F'). There is no need here to keep information available for several processing steps, and the different contexts set by the penultimate letters are sufficient to ensure that different predictions can be made for the last letter. Now consider Problem 3.

PSSS P   and   TSSS T   (3)

As can be seen, the presence of a final 'T' is contingent on the presence of an initial 'T', and a final 'P' on the presence of an initial 'P'. The shared 'S's do not supply any relevant information for disambiguating the last letter. Moreover, the predictions the network is required to make in the course of processing are identical in both sequences up to the last letter.

Obviously, the only way for the network to solve this problem is to develop *different internal representations* for *every* letter in the two sequences. Consider the fact that the network is required to make different predictions when presented with the last 'S'. As stated earlier, this will only be possible if the input presented at the penultimate time step produces different internal representations in the two sequences. However, this necessary difference cannot be due to the last 'S' itself, since it is presented in both sequences. Rather, the only way for different internal representations to arise when the last 'S' is presented is when the context pool holds different patterns of activation. Since the context pool holds a copy of the internal representations of the previous step, these representations must themselves be different. Recursively, we can apply the same reasoning up to the first letter. The network must therefore develop a different representation for all the letters in the sequence. Are initial different letters a sufficient condition to ensure that each letter in the sequences will be associated with different internal representations? The answer is twofold.

First, note that developing a different internal representation for each letter (including the different instances of the letter 'S') is provided *automatically* by the recurrent nature of the architecture, even without any training. Successive presentations of identical elements to a recurrent network generate different internal representations at each step because the context pool holds different patterns of activity at each step. In Problem 3, the first letters will generate different internal representations. On the following step, these patterns of activity will be fed back to the network and induce different internal representations again. This process will repeat itself up to the last 'S', and the network will therefore find itself in a state in which it is potentially able to correctly predict the last letter of the two sequences of Problem 3. Now, there is an important caveat to this observation. Another fundamental property of recurrent networks (and of finite-state automata as well; see Minsky, 1967) is convergence toward an attractor state when a long sequence of identical elements is presented. Even though, initially, different patterns of activation are produced on the hidden layer for each 'S' in a sequence of 'S's, eventually the network converges toward a stable state in which every new presentation of the same input produces the same pattern of activation on the hidden layer. The number of iterations required for the network to converge depends on the number of hidden units. With more degrees of freedom, it takes more iterations for the network to settle. Thus, increasing the number of hidden units provides the network with an increased *architectural* capacity of maintaining differences in its internal representations when the input elements are identical.[7]

Second, consider the way back-propagation interacts with this natural process of maintaining information about the first letter. In Problem 3, the predictions in each sequence are identical up to the last letter. As similar outputs are required on each time step, the weight adjustment procedure pushes the network into developing *identical* internal representations at each time step and for the two sequences—exactly the opposite of what is required. This "homogenizing" process can strongly hinder learning, as will be illustrated below. Note that if the network were trained to predict a successor only at the end of a sequence, its ability to master such sequences might be improved (see Jordan & Rumelhart, in press). This is a matter for further research.

From the above reasoning, we can infer that optimal learning conditions exist when both contexts and predictions are different in each sequence. If the sequences share identical sequences of predictions—as in Problem 3—the process of maintaining the differences between the internal representations generated by an (initial) letter can be disrupted by back-propagation itself. The very process of learning to predict correctly the intermediate shared elements of the sequence can even cause the total error to rise sharply in some cases after an initial decrease. Indeed, the more training the network gets on these intermediate elements, the more likely it is that their internal representations will become identical, thereby completely eliminating initial slight differences that could potentially be used to disambiguate the last element. Further training can only worsen this situation[8]. Note that in this sense back-propagation in the recurrent network is not guaranteed to implement gradient descent. Presumably, the ability of the network to resist the "homogenization" induced by the learning algorithm will depend on its representational power—the number of hidden units available for processing. With more hidden units, there is also less pressure on each unit to take on specified activation levels. Small but crucial differences in activation levels will therefore be allowed to survive at each time step, until they finally become useful at the penultimate step.

To illustrate this point, a network with 15 hidden units was trained on the two sequences of Problem 3. The network is able to solve this problem very accurately after approximately 10,000 epochs of training on the two patterns. Learning proceeds smoothly until a very long plateau in the error is reached. This plateau corresponds to a learning phase during which the weights are adjusted so that the network can take advantage of the small differences that remain in the representations induced by the last 'S' in the two strings in order to make accurate predictions about the identity of the last letter. These slight differences are of course due to the different context generated after presentation of the first letter of the string.

To understand further the relation between network size and problem size, four different networks (with 7, 15, 30, or 120 hidden units) were trained on each of four different versions of Problem 3 (with 2, 4, 6, or 12 intermediate elements). As predicted, learning was faster when the number of hidden units was larger. There was an interaction between the size of the network and the size of the problem: Adding more hidden units had little impact when the problem was small, but a much larger impact for larger numbers of intervening 'S's. We also observed that the relation between the size of the problem and the number of epochs to reach a learning criterion was exponential for all network sizes. These results suggest that for relatively short embedded sequences of identical letters, the difficulties encountered by the SRN can be alleviated by increasing the number of hidden units. However, beyond a certain range, maintaining different representations across the embedded sequence becomes exponentially difficult (see also Allen, 1988, 1990, for a discussion of how recurrent networks hold information across embedded sequences).

An altogether different approach to the question can also be taken. In the next section, we argue that some sequential problems may be less difficult than Problem 3. More precisely, we will show how very slight adjustments to the predictions the network is required to make in otherwise identical sequences can greatly enhance performance.

Spanning Embedded Sequences
The previous example is in several respects a limited test of the network's ability to preserve information during processing of an embedded sequence. Relevant information for making a prediction about the nature of the last letter is at a constant distance across all patterns, and elements inside the embedded sequence are all identical. To evaluate the performance of the SRN on a task that is more closely related to

natural language situations, we tested its ability to maintain information about long-distance dependencies on strings generated by the grammar shown in Figure 2.16. If the first letter encountered in the string is a 'T', the last letter of the string is also a 'T'. Conversely, if the first letter is a 'P', the last letter is also a 'P'. In between these matching letters, we interposed almost the same finite-state grammar that we had been using in previous experiments (Reber's) to play the role of an embedded sentence. We modified Reber's grammar by eliminating the 'S' loop and the 'T' loop in order to shorten the average length of strings.

In a first experiment, we trained the network on strings generated from the finite-state grammar with the same probabilities attached to corresponding arcs in the bottom and top versions of Reber's grammar. This version was called the *symmetrical grammar*: Contingencies inside the subgrammar are the same independently of the first letter of the string, and all arcs had a probability of 0.5. The average length of strings was 6.5 letters (*SD* = 2.1).

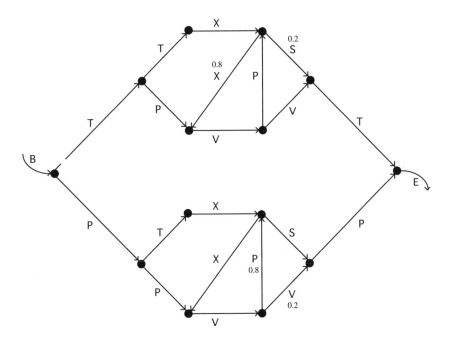

Figure 2.16
A complex finite-state grammar involving an embedded clause. The last letter is contingent on the first one, and the intermediate structure is shared by the two branches of the grammar. Some arcs in the asymmetrical version have different transitional probabilities in the top and bottom substructure, as explained in the text.

After training, the performance of the network was evaluated in the following way: 20,000 strings generated from the symmetrical grammar were presented, and for each string we looked at the relative activation of the predictions of 'T' and 'P' upon exit from the subgrammar. If the Luce ratio for the prediction witn the highest activation was below 0.6, the trial was treated as a "miss" (i.e., failure to predict one or the other distinctively).[9] If the Luce ratio was greater than or equal to 0.6 and the network predicted the correct alternative, a "hit" was recorded. If the incorrect alternative was predicted, the trial was treated as an "error." Following training on 900,000 exemplars, performance consisted of 75% hits, 6.3% errors, and 18.7% misses. Performance was best for shorter embeddings (i.e., three to four letters) and deteriorated as the length of the embedding increased (see Figure 2.17).

However, the fact that contingencies inside the embedded sequences are similar for both subgrammars greatly raises the difficulty of the task and does not necessarily reflect the nature of natural language. Consider a problem of number agreement illustrated by the following two sentences:

The **dog** *that chased the cat* **is** very playful.
The **dogs** *that chased the cat* **are** very playful.

We would contend that expectations about concepts and words forthcoming in the embedded sentence are different for the singular and plural forms. For example, the embedded clauses require different agreement morphemes—*chases* vs. *chase*—when the clause is in the present tense, and so on. Furthermore, even after the same word has

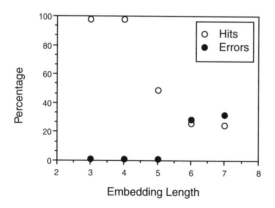

Figure 2.17
Percentage of hits and errors as a function of embedding length. All the cases with seven or more letters in the embedding were grouped together.

been encountered in both cases (e.g., *chased*), expectations about possible successors for that word would remain different (e.g., a single dog and a pack of dogs are likely to be chasing different things). As we have shown, if such differences in predictions do exist, the network is more likely to maintain information relevant to nonlocal context since that information is relevant at several intermediate steps.

To illustrate this point, in a second experiment, the same network—with 15 hidden units—was trained on a variant of the grammar shown in Figure 2.16. In this *asymmetrical* version, the second X arc had a 0.8 probability of being selected during training, whereas in the bottom subgrammar, the second P arc had a probability of 0.8 of being selected. Arcs stemming from all other nodes had the same probability attached to them in both subgrammars. The mean length of strings generated from this asymmetrical version was 5.8 letters (SD = 1.3).

Following training on the asymmetrical version of the grammar, the network was tested with strings generated from the symmetrical version. Its performance level rose to 100% hits. It is important to note that the performance of this network cannot be attributed to a difference in statistical properties of the test strings between the top and bottom subgrammars—such as the difference present during training—since the testing set came from the *symmetrical* grammar. Therefore, this experiment demonstrates that the network is better able to preserve information about the predecessor of the embedded sequence across identical embeddings as long as the ensemble of *potential* pathways is differentiated during training. Furthermore, differences in potential pathways may be only statistical and, even then, rather small. We would expect even greater improvements in performance if the two subgrammars included a set of nonoverlapping sequences in addition to a set of sequences that are identical in both.

It is interesting to compare the behavior of the SRN on this embedding task with the corresponding finite-state automaton that could process the same strings. The finite-state automaton would have the structure of Figure 2.16. It would only be able to process the strings successfully by having two distinct copies of all the states between the initial letter in the string and the final letter. One copy is used after an initial 'P', the other is used after an initial 'T'. This is inefficient since the embedded material is the same in both cases. To capture this similarity in a simple and elegant way, it is necessary to use a more powerful machine such as a recursive transition network. In this case, the embedding is treated as a subroutine that can be "called" from different places. A return from the call ensures that the grammar can correctly predict whether a 'T' or a 'P' will follow. This ability to handle long-distance dependencies without duplication of the representation of intervening material lies at the heart of the arguments that have led to the use of recursive formalisms to represent linguistic knowledge.

But the graded characteristics of the SRN allow the processing of embedded material as well as of the material that comes after the embedding, without duplicating the representation of intervening material, and without actually making a subroutine call. The states of the SRN can be used *simultaneously* to indicate where the network is inside the embedding and to indicate the history of processing prior to the embedding. The identity of the initial letter simply *shades* the representation of states inside the embedding, so that corresponding nodes have similar representations and are processed using overlapping portions of the knowledge encoded in the connection weights. Yet the shading that the initial letter provides allows the network to carry information about the early part of the string through the embedding, thereby allowing the network to exploit long-distance dependencies. This property of the internal representations used by the SRN is illustrated in Figure 2.18. We recorded some patterns of activation over the hidden units following the presentation of each letter inside the embeddings. The first letter of the string label in the figure ('t' or 'p') indicates whether the string corresponds to the upper or lower subgrammar. The figure shows that the patterns of activation generated by identical embeddings in the two different subgrammars are more similar to each other (e.g., 'tpvP' and 'ppvP') than to patterns of activation generated by different embeddings in the same subgrammar (e.g., 'tpvP' and 'tpV'). This indicates that the network is sensitive to the similarity of the corresponding nodes in each subgrammar, while retaining information about what preceded entry into the subgrammar.

Discussion

In this study, we attempted to understand better how the SRN could learn to represent and use contextual information when presented with structured sequences of inputs. Following the first experiment, we concluded that copying the state of activation on the hidden layer at the previous time step provided the network with the basic equipment of a finite-state machine. When the set of exemplars that the network is trained on comes from a finite-state grammar, the network can be

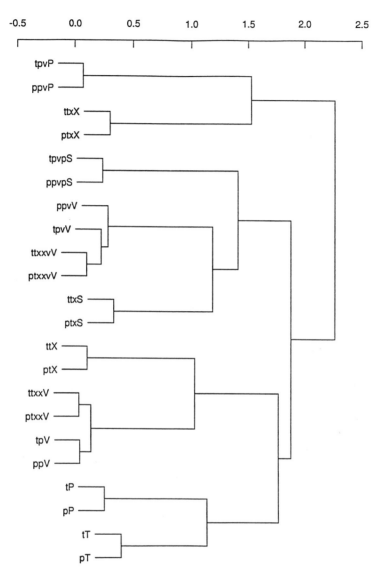

Figure 2.18
Hierarchical cluster analysis of hidden unit activation patterns following the presentation of identical sequences in each of the two subgrammars. Labels starting with the
letter 't' come from the top subgrammar; labels starting with the letter 'p' come from the
bottom sub-grammar.

used as a recognizer with respect to that grammar. When the representational resources are severely constrained, internal representations actually converge on the nodes of the grammar. Interestingly, though, this representational convergence is not a necessary condition for functional convergence: networks with more than enough structure to handle the prediction task sometimes represent the same node of the grammar using two quite different patterns, corresponding to different paths into the same node. This divergence of representations does not upset the network's ability to serve as a recognizer for well-formed sequences derived from the grammar.

We also showed that the mere presence of recurrent connections pushed the network to develop hidden layer patterns that capture information about sequences of inputs, even in the absence of training. The second experiment showed that back-propagation can be used to take advantage of this natural tendency when information about the path traversed is relevant to the task at hand. This was illustrated with predictions that were specific to particular subsequences in the training set or that took into account constraints on the length of sequences. Encoding of sequential structure depends on the fact that back-propagation causes hidden layers to encode task-relevant information. In the SRN, internal representations encode not only the prior event but also relevant aspects of the representation that was constructed in predicting the prior event from its predecessor. When fed back as input, these representations provide information that allows the network to maintain prediction-relevant features of an entire sequence. We illustrated this with cluster analyses of the hidden layer patterns.

Our description of the stages of learning suggested that the network initially learns to distinguish between events independently of the temporal context (e.g., simply distinguish between different letters). The information contained in the context layer is ignored at this point. At the end of this stage, each event is associated with a specific pattern on the hidden layer that identifies it for the following event. In the next phase, thanks to this new information, different occurrences of the same event (e.g., two occurrences of the same letter) are distinguished on the basis of immediately preceding events—the simplest form of a time tag. This stage corresponds to the recognition of the different "arcs" in the particular finite-state grammar used in the experiments. Finally, as the representation of each event progressively acquires a time tag, subsequences of events come to yield characteristic hidden layer patterns that can form the basis of further discriminations (e.g., between an early and a late 'T$_2$' in the Reber grammar). In this manner, and under appropriate conditions, the hidden unit patterns achieve an encoding of the entire sequence of events presented.

We do not mean to suggest that SRNs can learn to recognize *any* finite-state language. Indeed, we were able to predict two conditions under which performance of the SRN will deteriorate: (1) when different sequences may contain identical embedded sequences involving *exactly* the same predictions; and (2) when the number of hidden units is restricted and cannot support redundant representations of similar predictions, so that identical predictions following different events tend to be associated with very similar hidden unit patterns, thereby erasing information about the initial path. We also noted that when recurrent connections are added to a three-layer feedforward network, back-propagation is no longer guaranteed to perform gradient descent in the error space. Additional training, by improving performance on shared components of otherwise differing sequences, can eliminate information necessary to "span" an embedded sequence and result in a sudden rise in the total error. It follows from these limitations that the SRN could not be expected to learn sequences with a moderately complex recursive structure—such as context-free grammars—if contingencies inside the embedded structures do not depend on relevant information preceding the embeddings.

What is the relevance of this work with regard to language processing? The ability to exploit long-distance dependencies is an inherent aspect of human language-processing capabilities, and it lies at the heart of the general belief that a recursive computational machine is necessary for processing natural language. The experiments we have carried out with SRNs suggest another possibility: It may be that long-distance dependencies can be processed by machines that are simpler than fully recursive machines, as long as they make use of *graded* state information. This is particularly true if the probability structure of the grammar defining the material to be learned reflects—even very slightly—the information that needs to be maintained. As we noted previously, natural linguistic stimuli may show this property. Of course, true natural language is far more complex than the simple strings that can be generated by the machine shown in Figure 2.17, so we cannot claim to have shown that graded state machines will be able to process all aspects of natural language. However, our experiments indicate already that they are more powerful in interesting ways than traditional finite-state automata (see also the work of Allen and Riecksen, 1989;

Elman, in press; and Pollack, in press). Certainly, the SRN should be seen as a new entry into the taxonomy of computational machines. Whether the SRN—or rather some other instance of the broader class of graded state machines of which the SRN is one of the simplest—will ultimately turn out to prove sufficient for natural language processing remains to be explored by further research. As a very first step in that direction, the next chapter is an account of how the SRN may be applied to simulate human performance in situations that are considerably simpler, but that share some basic features with language processing: sequence-learning situations.

Chapter 3
Sequence Learning as a Paradigm for Studying Implicit Learning

Sequence-learning may be the best paradigm in which to study implicit learning processes, for the following reasons. First, the task demands are low in the sense that it is not necessary for subjects to encode relevant temporal information to perform according to task instructions. Second, the structure embedded in the material is of very low salience, since most of the information relevant to optimizing performance on the task is present in the context rather than in the manifest stimulus. As discussed in chapter 1, both factors would tend to lower subjects' attempts at using explicit learning strategies in typical implicit learning situations. A further feature of the specific kind of sequence-learning situation (choice reaction time) explored here is that it is fast-paced. Therefore, subjects have little time to develop explicit strategies or to ponder about the regularities present in the material. However, most sequence-learning situations explored until recently have used relatively simple material, such as repeating sequences only 5 to 10 elements in length. My work was aimed at establishing whether results obtained in these simple sequence-learning situations would transfer to a task involving more complex and noisy material. A second, and perhaps more important, goal was to develop a detailed information-processing model of sequence-learning that would be successful in accounting for subjects' behavior and in providing a plausible instantiation of the general principles of implicit learning outlined in chapter 1. The following section describes this work.

Most of the material contained in this chapter was adapted from work done with James L. McClelland (Cleeremans & McClelland, 1991). Again, to reflect the fact that the original paper was the result of collaborative work, the use of pronouns has not been changed in the text that follows.

This research was supported by a grant from the National Fund for Scientific Research (Belgium) to Axel Cleeremans and by an NIMH Research Scientist Career Development Award to James L. McClelland. We thank Emile and David Servan-Schreiber for several insightful discussions. Arthur Reber and an anonymous reviewer contributed many helpful comments. Copyright 1991 by the American Psychological Association. Adapted by permission of the publisher.

Learning the Structure of Event Sequences

An increasingly large number of empirical studies have begun to explore the conditions under which one might expect subjects to display sensitivity to sequential structure despite limited ability to verbalize their knowledge. In a series of studies, Lewicki and his collaborators (Lewicki, 1986; Lewicki, Czyzewska, & Hoffman, 1987; Lewicki, Hill, & Bizot, 1988) explored the implicit acquisition of knowledge about sequential patterns in choice reaction time and search tasks. Lewicki et al. (1987) presented subjects with the task of finding a target digit in a complex matrix. The material was organized in blocks of seven trials. The location of the target in the seventh trial of each block was predictable based on specific sequences of target locations in four of the six preceding trials. In the last experimental sessions, however, the pattern was reversed, so that any knowledge acquired by subjects about the location of the target in the seventh trial of each block became suddenly useless. The results indeed showed a significant increase in reaction time for those last sessions, thus indicating that subjects were using the temporal context set by previous elements of each block to anticipate their response on the last element. Pilot studies and postexperimental interviews indicated clearly that subjects were unable to identify the critical predictive elements of the sequence.

Lewicki et al. (1988) used a four-choice reaction time task during which the stimulus could appear in one of four quadrants of a computer screen on any trial. Unbeknownst to subjects, the sequential structure of the material was manipulated by generating sequences of five elements according to a set of simple rules. Each rule defined where the next stimulus could appear as a function of the locations at which the two previous stimuli had appeared. As the set of sequences was randomized, the first two elements of each sequence were unpredictable. By contrast, the last three elements of each sequence were determined by their predecessors. Lewicki et al. (1988) hypothesized that this difference would be reflected in response latencies to the extent that subjects are using the sequential structure to respond to successive stimuli. The results confirmed the hypothesis: A progressively widening difference between the number of fast and accurate responses elicited by predictable and unpredictable trials emerged with practice. Further, subjects were exposed to a different set of sequences in a later part of the experiment. These sequences were constructed using the same transition rules, but applied in a different order. Any knowledge about the sequential structure of the material acquired in the first part of the experiment thus became suddenly useless, and a sharp increase in response latency was expected. The results were consistent with this prediction. Yet, when asked after the task, subjects failed to report having noticed any pattern in the sequence of exposures, and none of them even suspected that the sequential structure of the material had been manipulated.

However, lack of awareness, or inability to recall the material, does not necessarily entail that these tasks require no attentional capacity. Nissen and Bullemer (1987) demonstrated that a task similar to that used by Lewicki et al. (1988) failed to elicit performance improvements with practice when a memory-intensive secondary task was performed concurrently. More recently, Cohen, Ivry, and Keele (1990) refined this result by showing that the ability to learn sequential material under attentional distraction interacts with sequence complexity. Only sequences composed entirely of ambiguous elements (i.e., elements that cannot be predicted solely based on their immediate predecessor) are difficult to learn when a secondary task is present.

As suggested in chapter 1, some of the conclusions from the above studies are not as definite as previously thought. In particular, recent studies by Perruchet and his collaborators (Perruchet, Gallego, & Savy, 1990; Perruchet & Amorim, 1992) suggest both that subjects may be aware of a significant part of knowledge acquired implicitly and that their performance does not necessarily reflect an abstract encoding of the rules by which the material was generated. Thus, Perruchet et al. suggested that performance in the Lewicki situation may be accounted for by simple sensitivity to the frequency of particular subsequences rather than by assuming that subjects induce the generation rules. Chapter 4 contains several simulations that directly address this issue. Perruchet and Amorim (1992) showed that subjects trained on a choice reaction time task similar to that used by Nissen and Bullemer (1987) rapidly develop an ability to freely generate fragments of the sequences used during training. This suggests that knowledge of at least some aspects of the training material is available to consciousness.

To sum up, there is clear evidence that subjects acquire specific procedural knowledge when exposed to structured material. When the material is sequential, this knowledge is about the temporal contingencies between sequence elements. Further, it appears that the learning processes underlying performance in sequential choice reaction experiments do not require awareness of the relevant contingencies, although attention is needed to learn even moderately complex material. Several important questions remain unanswered, however.

First, it is not clear how sensitivity to the temporal context develops over time. How do responses to specific sequence elements vary with practice? Does sensitivity to more or less distant contingencies develop in parallel, or in stages, with the shortest contingencies being encoded earlier than the longer ones? Is there an upper limit to the amount of sequential information that can be encoded, even after considerable practice?

Second, most recent research on sequence processing has used very simple material (but see Lewicki et al., 1987), sometimes even accompanied by explicit cues to sequence structure (Lewicki et al., 1988). Are the effects reported in these relatively simple situations also observed when subjects are exposed to much more complex material involving, for instance, some degree of randomness, or sequence elements that differ widely in their predictability?

Third, and perhaps most importantly, no detailed information-processing model of the mechanisms involved has been developed to account for the empirical findings reviewed above. In other words: What kind of mechanisms may underlie sequence-learning in choice reaction time situations?

In the rest of this chapter, we explore the first two questions by proposing an answer to the third. We first describe how the SRN model may be used to simulate human performance in sequence-learning situations. As discussed in chapter 2, the model learns to develop its own internal representations of the temporal context despite very limited processing resources, and it produces responses that reflect the likelihood of observing specific events in the context of an increasingly large temporal "window." We then report on two experiments using a choice reaction time task. Unbeknownst to subjects, successive stimuli followed a sequence derived from a "noisy" finite-state grammar, in which random stimuli were interspersed with structured stimuli in a small proportion of the trials throughout training. This procedure allowed us to obtain detailed data about subjects' expectations after specific stimuli at any point in training. After considerable practice (60,000 exposures) with Experiment 1, subjects acquired a complex body of procedural knowledge about the sequential structure of the material. We analyze these data in detail. Experiment 2 attempted to identify limits on subjects' ability to encode the temporal context by using more distant contingencies that spanned irrelevant material.

Next, we argue that the mechanisms implemented in our model may constitute a viable model of implicit learning in sequence-learning situations, and we support this claim by a detailed analysis of the correspondence between the model and our experimental data.

Psychological Models of Sequence-Learning
Early research on sequence processing has addressed two related but distinct issues: probability-learning situations, in which subjects are asked to *generate* successive events of sequences they have previously observed; and choice reaction situations, in which subjects simply respond to the current stimulus (but nevertheless display sensitivity to the sequential structure of the material). Most of the work in the latter area has concentrated on relatively simple experimental situations, such as two-choice reaction time paradigms, and relatively simple effects, such as repetition and stimulus frequency effects. In both cases, most early models of sequence processing (e.g., Estes, 1976; Falmagne, 1965; Laming, 1969; Restle, 1970) have typically assumed that subjects somehow base their performance on an estimate of the conditional probabilities characterizing the transitions between sequence elements, but have failed to show how subjects might come to represent or compute them. Laming (1969), for instance, assumes that subjects continuously update "running average" estimates of the probability of occurrence of each stimulus, based on an arbitrarily limited memory of the sequence. Restle (1970) has emphasized the role that explicit recoding strategies play in probability learning, but presumably this work is less relevant in situations for which no explicit prediction responses are expected from the subjects.

Two points seem problematic with these early models. First, it seems dubious to assume that subjects actually base their performance on some kind of explicit computation of the optimal conditional probabilities, except possibly in situations where such computations are required by the instructions (such as in probability learning experiments). In other words, these early models are not process models. They may be successful in providing good descriptions of the data, but fail to give any insights into how processing is actually conducted.

Second, it is not clear how the temporal context gets integrated in these early models. Often, an assumption is made that subjects estimate the conditional probabilities of the stimuli given the relevant temporal context information, but no functional account of how the context information—and how much of it—is allowed to influence processing of the current event is provided.

The SRN model described in chapter 2 is clearly a process model. At first sight, this architecture—as well as other connectionist architectures with which the SRN shares several basic features—appears to be a good candidate for modeling implicit learning phenomena. For instance, because all the knowledge of the system is stored in its connections, this knowledge may only be expressed through performance— a central characteristic of implicit learning. Further, the back-propagation learning procedure implements the kind of elementary associative learning that also seems characteristic of many implicit learning processes. However, there is also substantial evidence that knowledge acquired implicitly is very complex and structured (Reber, 1989)—not the kind of knowledge one thinks would emerge from associative learning processes. As discussed in chapter 2, however, the work of Elman (1990, in press), in which the SRN architecture was applied to language processing, has demonstrated that the representations developed by the network are highly structured and accurately reflect subtle contingencies, such as those entailed by pronominal reference in complex sentences. Thus, it appears that the SRN embodies two important aspects of implicit learning performance: elementary learning mechanisms that yield complex and structured knowledge. The SRN model shares these characteristics with many other connectionist models, but its specific architecture makes it particularly suitable for processing sequential material.

To summarize, learning and processing in the SRN model have several properties that make it attractive as an architecture for implicit sequence-learning. First, the model has the potential to encode contextual information (Principle 4), but will develop sensitivity to the temporal context only if it is relevant in optimizing performance on the current element of the sequence (Principles 2 and 3). As a result, there is no need to make specific assumptions regarding the size of the temporal window that the model is allowed to receive input from. Rather, the size of this self-developed window appears to be essentially limited by the complexity of the sequences to be learned by the network. Representational resources (i.e., the number of hidden units available for processing) are also a limiting factor, but only a marginal one. Second, the model makes minimal assumptions regarding processing resources: Its architecture is elementary, and all computations are local to the current element (Principle 1). Processing is therefore strongly driven by the constraints imposed by the prediction task. As a consequence, the model tends to become sensitive to the temporal context in a very gradual way (Principle 3 again) and will tend to fail to discriminate between the successors of identical subsequences preceded by disambiguating predecessors when the embedded material is not itself dependent on the preceding information. I will return to this point in the last section of the chapter.

To evaluate the model as a theory of human learning in sequential choice reaction time situations, we assumed (1) that the activations of the output units represent response tendencies, and (2) that the reaction time associated with a particular response is proportional to some function of the activation of the corresponding output unit. The specific instantiations of these assumptions that were adopted in this research will be detailed later. With these assumptions in place, the model produces responses that can be directly compared to experimental data. In the following, I report on two experiments that were designed to allow such detailed comparisons to be conducted.

Experiment 1

Subjects were exposed to a six-choice reaction time task. The entire experiment was divided into 20 sessions. Each session consisted of 20 blocks of 155 trials. On any of the 60,000 recorded trials (see below), a stimulus could appear at one of six positions arranged in a horizontal line on a computer screen. The task consisted of pressing as fast and as accurately as possible on one of six corresponding keys. Unbeknownst to subjects, the sequential structure of the stimulus material was manipulated. Stimuli were generated using a small finite-state grammar that defined legal transitions between successive trials. Some stimuli, however, were not "grammatical." On each trial, there was a 15% chance of substituting a random stimulus for the one prescribed by the grammar. This "noise" served two purposes. First, it ensured that subjects could not simply memorize the sequence of stimuli and hindered their ability to detect regularities in an explicit way. Second, since each stimulus was possible on every trial (if only in a small proportion of the trials), we could obtain detailed information about which stimuli subjects did or did not expect at each step.

If subjects become increasingly sensitive to the sequential structure of the material over training, one would thus predict an increasingly large difference in the reaction times (RTs) elicited by predictable and unpredictable stimuli. Further, detailed analyses of the RTs to particular stimuli in different temporal contexts should reveal differences that reflect subjects' progressive encoding of the sequential structure of the material.

Method

Subjects   Six subjects (Carnegie Mellon University staff and students) aged 17–42 participated in the experiment. Subjects were each paid $100 for their participation in the 20 sessions of the experiment and received a bonus of up to $50 based on speed and accuracy.

Apparatus and Display   The experiment was run on a Macintosh II computer. The display consisted of six dots arranged in a horizontal line on the computer's screen and separated by intervals of 3 cm. At a viewing distance of 57 cm, the distance between any two dots subtended a visual angle of 3°. Each screen position corresponded to a key on the computer's keyboard. The spatial configuration of the keys was entirely compatible with the screen positions (i.e., the leftmost key corresponded to the leftmost screen position). The stimulus was a small black circle 0.40 cm in diameter that appeared centered 1 cm below one of the six dots. The timer was started at the onset of the stimulus and stopped by the subject's response. The response-stimulus interval was 120 msec.

Procedure   Subjects received detailed instructions during the first meeting. They were told that the purpose of the experiment was to "learn more about the effect of practice on motor performance." Both speed and accuracy were stressed as important. After receiving the instructions, subjects were given three practice blocks of 15 random trials each at the task. A schedule for the 20 experimental sessions was then set up. Most subjects followed a regular schedule of 2 sessions per day.

The experiment itself consisted of 20 sessions of 20 blocks of 155 trials each. Each block was initiated by a *get ready* message and a warning beep. After a short delay, 155 trials were presented to the subject. The first 5 trials of each block were entirely random to eliminate initial variability in the responses. These data points were not recorded. The next 150 trials were generated according to the procedure described below under "Stimulus Material." Errors were signaled to the subject by a short beep. After each block, the computer paused for approximately 30 seconds. The message *rest break* was displayed on the screen, along with information about the subject's performance. This feedback consisted of the mean RT and accuracy values for the last block and of information about how these values compared to those for the next-to-last block. If the mean RT for the last block was within a 20-msec interval of the mean RT for the next-to-last block, the words *as before* were displayed; otherwise, either *better* or *worse* appeared. A 2% interval was used for accuracy. Finally, subjects were also told about how much they had earned during the last block and during the entire session up to the last block. Bonus money was allocated as follows: Each reaction time under 600 msec was rewarded by 0.078 cents, and each error entailed a penalty of 1.11 cents. These values were calculated to yield a maximum of $2.50 per session.

Stimulus Material Stimuli were generated based on the small finite-state grammar shown in Figure 3.1. Finite-state grammars consist of nodes connected by labeled arcs. Expressions of the language are generated by starting at Node #0, choosing an arc, recording its label, and repeating this process with the next node. Note that the grammar loops onto itself: The first and last nodes, both denoted by the digit 0, are actually the same. The vocabulary associated with the grammar consists of six letters ('T', 'S', 'X', 'V', 'P', and 'Q'), each represented twice on different arcs (as denoted by the subscript on each letter). This results in highly context-dependent transitions, since identical letters can be followed by different sets of successors as a function of their position in the grammar (for instance, 'S_1' can only be followed by 'Q', but 'S_2' can be followed by either 'V' or 'P'). Finally, the grammar was designed to exclude direct repetitions of a particular letter, since it is known (Bertelson, 1961; Hyman, 1953) that repeated stimuli elicit

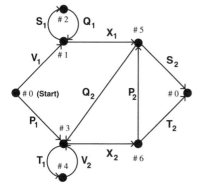

Figure 3.1
The finite-state grammar used to generate the stimulus sequence in Experiment 1. Note that the first and last nodes are one and the same.

shorter reaction times independently of their probability of presentation. (Direct repetitions can still occur because a small proportion of the trials were generated randomly, as described below.)

Stimulus generation proceeded as follows. On each trial, three steps were executed in sequence. First, an arc was selected at random among the possible arcs coming out of the current node, and its corresponding letter recorded. The current node was set to be Node #0 on the sixth trial of any block and was updated on each trial to be the node pointed to by the selected arc. Second, in 15% of the cases, another letter was substituted for the letter recorded at the first step by choosing it at random among the five remaining letters in the grammar. Third, the selected letter was used to determine the screen position at which the stimulus would appear. A 6 × 6 Latin square design was used, so that each letter corresponded to each screen position for exactly 1 of the 6 subjects. (Note that subjects were never presented with the actual letters of the grammar.)

Postexperimental Interviews   All subjects were interviewed after completion of the experiment. The experimenter asked a series of increasingly specific questions in an attempt to gain as much information about subjects' explicit knowledge of the manipulation and the task.

Results and Discussion

Task Performance   Figure 3.2 shows the average reaction times on correct responses for each of the 20 experimental sessions, plotted separately for predictable and unpredictable trials. We discarded responses to repeated stimuli (which are necessarily ungrammatical) since they elicit fast RTs independently of their probability of presentation, as discussed above. The figure shows that a general practice effect is readily apparent, as well as an increasingly large difference between predictable and unpredictable trials. A two-way analysis of variance (ANOVA) with repeated measures on both factors (practice [20 levels] by trial type [grammatical vs. ungrammatical]) revealed significant main effects of practice, $F(19, 95) = 9.491$, $p < .001$, $MS_e = 17710.45$; and of trial type, $F(1, 5) = 105.293$, $p < .001$, $MS_e = 104000.07$; as well as a significant interaction, $F(19, 95) = 3.022$, $p < .001$, $MS_e = 183.172$. It appears that subjects become increasingly sensitive to the sequential structure of the material. To assess whether the initial difference between grammatical and ungrammatical trials was significant, a similar analysis was conducted on the data from the first session only,

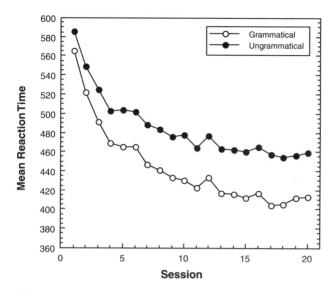

Figure 3.2
Mean reaction times for grammatical and ungrammatical trials for each of the 20 sessions of Experiment 1.

using the 20 blocks of this session as the levels of the practice factor. This analysis revealed that there were significant main effects of practice, $F(19, 95) = 4.006$, $p < .001$, $MS_e = 2634.295$; and of trial type, $F(1, 5) = 8.066$, $p < .05$, $MS_e = 3282.914$; but no interaction, $F(19, 95) = 1.518$, $p > .05$, $MS_e = 714.558$. We will provide an interpretation for this initial difference when examining the model's performance.

Accuracy averaged 98.12% over all trials. Subjects were slightly more accurate on grammatical trials (98.40%) than on ungrammatical trials (96.10%) throughout the experiment. A two-way ANOVA with repeated measures on both factors (practice [20 levels] by trial type [grammatical vs. ungrammatical]) confirmed this difference, $F(1, 5) = 7.888$, $p < .05$, $MS_e = .004$. The effect of practice did not reach significance, $F(19, 95) = .380$, $p > .05$, $MS_e = .0003$; neither did the interaction, $F(19, 95) = .727$, $p > .05$, $MS_e = .0002$.

Postexperimental Interviews   Each subject was interviewed after completion of the experiment. We loosely followed the scheme used by Lewicki et al. (1988). Subjects were first asked about "whether they had anything to report regarding the task." All subjects reported that they felt their performance had improved a lot during the 20 sessions, but much less so in the end. Two subjects reported that they felt frustrated because of the lack of improvement in the last sessions.

Next, subjects were asked "if they had noticed anything special about the task or the material." This question failed to elicit more detailed reports. All subjects tended to repeat the comments they had given in answering the first question.

Finally, subjects were asked directly "if they had noticed any regularity in the way the stimulus was moving on the screen." All subjects reported noticing that short sequences of alternating stimuli did occur frequently. When probed further, 5 subjects could specify that they had noticed two pairs of positions between which the alternating pattern was taking place. Upon examination of the data, it appeared that these reported alternations corresponded to the two small loops on Nodes #2 and #4 of the grammar. One subject also reported noticing another, more complex pattern between three positions, but was unable to specify the exact locations when asked. All subjects felt that the sequence was random when not involving these salient patterns. When asked if they "had attempted to take advantage of the patterns they had noticed to anticipate subsequent events," all subjects reported that they had attempted to do so at times (for the shorter patterns), but that they felt it was detrimental to their performance since it resulted in more errors and slower responses. Thus, it appears that subjects had only limited reportable knowledge of the sequential structure of the material and that they tried not to use what little knowledge they had.

Gradual Encoding of the Temporal Context   As discussed above, one mechanism that would account for the progressive differentiation between predictable and unpredictable trials consists of assuming that subjects, in attempting to optimize their responses, progressively come to prepare for successive events based on an increasingly large temporal context set by previous elements of the sequence. In the grammar we used, the uncertainty associated with the next element of the sequence can, in most cases, be optimally reduced by encoding two elements of temporal context. However, some sequence elements require three or even four elements of temporal context to be optimally disambiguated. For instance, the path 'SQ' (leading to Node #1) occurs only once in the grammar and can only be legally followed by 'S' or by 'X'. In contrast, the path 'TVX' can lead to either Node #5 or Node #6 and is therefore not sufficient to distinguish perfectly between stimuli that occur only (according to the grammar) at Node #5 ('S' or 'Q') and stimuli that occur only at Node #6 ('T' or 'P'). One would assume that subjects initially respond to the contingencies entailed by the shortest paths and progressively become sensitive to the higher-order contingencies as they encode more and more temporal context. A simple analysis that would reveal whether subjects are indeed basing their performance on an encoding of an increasingly large temporal context was conducted. Its general principle consists of comparing the data with the probability of occurrence of the stimuli given different amounts of temporal context.

First, we estimated the overall probability of observing each letter, as well as the conditional probabilities (CPs) of observing each letter as the successor of every grammatical path of length 1, 2, 3, and 4 respectively. This was achieved by generating 60,000 trials in exactly the same way as during the experiment and by recording the probability of observing every letter after every observed sequence of every length up to four elements. Only grammatical paths (i.e., sequences of letters that conform to the grammar) were then retained for further analysis. There are 70 such paths of length 4, each possibly followed by each of the six letters, thus yielding a total of 420 data points. There are fewer types of shorter paths, but each occurs more often.

Next, the set of average correct RTs for each successor to every grammatical path of length 4 was computed, separately for groups of four successive experimental sessions.

Finally, 25 separate regression analyses were conducted, using each of the five sets of CPs (0–4) as predictor, and each of the five sets of mean RTs as dependent variable. Since the human data are far from being perfectly reliable at this level of detail, the obtained correlation coefficients were then corrected for attenuation (Carmines & Zeller, 1987). This correction consists of estimating the reliability of each variable and of using these estimates to determine what the correlation between the two variables would be if they were perfectly reliable. We estimated the experimental data's reliability by using the split-halves method on the reaction times from even and odd experimental blocks. Estimating the reliability of the model's responses is not necessary because it is deterministic for any given set of parameters.

Figure 3.3 illustrates the results of these analyses. Each point on the figure represents the corrected r^2 of a specific regression analysis. Points corresponding to analyses conducted with the same amount of temporal context (0–4 elements) are linked together. If subjects are encoding increasingly large amounts of temporal context, we would expect the variance in the distribution of their responses at successive points in training to be better explained by CPs of increasingly higher statistical

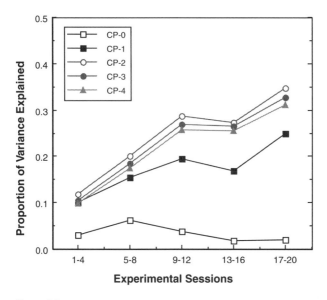

Figure 3.3
Correspondence between the human responses and conditional probabilities (CPs) after paths of length 0–4 during successive blocks of four simulated sessions.

orders. Although the overall fit is rather low (note that the vertical axis only extends to 0.5), the figure nevertheless reveals the expected pattern: First, the correspondence between human responses and the overall probability of appearance of each letter (CP-0) is very close to zero. This clearly indicates that subjects are responding based on an encoding of the constraints imposed by previous elements of the sequence. Second, the correspondence to the first-order CPs tends to level off below the fits for the second, third, and fourth orders early in training. By contrast, the correspondence between the data and the higher-order CPs keeps increasing throughout the experiment. The fits to the second-, third-, and fourth-order paths are highly similar in part because their associated CPs are themselves highly similar. This, in turn, is because only a few sequence elements are ambiguous up to the third or fourth position. Further, even though the data may appear to be most closely consistent with the second-order CPs throughout the task, a separate analysis restricted to the first four sessions of training indicated that the first-order CPs were the best predictor of the data in the first two sessions. Finally, it is still possible that deviations from the second-order CPs are influenced by the constraints reflected in the third- or even fourth-order CPs. The next section addresses this issue.

Sensitivity to Long-Distance Temporal Contingencies   To assess more directly whether subjects can encode three or four letters of temporal context, several analyses on specific successors of specific paths were conducted. One such analysis involved several paths of length 3. These paths were the same in their last two elements, but differed in their first element as well as in their legal successors. For example, we compared 'XTV' with 'PTV' and 'QTV' and examined RTs for the letters 'S' (legal only after 'XTV') and 'T' (legal only after 'PTV' or 'QTV'). If subjects are sensitive to three letters of context, their response to an 'S' should be relatively faster after 'XTV' than in the other cases, and their response to a 'T' should be relatively faster after 'PTV' or 'QTV' than after 'XTV'. Similar contrasting contexts were selected in the following manner: First, as described above, we considered only *grammatical* paths of length 3 that were identical but for their first element. Specific ungrammatical paths are too infrequent to be represented often enough in each individual subject's data. Second, some paths were eliminated to control for priming effects to be discussed later. For instance, the path 'VTV' was eliminated from the analysis because the alternation between 'V' and 'T' favors a subsequent 'T'. This effect is absent in contrasting cases, such as 'XTV', and may thus introduce biases in the comparison. Third, specific successors to the remaining paths were eliminated for similar reasons. For instance, we eliminated 'S' from comparisons on the successors of 'SQX' and 'PQX' because both 'Q' and 'S' prime 'S' in the case of 'SQX' but not in the case of 'PQX'. As a result of this residual priming, the response to 'S' after 'SQX' tends to be somewhat faster than what would be predicted based on the grammatical constraints only, and the comparison is therefore contaminated. These successive eliminations left the following contrasts available for further analysis: 'SQX-Q' and 'PQX-T' (grammatical) versus 'SQX-T' and 'PQX-Q' (ungrammatical); 'SVX-Q' and 'TVX-P' versus 'SVX-P' and 'TVX-Q'; and 'XTV-S', 'PTV-T', and 'QTV-T' versus 'XTV-T', 'PTV-S', and 'QTV-S'.

Figure 3.4 shows the RTs elicited by grammatical and ungrammatical successors of these remaining paths, averaged over blocks of four successive experimental sessions. The figure reveals that there is a progressively widening difference between the two curves, thereby suggesting that subjects become increasingly sensitive to the contingencies entailed by elements of the temporal context as distant as three elements from the current trial. A two-way ANOVA with repeated measures on both factors (practice [4 levels] by successor type [gram-

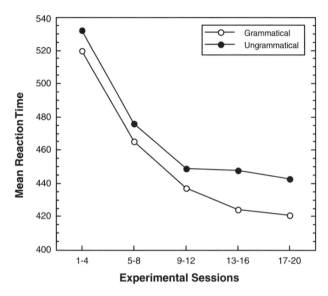

Figure 3.4
Mean reaction times for predictable and unpredictable successors of selected paths of
length 3, and for successive blocks of four experimental sessions.

matical vs. ungrammatical]) was conducted on these data and revealed
significant main effects of successor type, $F(1, 5) = 7.265$, $p < .05$, MS_e
$= 530.786$; and of practice, $F(4, 20) = 11.333$, $p < .001$, $MS_e = 1602.862$.
The interaction just missed significance, $F(4, 20) = 2.530$, $p < .07$, MS_e
$= 46.368$, but it is obvious that most of the effect is located in the later
sessions of the experiment. This was confirmed by the results of a
paired, one-tailed t test conducted on the difference between grammatical and ungrammatical successors, pooled over the first eight and the
last eight sessions of training. The difference score averaged -11.3 msec
early in training and -22.8 msec late in training. It was significantly
larger late in training, $t(5) = -5.05$, $p < .005$. Thus, there appears to be
evidence of a gradually increasing sensitivity to at least three elements
of temporal context.

A similar analysis was conducted on selected paths of length 4. After
candidate contexts were selected as described above, the following
paths remained available for further analysis: 'XTVX-S', 'XTVX-Q',
'QTVX-T', 'QTVX-P', 'PTVX-T', and 'PTVX-P' (grammatical) versus
'XTVX-T', 'XTVX-P', 'QTVX-S', 'QTVX-Q', 'PTVX-S', and 'PTVX-Q'
(ungrammatical). No sensitivity to the first element of these otherwise
identical paths of length 4 was found, even during Sessions 17–20: a

paired, one-tailed t test on the difference between grammatical and ungrammatical successors failed to reach significance, $t(5) = .076$, $p > .1$. Although one cannot reject the idea that subjects would eventually become sensitive to the constraints set by temporal contingencies as distant as four elements, there is no indication that they do so in this situation.

Experiment 2

Experiment 1 demonstrated that subjects progressively become sensitive to the sequential structure of the material and seem to be able to maintain information about the temporal context for up to three steps. The temporal contingencies characterizing this grammar were relatively simple, however, since in most cases, only two elements of temporal context are needed to disambiguate the next event perfectly. Further, contrasting long-distance dependencies were not controlled for their overall frequency. In Experiment 2, a more complex grammar (Figure 3.5) was used in an attempt to identify limits on subjects' ability to maintain information about more distant elements of the sequence. This grammar was inspired by the simulations described in chapter 2 and is almost identical with the grammar represented in Figure 2.16. In this grammar, the last element ('A' or 'X') is contingent on the first one (also 'A' or 'X'). Information about the first element, however, has

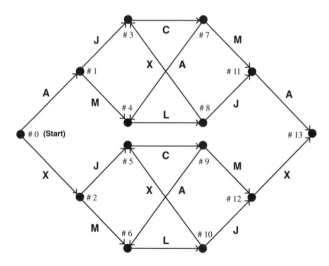

Figure 3.5
The finite-state grammar used to generate the stimulus sequence in Experiment 2.

to be maintained across either of the two identical embeddings in the grammar and is totally irrelevant for predicting the elements of the embeddings. Thus, to prepare optimally for the last element at Nodes #11 or #12, one needs to maintain information for a minimum of four steps. Accurate expectations about the nature of the last element would be revealed by a difference in the RT elicited by the letters 'A' and 'X' at Nodes #11 and #12 ('A' should be faster than 'X' at Node #11, and vice versa). Naturally, there was again a 15% chance of substituting another letter for the one prescribed by the grammar. Further, a small loop was inserted at Node #13 to avoid direct repetitions between the letters that precede and follow Node #13. One random letter was always presented at this point, after which there was a 40% chance of staying in the loop on subsequent steps. Finally, to obtain more direct information about subjects' explicit knowledge of the training material, we asked them to try to generate the sequence after the experiment was completed. This "generation" task involved exactly the same stimulus sequence generation procedure as during training. On every trial, subjects had to press the key corresponding to the location of the next event.

Method
The design of Experiment 2 was almost identical with that of Experiment 1. The following subsections detail the changes.

Subjects   Six new subjects (Carnegie Mellon University undergraduates and graduate students, aged 19–35) participated in Experiment 2.

Generation Task   Experiment 1 did not include any strong test of subjects' verbalizable knowledge about the stimulus material. In the present experiment, we attempted to remedy this situation by using a *generation task* inspired by Nissen and Bullemer (1987). After completing the 20 experimental sessions, subjects were informed of the nature of the manipulation and asked to try to predict the successor of each stimulus. The task consisted of three blocks of 155 trials of events generated in exactly the same way as during training. (As during the experiment itself, the 5 initial random trials of each block were not recorded.) On each trial, the stimulus appeared below one of the six screen positions, and subjects had to press the key corresponding to the position at which they expected the *next* stimulus to appear. Once a response had been typed, a cross 0.40 cm in width appeared centered 1 cm above the screen position corresponding to the subject's prediction, and the stimulus was moved to its next location. A short beep was emitted by the computer on each error. Subjects were encouraged to be as accurate as possible.

Results and Discussion

Task Performance   Figure 3.6 shows the main results of Experiment 2. They closely replicate the general results of Experiment 1, although subjects were a little faster overall in Experiment 2. A two-way ANOVA with repeated measures on both factors (practice [20 levels] by trial type [grammatical vs. ungrammatical]) again revealed significant main effects of practice, $F(19, 95) = 32.011, p < .001, MS_e = 21182.79$; and of trial type, $F(1, 5) = 253.813, p < .001, MS_e = 63277.53$; as well as a significant interaction, $F(19, 95) = 4.670, p < .001, MS_e = 110.862$. A similar analysis conducted on the data from the first session only again revealed significant main effects of practice, $F(19, 95) = 4.631, p < .001, MS_e = 1933.331$; and of trial type, $F(1, 5) = 19.582, p < .01, MS_e = 861.357$; but no interaction, $F(19, 95) = 1.383, p > .1, MS_e = 343.062$.

Accuracy averaged 97.00% over all trials. Subjects were again slightly more accurate on grammatical (97.60%) than on ungrammatical (95.40%)

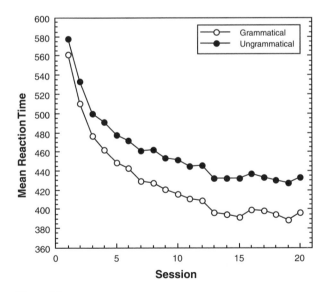

Figure 3.6
Mean reaction times for grammatical and ungrammatical trials for each of the 20 sessions of Experiment 2.

trials. However, a two-way ANOVA with repeated measures on both factors (practice [20 levels] by trial type [grammatical vs. ungrammatical]) failed to confirm this difference, $F(1, 5) = 5.351, p > .05, MS_e = .005$. The effect of practice did reach significance, $F(19, 95) = 4.112, p < .001, MS_e = .00018$; but the interaction did not, $F(19, 95) = 1.060, p > .05, MS_e = .00008$. Subjects became more accurate on both grammatical and ungrammatical trials as the experiment progressed.

Sensitivity to Long-Distance Temporal Contingencies   Of greater interest are the results of analyses conducted on the responses elicited by the successors of the four shortest paths starting at Node #0 and leading to either Node #11 or Node #12 ('AJCM', 'AMLJ', 'XJCM', and 'XMLJ'). Among those paths, those beginning with 'A' predict 'A' as their only possible successor, and vice versa for paths starting with 'X'. Since the subpaths 'JCM' and 'MLJ' undifferentially predict 'A' or 'X' as their possible successors, subjects need to maintain information about the initial letter to prepare accurately for the successors. The RTs on legal successors of each of these four paths (i.e., 'A' for 'AJCM' and 'AMLJ', and 'X' for 'XJCM' and 'XMLJ') were averaged together and compared to the average RT on the illegal successors (i.e., 'X' for 'AJCM' and 'AMLJ', and 'A' for 'XJCM' and 'XMLJ'), thus yielding two scores. Any significant difference between these two scores would mean that subjects are discriminating between legal and illegal successors of these four paths, thereby suggesting that they have been able to maintain information about the first letter of each path over three irrelevant steps. The mean RT on legal successors over the last four sessions of the experiment was 385 msec, and the corresponding score for illegal successors was 388 msec. A paired, one-tailed t test on this difference failed to reach significance, $t(5) = 0.57, p > .05$. Thus, there is no indication that subjects were able to encode even the shortest long-distance contingency of this type.

Generation Task   To find out whether subjects were better at predicting grammatical elements than ungrammatical elements after training, we conducted a two-way ANOVA with repeated measures on both factors (practice [3 levels] by trial type [grammatical vs. ungrammatical]) on the accuracy data of 5 subjects (1 subject had to be eliminated because of a technical failure).

For grammatical trials, subjects averaged 23.00%, 24.40%, and 26.20% correct predictions for the three blocks of practice respectively. The corresponding data for the ungrammatical trials were 18.4%, 13.8%, and 20.10%. Chance level was 16.66%. It appears that subjects are indeed better at predicting grammatical events than ungrammatical events. The ANOVA confirmed this effect: There was a significant main effect of trial type, $F(1, 4) = 10.131$, $p < .05$, $MS_e = .004$; but no effect of practice, $F(2, 8) = 1.030$, $p > .05$, $MS_e = .004$; and no interaction, $F(2, 8) = .1654$, $p > .05$, $MS_e = .001$. Although overall accuracy scores are very low, these results nevertheless clearly indicate that subjects have acquired some explicit knowledge about the sequential structure of the material during training. This is consistent with previous studies (A. Cohen et al., 1990; Willingham, Nissen, & Bullemer, 1989); and it is not surprising given the extensive training subjects have been exposed to. At the same time, it is clear that whatever knowledge was acquired during training is of limited use in predicting grammatical elements, since subjects were able to do so in only about 25% of the trials of the generation task.

In the following section, we describe how the SRN model may be used to account for human performance in this paradigm.

Simulation of the Experimental Data

Taken together, the results of both experiments suggest that subjects do not appear to be able to encode long-distance dependencies when they involve four elements of temporal context (i.e., three items of embedded independent material); at least, they cannot do so under the conditions used here. However, there is clear evidence of sensitivity to the last three elements of the sequence (Experiment 1). Further, there is evidence for a progressive encoding of the temporal context information: Subjects rapidly learn to respond on the basis of more information than the overall probability of each stimulus and only gradually become sensitive to the constraints entailed by higher-order contingencies.

Application of the SRN Model
To model our experimental situation, we used an SRN with 15 hidden units and local representations on both the input and output pools (i.e., each unit corresponded to one of the six stimuli). The network was trained to predict each element of a continuous sequence of stimuli generated in exactly the same conditions as for human subjects in Experiment 1. On each step, a letter was generated from the grammar as described in the "Method" section of Experiment 1 and was pre-

sented to the network by setting the activation of the corresponding input unit to 1.0. Activation was then allowed to spread to the other units of the network, and the error between its response and the actual successor of the current stimulus was used to modify the weights.

During training, the activation of each output unit was recorded on every trial and transformed into Luce ratios (Luce, 1963) to normalize the responses.[1] To compare human and simulated responses, we assumed (1) that the normalized activations of the output units represent response tendencies, and (2) that there is a linear reduction in RT proportional to the relative strength of the unit corresponding to the correct response.

These data were first analyzed in the same way as for Experiment 1 subjects and compared to the CPs of increasingly higher statistical orders in 20 separate regression analyses. The results are illustrated in Figure 3.7.

In stark contrast with the human data (Figure 3.3; note the scale difference), the variability in the model's responses appears to be very strongly determined by the probabilities of particular successor letters given the temporal context. The figure also reveals that the model's behavior is dominated by the first-order CPs for most of the training,

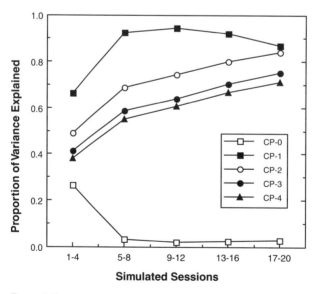

Figure 3.7
Correspondence between the simple recurrent network's (SRN's) responses and conditional probabilities (CPs) after paths of length 0–4 during successive blocks of four simulated sessions.

but that it becomes progressively more sensitive to the second-order and higher-order CPs. Beyond 60,000 exposures, the model's responses come to correspond most closely to the second-, then third-, and finally fourth-order CPs, in a way similar to that illustrated in Figure 2.15.

Figure 3.8 illustrates a more direct comparison between the model's responses at successive points in training and the corresponding human data. We compared human and simulated responses after paths of length 4 in 25 separate analyses, each using one of the five sets of simulated responses as predictor variable and one of the five sets of experimental responses as dependent variable. The obtained correlation coefficients were again corrected for attenuation. Each point in Figure 3.8 represents the corrected r^2 of a specific analysis. One would expect the model's early performance to be a better predictor of the subjects' early behavior, and vice versa for later points in training.

It is obvious that the model is not very good at capturing subjects' behavior: The overall fit is relatively low (note that the vertical axis only goes up to 0.5) and reflects only weakly the expected progressions. It appears that too much of the variance in the model's performance is accounted for by sensitivity to the temporal context. However, exploratory examination of the data revealed that factors other than the

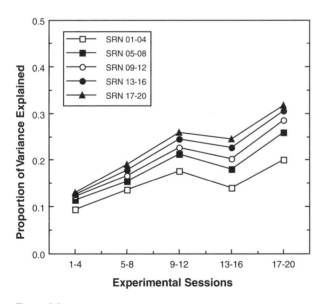

Figure 3.8
Correspondence between the simple recurrent network's (SRN's) responses and the human data during successive blocks of four sessions of training (Experiment 1).

conditional probability of appearance of a stimulus exert an influence on performance in our task. We identified three such factors and incorporated them in a new version of the simulation model.

The Augmented SRN Model

First of all, it appears that a response that is actually executed remains primed for a number of subsequent trials (Bertelson, 1961; Hyman, 1953; Remington, 1969). In the last sessions of our data, we found that if a response follows itself immediately, there is about 60 to 90 msec of facilitation, depending on other factors. If it follows after a single intervening response (as in 'VT-V' in Experiment 1, for example), there is about 25 msec of facilitation if the letter is grammatical at the second occurrence, and 45 msec if it is ungrammatical.

The second factor may be related: responses that are grammatical at Trial t but do not actually occur remain primed at Trial $t + 1$. The effect is somewhat weaker, averaging about 30 msec.

These two factors may be summarized by assuming (1) that activations at Time t decay gradually over subsequent trials, and (2) that responses that are actually executed become fully activated, whereas those that are not executed are only partially activated.

The third factor is a priming, not of a particular response, but of a particular sequential pairing of responses. This can best be illustrated by a contrasting example, in which the response to the second 'X' is compared in 'QXQ-X' and 'VXQ-X'. Both transitions are grammatical; yet the response to the second 'X' tends to be about 10 msec faster in cases like 'QXQ-X', where the 'X' follows the same predecessor twice in a row, than it is in cases like 'VXQ-X', where the first 'X' follows one letter and the second follows a different letter.

This third factor can perhaps be accounted for in several ways. We have explored the possibility that it results from a rapidly decaying component to the increment to the connection weights mediating the associative activation of a letter by its predecessor. Such "fast" weights have been proposed by a number of investigators (McClelland & Rumelhart, 1985; Hinton & Plaut, 1987). The idea is that when 'X' follows 'Q', the connection weights underlying the prediction that 'X' will follow 'Q' receive an increment that has a short-term component in addition to the standard long-term component. This short-term increment decays rapidly, but is still present in sufficient force to influence the response to a subsequent 'X' that follows an immediately subsequent 'Q'. In light of these analyses, one possibility for the relative failure of the original model to account for the data is that the SRN model is partially correct, but that human responses are also affected by rapidly decaying activations and adjustments to connection weights from preceding trials. To test this idea, we incorporated both kinds of mechanisms into a second version of the model. This new simulation model was exactly the same as before, except for two changes.

First, it was assumed that preactivation of a particular response was based, not only on activation coming from the network but also on a decaying trace of the previous activation:

$$\text{ravact}[i](t) = \text{act}[i](t) + (1 - \text{act}[i](t)) * k * \text{ravact}[i](t - 1)$$

where $act[i](t)$ is the activation of the ith unit based on the network at Time t, and $ravact[i](t)$ (running average activation at Time t) is a nonlinear running average that remains bounded between 0 and 1. After a particular response had been executed, the corresponding $ravact$ was set to 1.0. The other $ravact$s were left at their current values. The constant k was set to 0.5, so that the half-life of a response activation is one time step.

The second change consisted of assuming that changes imposed on the connection weights by the back-propagation learning procedure have two components. The first component is a small (*slow* $\eta = 0.15$) but effectively permanent change (i.e., a decay rate slow enough to ignore for present purposes), and the other component is a slightly larger (*fast* $\eta = 0.2$) change, but one that has a half-life of only a single time step. (The particular values of η were chosen by trial and error, but without exhaustive search.)

With these changes in place, we observed that, of course, the proportion of the variance in the model accounted for by predictions based on the temporal context is dramatically reduced, as illustrated in Figure 3.9 (compare with Figure 3.7). More interestingly, the pattern of change in these measures, as well as the overall fit, is now quite similar to that observed in the human data (Figure 3.3). Indeed, there is a similar progressive increase in the correspondence to the higher-order CPs, with the curve for the first-order CPs leveling off relatively early with respect to those corresponding to CPs based on paths of length 2, 3, and 4.

A more direct indication of the good fit provided by the current version of the model is given by the fact that it now correlates very well with the performance of the subjects (Figure 3.10; compare with the same analysis illustrated in Figure 3.8 but note the scale difference). Late

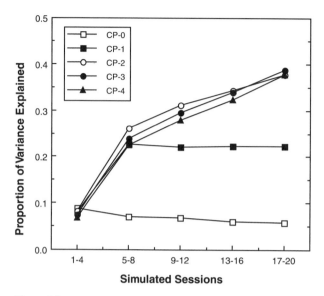

Figure 3.9
Correspondence between the augmented simple recurrent network's (SRN's) responses and conditional probabilities (CPs) after paths of length 0–4 during successive blocks of four simulated sessions.

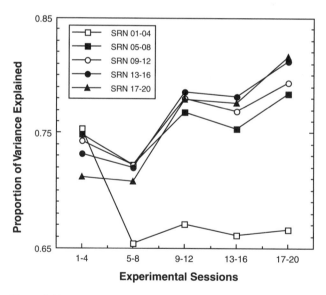

Figure 3.10
Correspondence between the augmented simple recurrent network's (SRN's) responses and the human data during successive blocks of four sessions of training (Experiment 1).

in training, the model explains about 81% of the variance of the corresponding human data. Close inspection of the figure also reveals that, as expected, the SRN's early distribution of responses is a slightly better predictor of the corresponding early human data. This correspondence gets inverted later on, suggesting that the model now captures key aspects of acquisition as well. Indeed, at almost every point, the best predictor of the human data is the simulation of the corresponding point in training.

Two aspects of these data need some discussion. First, the curves corresponding to each set of CPs are close to each other because most of the model's responses retain their relative distribution as training progresses. This is again a consequence of the fact that only a few elements of the sequence require more than two elements of temporal context to be perfectly disambiguated. Second, the model's responses correlate very well with the data, but not perfectly. This raises the question of whether there are aspects of the data that cannot be accounted for by the postulated mechanisms. There are three reasons why this need not be the case. First, the correction for attenuation assumes homogeneity, but because of different numbers of trials in different cells there is more variability in some cells than in others (typically, the cells corresponding to grammatical successors of paths of length 4 are much more stable than those corresponding to ungrammatical successors). Second, the set of parameters we used is probably not optimal. Although we examined several combinations of parameter values, the possibility of better fits with better parameters cannot be excluded. Finally, in fitting the model to the data, we have assumed that the relation between the model's responses and reaction times was linear, whereas in fact it might be somewhat curvilinear. These three facts would all tend to reduce the r^2 well below 1.0 even if the model is in fact a complete characterization of the underlying processing mechanisms.

The close correspondence between the model and the subjects' behavior during learning is also supported by an analysis of the model's responses to paths of length 3 and 4 (Experiment 1). Using exactly the same selection of paths as for the subjects in each case, we found that a small but systematic difference between the model's responses to predictable and unpredictable successors to paths of length 3 emerged in Sessions 9–12 and kept increasing over Sessions 13–16 and 17–20. The difference was .056 (i.e., a 5.6% difference in the mean response strength) when averaged over the last four sessions of training. By contrast, this difference score for paths of length 4 was only .003 at the same point in training, thereby clearly indicating that the model was not sensitive to the fourth-order temporal context.

Finally, to further illustrate the correspondence between the model and the experimental data, we wanted to compare human and simulated responses on an ensemble of specific successors of specific paths, but the sheer number of data points renders an exhaustive analysis virtually intractable. There are 420 data points involved in each of the analyses discussed above. However, one analysis that is more parsimonious but preserves much of the variability of the data consists of comparing human and simulated responses for each letter *at each node* of the grammar. Since the grammar used in Experiment 1 counts seven nodes (0–6), and since each letter can occur at each node because of the noise, this analysis yields 42 data points, a comparatively small number. Naturally, some letters are more likely to occur at some nodes than at others, and therefore one expects the distribution of average RTs over the six possible letters to be different for different nodes. For instance, the letters 'V' and 'P' should elicit relatively faster responses at Node #0, where both letters are grammatical, than at Node #2, where neither of them is. Figure 3.11 represents the results of this analysis. Each individual graph shows the response to each of the six letters at a particular node, averaged over the last four sessions of training, for both human and simulated data. Since there is an inverse relationship between activations and RTs, the model's responses were subtracted from 1. All responses were then transformed into standard scores to allow for direct comparisons between the model and the experimental data, and the figures therefore represent deviations from the general mean. Visual examination reveals that the correspondence between the model and the data is very good. This was confirmed by the high degree of association between the two data sets: The corrected r^2 was .88. Commenting in detail on each of the figures seems unnecessary, but some aspects of the data are worth remarking on. For instance, one can see that the fastest response overall is elicited by a 'V' at Node #4. This is not surprising, since the 'T-V' association is both frequent (note that it also occurs at Node #0) and consistent (i.e., the letter 'T' is a relatively reliable cue to the occurrence of a subsequent 'V'). Further, 'V' also benefits from its involvement in a 'TVT-V' alternation in a number of cases. On the same figure, one can also see that 'T' elicits a relatively fast response, even though it is ungrammatical at Node #4. This is a direct consequence of the fact that a 'T' at Node #4 follows itself immediately. It is therefore primed despite its ungrammaticality. The augmented SRN model captures both effects quite adequately, if not perfectly.

The impact of the short-term priming effects is also apparent in the model's overall responses. For instance, the initial difference between grammatical and ungrammatical trials observed in the first session of both experiments is also present in the simulation data. In both cases, this difference results from the fact that responses to first-order repetitions (which are necessarily ungrammatical) were eliminated from the ungrammatical trials, whereas second-order repetitions and trials involved in alternations were not eliminated from the grammatical trials.

Each of these two factors contributes to widening the difference between responses to grammatical and ungrammatical trials, even though learning of the sequential structure is only minimal at that point. The fact that the SRN model also exhibits this initial difference is a further indication of its aptness at accounting for the data.

General Discussion

In Experiment 1, subjects were exposed to a six-choice serial reaction time task for 60,000 trials. The sequential structure of the material was manipulated by generating successive stimuli based on a small finite-state grammar. On some trials, random stimuli were substituted for those prescribed by the grammar. The results clearly support the idea that subjects become increasingly sensitive to the sequential structure of the material. Indeed, the smooth differentiation between grammatical and ungrammatical trials can only be explained by assuming that the temporal context set by previous elements of the sequence facilitates or interferes with the processing of the current event. Subjects progressively come to encode more and more temporal context by attempting to optimize their performance on the next trial. Experiment 2 showed that subjects were relatively unable to maintain information about long-distance contingencies that span irrelevant material. Taken together, these results suggest that in this type of task subjects gradually acquire a complex body of procedural knowledge about the sequential structure of the material. Several issues may be raised regarding the form of this knowledge and the mechanisms that underlie its acquisition.

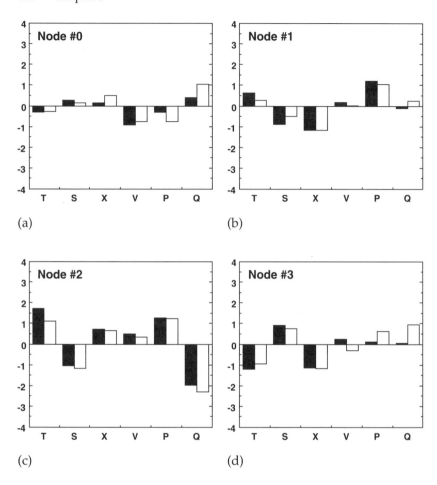

(a)

(b)

(c)

(d)

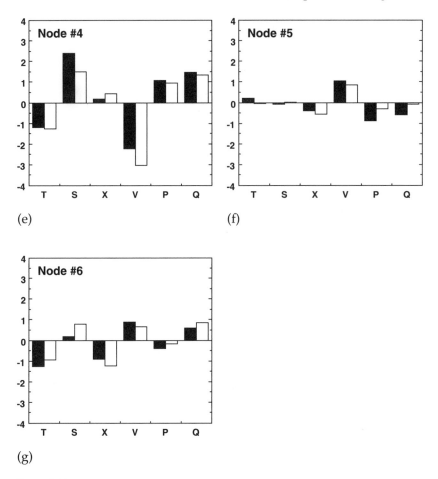

(e)   (f)

(g)

Figure 3.11
Human (black bars) and simulated (white bars) responses to each of the six letters,
plotted separately for each node (#0–#6) of the grammar (Experiment 1). All responses
have been transformed into standard scores with respect to the mean of the entire
distribution.

Sensitivity to the Temporal Context and Sequence Representation
Subjects are clearly sensitive to more than just the immediate predecessor of the current stimulus; indeed, there is evidence of sensitivity
to differential predictions based on two and even three elements of
context. However, sensitivity to the temporal context is also clearly
limited: Even after 60,000 trials of practice, there is no evidence that
subjects discriminate between the different possible successors entailed
by elements of the sequence four steps away from the current trial. The
question of how much temporal context subjects may be able to encode
has not been thoroughly explored in the literature, and it is therefore
difficult to compare our results with the existing evidence. Remington
(1969) has demonstrated that subjects' responses in a simple two-choice
reaction task were affected by elements as far removed as five steps,
but the effects were very small and did not depend on the sequential
structure of the material. Rather, they were essentially the result of
repetition priming. Early studies by Millward and Reber (1968, 1972),
however, documented sensitivity to as many as seven elements of
temporal context in a two-choice probability learning paradigm that
used structured material. In the Millward and Reber (1972) study, the
sequences were constructed so that the event occurring on Trial t was
contingent on an earlier event occurring at Trial $t - L$. The lag L was
progressively increased from 1 to 7 over successive experimental sessions. The results indicated that subjects were slightly more likely to
produce the contingent response on the trial corresponding to the lag
than on any other trial, thereby suggesting that they encoded the
contingency. A number of factors make this result hard to generalize
to our situation, however. First, subjects were asked to predict the next
element of a sequence, rather than simply react to it. It is obvious that
this requirement will promote explicit encoding of the sequential structure of the material much more than in our situation. Second, the task
involved only two choices—far fewer than the six choices used here.
There is little doubt that detecting contingencies is facilitated when the
number of stimuli is reduced. Third, the training schedule (in which
the lag between contingent events was progressively increased over
successive practice sessions) used in this study is also likely to have
facilitated encoding of the long-distance contingencies. Finally, the
differences in response probabilities observed by Millward and Reber
(1972) were relatively small for the longer lags (for instance, they
reported a .52 probability of predicting the contingent event at Lag 7,
versus .47 for the noncontingent event).

More recently, Lewicki et al. (1987), and also Stadler (1989), reported that subjects seemed to be sensitive to six elements of temporal context in a search task in which the location of the target on the seventh trial was determined by the locations of the target on the six previous trials. This result may appear to contrast with ours, but close inspection of the structure of the sequences used by Lewicki et al. (1987) revealed that 50% of the uncertainty associated with the location of the target on the seventh trial may be removed by encoding just three elements of temporal context. This could undoubtedly account for the facilitation observed by Lewicki et al. and is totally consistent with the results obtained here.

In summary, none of the above studies provide firm evidence that subjects become sensitive to more than three or four elements of temporal context in situations that do not involve explicit prediction of successive events. It is interesting to speculate on the causes of these limitations. Long-distance contingencies are necessarily less frequent than shorter ones. However, this should not per se prevent them from becoming eventually encoded, should the regularity detection mechanism be given enough time and resources. A more sensible interpretation is that memory for sequential material is limited and that the traces of individual sequence elements decay with time. More recent traces would replace older ones as they are processed. This notion is at the core of many early models of sequence processing (e.g., Laming, 1969). In the SRN model, however, sequence elements are not represented individually, nor does memory for context spontaneously decay with time. The model nevertheless has clear limitations in its ability to encode long-distance contingencies. The reason for these limitations is that the model develops representations that are strongly determined by the constraints imposed by the prediction task. That is, the current element is represented *together* with a representation of the prediction-relevant features of previous sequence elements. As learning progresses, representations of subsequences followed by identical successors tend to become increasingly similar. For instance, the simulation work described in chapter 2 indicates that an SRN with three hidden units may develop internal representations that correspond exactly to the nodes of the finite-state grammar from which the stimulus sequence was generated. This is a direct consequence of the fact that all the subsequences that entail the same successors (i.e., that lead to the same node) tend to be represented together. As a result, it also becomes increasingly difficult for the network to produce different responses to

otherwise identical subsequences preceded by disambiguating elements. In a sense, more distant elements are subject to a loss of resolution, the magnitude of which depends exponentially on the number
of hidden units available for processing (see Chapter 2 for a detailed
discussion of this point). Encoding long-distance contingencies is considerably facilitated when each element of the sequence is relevant—
even only in a probabilistic sense—for predicting the next one. Whether
subjects also exhibit this pattern of behavior is a matter for further
research, which I start exploring in chapter 5.

Awareness of the Sequential Structure
It is often claimed that learning can proceed without explicit awareness
(e.g., Reber, 1989; Willingham et al., 1989). However, in the case of
sequence-learning, as in most other implicit learning situations, it
appears that subjects become aware of at least some aspects of the
structure inherent in the stimulus material. Our data suggest that
subjects do become aware of the alternations that occur in the grammar
(e.g., 'SQSQ' and 'VTVT' in Experiment 1), but have little reportable
knowledge of any other contingencies. The loops also produced marked
effects on performance. Indeed, as Figure 3.11 illustrates, the greatest
amount of facilitation occurs at Nodes #2 and #4, and for the letters
involved in the loops ('Q' at Node #2 and 'V' at Node #4). However,
this does not necessarily entail that explicit knowledge about these
alternations played a significant role in learning the sequential structure of the material. Indeed, a great part of the facilitation observed for
these letters results from the fact that they are subject to associative
priming effects because of their involvement in alternations. Further,
our data contain many instances of cases where performance facilitation resulting from sensitivity to the sequential structure was not
accompanied by corresponding explicit knowledge. For instance, the
results of the analysis on differential sensitivity to the successors of
selected paths of length 3 (Experiment 1) clearly demonstrate that
subjects are sensitive to contingencies they are unable to elaborate in
their explicit reports. In other words, we think that awareness of some
aspects of the sequential structure of the material emerges as a side
effect of processing and plays no significant role in learning itself. As
it stands, the SRN model does not address this question directly.
Indeed, it incorporates no mechanism for verbalizing knowledge or for
detecting regularities in a reportable way. However, the model implements a set of principles that are relevant to the distinction between

implicit and explicit processing. For instance, even though the internal representations of the model are structured and reflect information about the sequence, the relevant knowledge is embedded in the connection weights. As such, this knowledge is relatively inaccessible to observation. By contrast, the internal representations of the model may be made available to some other component of the system. This other component of the system may then be able to detect and report on the covariations present in these internal representations, even though it would play but a peripheral role in learning or in processing. Even so, the internal representations of the model may be hard to describe because of their graded and continuously varying nature.

Other aspects of the data support the view that explicit knowledge of the sequence played but a minimal role in this task. For instance, even though the results of the generation task, which followed training in Experiment 2, clearly indicate that subjects were able to use their knowledge of the sequence to predict the location of some grammatical events, overall prediction performance was very poor, particularly when compared with previous results. A. Cohen et al. (1990), for instance, showed that subjects were able to achieve near perfect prediction performance in as few as 100 trials. In stark contrast, our subjects were able to predict correctly only about 25% of the grammatical events after 450 trials of the generation task and 60,000 trials of training! This difference further highlights the complexity of our experimental situation and suggests that the presence of the noise and the number of different possible grammatical subsequences make it very hard to process the material explicitly. This was corroborated by subjects' comments that they had sometimes tried to predict successive events but had abandoned this strategy because they felt it was detrimental to their performance.

In short, these observations lead us to believe that subjects had very little explicit knowledge of the sequential structure in this situation and that explicit strategies played but a negligible role during learning. One may wonder, however, about the role of explicit recoding strategies in task settings as simple as those used by Lewicki et al. (1988) or A. Cohen et al. (1990). In both these situations, subjects were exposed to extremely simple repeating sequences of no more than six elements in length. But the work of Willingham et al. (1989) has demonstrated that a sizable proportion of subjects placed in a choice reaction situation involving sequences of 10 elements do become aware of the full sequence. These subjects were also faster in the sequence-learning task and more accu-

rate in predicting successive sequence elements in a follow-up generation task. By the same token, a number of subjects also failed to show
any declarative knowledge of the task despite good performance during
the task. These results highlight the fact that the relationship between
implicit and explicit learning is complex and subject to individual
differences. Claims that acquisition is entirely implicit in simple sequence-learning situations must be taken with caution. Recent experiments by Perruchet and Amorim (1992) even suggest that awareness
of the sequence may develop in parallel to sequence-learning performance, as opposed to after it or not at all. The authors used a simple
sequence-learning situation based on the design introduced by Nissen
and Bullemer (1987), but modified the subsequent generation task.
Instead of having to predict each successive location at which the
stimulus may appear, subjects were simply asked to generate sequences
similar to those they had been exposed to during training. This procedure differs from the standard one in two important ways. First,
subjects are made aware of the fact that the experimenters want to know
more about their knowledge of the training sequence, and second, they
receive no feedback, which prevents learning during the generation
task but also ensures that performance is minimally disrupted. The
results revealed that subjects generated more fragments of sequences
that they had previously seen than control subjects who received only
random material during training. Further, in a new recognition test
during which subjects were presented with fragments of grammatical
or ungrammatical sequences, there was clear evidence that fragments
that were part of training were best recognized. Finally, those sequence
fragments that were best recognized are also those that elicited the
fastest reaction times during training and that were most generated by
subjects. A particularly important aspect of this study is that these
associations between explicit knowledge and performance on the sequence-learning task were observed even after very little training. Of
course, the material used in this experiment is so elementary (e.g.,
repetitions of a sequence of 10 elements, each of which may appear at
four different locations) that it is not clear how the results would
generalize to more complex situations like ours.

    To summarize, although it is likely that some subjects used explicit
recoding strategies during learning, the complexity of the material we
used—as well as the lack of improvement in the generation task—
makes it unlikely that they did so in any systematic way. Further
experimental work is needed to assess in greater detail the impact of
explicit strategies on sequence-learning, using a range of material of

differing complexity, before simulation models that incorporate these effects can be elaborated.

Short-Term and Long-Term Learning
The augmented SRN model provides a detailed, mechanistic, and fairly good account of the data. Although the correspondence is not perfect, the model nevertheless captures much of the variability of human responses. The model's core learning mechanism implements the notion that sensitivity to the temporal context emerges as the result of optimizing preparation for the next event based on the constraints set by relevant (i.e., predictive) features of the previous sequence. However, this core mechanism alone is not sufficient to account for all aspects of performance. Indeed, as discussed above, our data indicate that in addition to the long-term and progressive facilitation obtained by encoding the sequential structure of the material, responses are also affected by a number of other short-term (repetition and associative) priming effects.

It is interesting to remark that the relative contribution of these short-term priming effects tends to diminish with practice. For instance, an ungrammatical but repeated 'Q' that follows an 'SQ-' at Node #1 in Experiment 1 elicits a mean RT of 463 msec over the first four sessions of training. This is much faster than the 540 msec elicited by a *grammatical* 'X' that follows 'SQ-' at the same node. By contrast, this relationship becomes inverted in the last four sessions of the experiment: The 'Q' now evokes a mean RT of 421 msec, whereas the response to an 'X' is 412 msec. Thus, through practice, the sequential structure of the material comes to exert a growing influence on response times and tends to become stronger than the short-term priming effects.

The augmented SRN model captures this interaction in a simple way: Early in training, the connection weights underlying sensitivity to the sequential structure are very small and can exert only a limited influence on the responses. At this point, responses are quite strongly affected by previous activations and adjustments to the fast weights from preceding trials. Late in training, however, the contribution of these effects in determining the activation of the output units ends up being dominated by the long-term connection weights, which, through training, have been allowed to develop considerably[2]. With both these short-term and long-term learning mechanisms in place, we found that the augmented SRN model captured key aspects of sequence-learning and processing in our task.

Conclusion

Subjects placed in a choice reaction time situation acquire a complex body of procedural knowledge about the sequential structure of the material and gradually come to respond based on the constraints set by the last three elements of the temporal context. It appears that the mechanisms underlying this progressive sensitivity operate in conjunction with short-term and short-lived priming effects. Encoding of the temporal structure seems to be primarily driven by anticipation of the next element of the sequence. A connectionist model that incorporates both of these mechanisms in its architecture was described and found to be useful in accounting for key aspects of acquisition and processing. This class of model therefore appears to offer a viable framework for modeling unintentional learning of sequential material.

Chapter 4
Sequence Learning: Further Explorations

Can the SRN model also yield insights into other aspects of sequence-learning? A number of recent studies have begun to explore the effects of important variables on sequence-learning performance. For instance, the study of Lewicki, Hill, and Bizot (1988) raises—although in a somewhat indirect manner—the issue of the role played by explicit knowledge in sequence-learning. Cohen, Ivry, and Keele (1990) have examined the interactions between attention and sequence complexity. Kushner and Reber (see Kushner, Cleeremans, & Reber, 1991) have explored a situation in which the underlying regularities are very complex, and in which subjects are required to make explicit predictions about the successor of the sequences (this task is different enough from the others that it deserves a chapter of its own: see chapter 6). In the following sections, I describe how the SRN model may be used to simulate these different experimental situations. In some cases, the results of these simulations allow discrepant interpretations of the same data to be reconciled, or new predictions to be generated. In some other cases, current shortcomings of the model are highlighted. Taken together, however, these different simulations provide additional insights into the effects of various variables on sequence-learning and constitute further support for the SRN model.

Finally, I also took advantage of the smaller scale of some of these simulations to explore the effects of different parameters on learning performance. For instance, I discuss the effects of introducing noise in the weight updates, or the effects of using different learning rates on performance. These explorations further our understanding of how the parameters characterizing connectionist systems affect their performance, and of how some of them may be used to model the effects of psychological variables.

Another way to provide support for the notion that sequence-learning involves the kind of elementary and implicit mechanisms that the SRN model implements is to explore how well subjects who present with specific deficits in their ability to maintain explicit information in memory perform in the Cleeremans and McClelland (1991) sequence-learning situation. The next section describes preliminary work that addresses this issue.

Sequence Learning and Memory Disorders

Many studies (e.g., Schacter & Graf, 1986; see Schacter, 1987, for a review) have documented that severely amnesic patients may exhibit normal skill learning and repetition effects despite poor performance on recall and recognition memory tasks. Such dissociations between *explicit memory* (i.e., conscious recollection) and *implicit memory* (i.e., a facilitation of performance without conscious recollection) are generally attributed to the existence of separate memory mechanisms and/ or structures that support distinct functions. Schacter (1987) distinguishes three main models to account for the implicit memory/explicit memory distinction: *activation* models, which assume that "priming effects . . . are attributable to the temporary activation of preexisting representations"; *processing* models, for which differences between implicit and explicit memory performance are related to the type of processing subjects are engaged in (conceptually driven vs. data-driven processes); and *multiple memory systems* models, which "ascribe differences between implicit and explicit memory to the different properties of hypothesized underlying [memory] systems" (p. 511). Some authors (Sherry & Schacter, 1987) even argue that different memory systems have evolved as the result of incompatibilities between their functions (e.g., the need to maintain specific information vs. the need to maintain general information). Whatever the final word will be on the validity of each of these models, it is clear that the pattern of dissociation exhibited by amnesic patients is strongly indicative of a functional dissociation between declarative and procedural memory systems. Because of this, amnesic patients are particularly interesting subjects to study in implicit learning experiments. Indeed, one would expect such patients to exhibit almost normal performance (when controlled for age and other similar variables) despite dramatic deficits in acquiring and storing new material, thereby indirectly confirming (or disconfirming) the implicit nature of the task. Sequence-learning tasks are particularly adequate in this context because of their nonverbal and elementary character. Most of the relevant research is quite recent. Nissen and Bullemer (1987) demonstrated that amnesic patients exposed to a repeating sequence of 10 elements were able to learn to respond based on the contingencies present in the material, despite their obvious inability to recall the material or the experience itself. This basic result clearly indicated that amnesic patients may exhibit some preserved learning abilities for new associations, and it provided indirect confirmation that awareness plays but a minor role in the learning processes involved in sequence acquisition.

The following is a brief account of my own work with amnesic patients. This work is obviously preliminary, since only one patient was available for testing. Further, the results do not go much beyond establishing that this experimental material is learnable by amnesics. Nevertheless, it is the first demonstration of the phenomenon with such complex and noisy material.

Subject E.R. is a 57-year-old male patient who suffered a herpes simplex encephalitis in 1969, which resulted in a severe anterograde amnesia[1]. The diagnosis was confirmed by a CT scan conducted in 1985, which showed areas of low attenuation in both temporal lobes. Intellectual assessment on the Wechsler Adult Intelligence Scale, Revised (WAIS-R) revealed an overall normal IQ of 97 (verbal: 95; performance: 101). Performance was also normal on a series of standard performance (e.g., Wisconsin Card Sorting Test, Token Test) and perceptual (e.g., Rey-Osterrieth Figure Test) tests. Apparent normality in these functions contrasts sharply with E.R.'s amnesic syndrome. The patient is disoriented with respect to time and place and exhibits severely impaired memory for ongoing events, as confirmed by his extremely poor performance on the Wechsler Logical Memory test (3/24), on the Wechsler Paired-Associates Learning test (2/30), and on the Benton Visual Retention test (4/15 on recognition).

Method E.R. was tested in the same conditions as subjects in Experiment 1 described above. The patient refused to continue the experiment beyond the eighth session, complaining that the situation was boring and that he had already participated in this study. Since the patient was very reluctant to continue, testing was stopped. It is interesting to note that the patient obviously *recognized* the situation (but with only low confidence), although when asked later, he could not recall having participated in the experiment.

Results Figure 4.1 presents a comparison between E.R.'s performance over the first eight sessions of the experiment with normal subjects' performance over the entire experiment. Although his overall performance level is (not surprisingly) much lower than that of younger normals, E.R. exhibits about as much sequence-learning, as evidenced by the typical widening difference between the curves corresponding to grammatical and ungrammatical events.

Discussion   This work established that amnesic patients appear to be able to acquire specific procedural knowledge about the sequential contingencies present in the stimulus material, even when the material is complex and noisy. Thus, it extends previous results (e.g., Nissen & Bullemer, 1987). At this point, not much more can be done with this work, short of testing additional patients. With only 1 subject, specific comparisons between grammatical and ungrammatical elements are obviously too noisy to lend themselves to reliable interpretation.

Attention and Sequence Structure

If awareness has always attracted much interest in its relationship with implicit learning phenomena, it is only recently that studies addressing the role of attention in implicit learning have begun to appear. Such a study was conducted by A. Cohen et al. (1990). The authors reported that sequence structure interacts with attentional requirements. Sub-

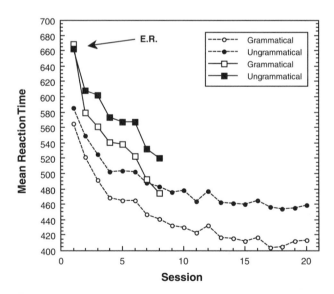

Figure 4.1
Mean correct reaction times for grammatical and ungrammatical trials for patient E.R. (solid lines) and for normal subjects (dashed lines).

jects placed in a choice reaction situation were found to be able to learn sequential material under attentional distraction, but only when it involved simple sequences in which each element has a unique successor (as in '12345...'). More complex sequences involving ambiguous elements (i.e., elements that could be followed by several different successors, as in '123132...') could only be learned when no secondary task was performed concurrently. A third type of sequence—hybrid sequences—in which some elements were uniquely associated with their successor and other elements were ambiguous (as in '143132...'), elicited intermediate results. A. Cohen et al. hypothesized that the differential effects of the secondary task on the different types of sequences might be due to the existence of two different learning mechanisms: one that establishes direct pairwise associations between an element of the sequence and its successor, and another that creates hierarchical representations of entire subsequences of events. The first mechanism would require fewer attentional resources than the second and would thus not suffer as much from the presence of a secondary task. A. Cohen et al. further point out that there is no empirical basis for distinguishing between this hypothesis and a second one, namely that all types of sequences are processed hierarchically, but that ambiguous sequences require a more complex "parsing" than unique sequences. Distraction would then have differential effects on these two kinds of hierarchical coding.

I propose a third possibility: that sequence-learning may be based solely on associative learning processes of the kind found in the SRN[2]. Through these learning mechanisms, associations are established between prediction-relevant features of previous elements of the sequence and the next element. If two subsequences have the same successors, the model will tend to develop identical internal representations in each case. If two otherwise identical subsequences are followed by different successors as a function of their predecessors, however, the network will tend to develop slightly different internal representations for each subsequence. This ability of the network to represent simultaneously similarities and differences led McClelland, Cleeremans, and Servan-Schreiber (1990) to refer to the SRN model as an instantiation of a *graded state machine* (see also chapter 2). This notion emphasizes the fact that, although there is no explicit representation of the hierarchical nature of the material, the model nevertheless develops internal representations that are *shaded* by previous elements of the sequence.

The key point in the context of this discussion is that the representations of sequence elements that are uniquely associated with their successors are not different in kind from those of elements that can be followed by different successors as a function of their own predecessors. How, then, might the model account for the interaction between attention and sequence structure reported by A. Cohen et al. (1990)? One possibility is that the effect of the presence of a secondary task is to hamper processing of the sequence elements. A simple way to implement this notion in the SRN model consists of adding normally distributed random noise to the input of specific units of the network (Cohen and Servan-Schreiber [1989] explored a similar idea by manipulating gain to model processing deficits in schizophrenia). The random variability in the net input of units in the network tends to disrupt processing, but in a graceful way (i.e., performance does not break down entirely). The intensity of the noise is controlled by a scale parameter, σ. I explored how well changes in this parameter, as well as changes in the localization of the noise, captured the results of Experiment 4 of A. Cohen et al. (1990).[3]

A Simulation of Attentional Effects in Sequence Learning
In this experiment, subjects were exposed to 14 blocks of either 100 trials for the unique sequence ('12345...') condition, or of 120 trials for the ambiguous sequence ('123132...') and hybrid sequence ('143132...') conditions. Half the subjects receiving each sequence performed the task under attentional distraction (in the form of a tone-counting task); the other half performed only the sequence-learning task. In each of these six conditions, subjects first received two blocks of random material (Blocks 1–2), followed by eight blocks of structured material (Blocks 3–10), then another two blocks of random material (Blocks 11–12), and a final set of two blocks of structured material (Blocks 13–14). The interesting comparisons are between performance on the last two random blocks (Blocks 11–12), on the one hand, and the four last structured blocks (Blocks 9–10 and 13–14), on the other hand. Any positive difference between the average RTs on these two groups of blocks would indicate interference when the switch to random material occurred, thereby suggesting that subjects have become sensitive to the sequential structure of the material.

I have represented the standard scores of the six relevant RT differences in Figure 4.2a. When the sequence-learning task is performed alone (*single* condition), unique and hybrid sequences are better learned

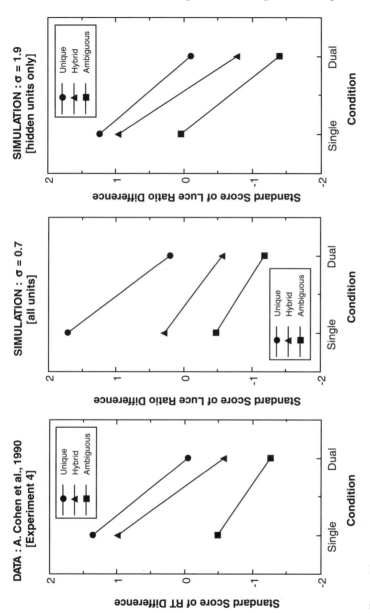

Figure 4.2
Standard scores of human and simulated mean difference scores between responses on random and structured material, for unique, hybrid, and ambiguous sequences, and under single- or dual-task conditions.

than ambiguous sequences, as indicated by the larger difference between random and structured material elicited by unique and hybrid
sequences. The same pattern is observed when the sequence-learning
task is performed concurrently with the tone-counting task (*dual* condition), but overall performance is much lower. In the actual data, there
is almost no difference between the reaction times elicited by random
and structured material, for the ambiguous sequence. In other words,
the ambiguous sequence is not learned at all under dual-task conditions. The crucial point that this analysis reveals, however, is that
learning of the unique and hybrid sequences is also hampered by the
presence of the secondary task.

To capture this pattern of results, an SRN with 15 hidden units was
trained in exactly the same conditions as the subjects in the study of
A. Cohen et al. (1990). The response of the network to each stimulus
was recorded and these responses were averaged separately over the
last random and structured blocks, as described above. These mean
responses were then subtracted from 1 and transformed into standard
scores to allow for direct comparisons with the data.

I explored three different ways of modeling the secondary task by
using noise. One consists of adding noise to the connections from the
context units to the hidden units only. I found that this resulted in
specific interference with acquisition of the ambiguous sequence. Basically, the network learns to ignore the noisy information coming from
the context units and minimizes the error using the main processing
pathway only. However, this is not what is observed in the data: The
presence of the secondary task also hampers learning of the unique and
hybrid sequences. Therefore, I focused on two other ways of allowing
noise to interfere with processing: adding noise to the net input of each
unit of the network, or adding noise to the net input of each hidden
unit only. In both cases, activation propagating from the context units
and from the input units to the rest of the network was affected equally.

In a first simulation, the secondary task was modeled by adding
normally distributed random noise ($\sigma = 0.7$) to the net input of each
unit in the network. The learning rates were set to 0.35 (*slow* η) and to
0.45 (*fast* η). The values of the other parameters were identical with
those used in the simulations described in chapter 3. The results are
illustrated in Figure 4.2b. The response pattern produced by the network is quite similar to the human data. In particular, (1) the noise
affected learning of all three types of sequences, and (2) it virtually
eliminated learning of the ambiguous sequence. Indeed, the difference
score for the ambiguous sequence was 0.019 in the dual condition—only

1.9%. Thus, at this level of noise, learning of the ambiguous sequence is almost entirely blocked, as for subjects in the study of A. Cohen et al. (1990). By contrast, learning of the unique and hybrid sequences is relatively preserved, although the hybrid sequence was not learned as well by the model as by the subjects.

Figure 4.2c illustrates the results of a similar analysis conducted on a simulation using higher learning rates (*slow* η = 0.7, *fast* η = 0.8) and in which noise (σ = 1.9) was only allowed to affect the net input to each hidden unit of the network. The figure shows that with these very different parameters, the model still captures the basic pattern of results observed in the data. The difference score for the ambiguous sequence in the dual condition was 0.023—again very close to zero. In contrast with the previous simulation, however, the hybrid sequence now appears to be learned as well as by human subjects. The ambiguous sequence, on the other hand, seems to be learned somewhat too well with this particular set of parameters.

The important result is that both simulations produced an interference pattern qualitatively similar to the empirical data. I found that quite a wide range of parameter values would produce this effect. For instance, the basic pattern is preserved if the learning rates and the noise parameter are varied proportionally, or, as the two simulations illustrate, if the noise is allowed to interfere with all the units in the network or with only the hidden units. This just shows that fitting simulated responses to empirical data ought to be done at a fairly detailed level of analysis. A precise, quantitative match with the data seems inappropriate at this relatively coarse level of detail. Indeed, there is no indication that *exactly* the same pattern of results would be obtained in a replication, and overfitting is always a danger in simulation work. The central point is that I was able to reproduce this pattern of results by manipulating a single parameter in a system that makes no processing or representational distinction between unique, hybrid, and ambiguous sequences.

To summarize, these results have two important implications. First, it appears that the secondary task exerts similar detrimental effects on both types of sequences. Learning of ambiguous sequences is almost entirely blocked when performed concurrently with the tone-counting task. Unique and hybrid sequences can be learned under attentional distraction, but to a lesser extent than under single-task conditions. Both of these effects can be simulated by varying the level of noise in the SRN model.

Second, these simulations suggest that unique and ambiguous sequences are represented and processed in the same way. Therefore, a distinction between associative and hierarchical sequence representations does not appear to be necessary to explain the interaction between sequence structure and attention observed by A. Cohen et al. (1990).

Discussion

The SRN model captures the effects of attention on sequence-learning reported by A. Cohen et al. (1990). Even though ambiguous sequences are not processed by separate mechanisms in the SRN model, they are nevertheless harder to learn than unique and hybrid sequences because they require more temporal context information to be integrated. So the basic difference among the three sequence types is produced naturally by the model. Further, when processing is disturbed by means of noise, the model produces an interference pattern very similar to the human data. Presumably, a number of different mechanisms could produce this effect. For instance, Jennings and Keele (1990) explored the possibility that the absence of learning of the ambiguous sequence under attentional distraction was the result of impaired "parsing" of the material. The authors trained a sequential back-propagation network (Jordan, 1986) to predict successive elements of a sequence and measured how the prediction error varied with practice under different conditions and for different types of sequences. The results showed that learning of ambiguous sequences progressed more slowly than for unique or hybrid sequences when the input information did not contain any cues about the structure of the sequences. By contrast, learning of ambiguous sequences progressed at basically the same rate as for the other two types of sequences when the input to the network did contain information about the structure of the sequence, such as the marking of sequence boundaries or an explicit representation of its subparts. If one assumes that attention is required for this explicit parsing of the sequence to take place and that the effect of the secondary task is to prevent such mechanisms from operating, then indeed learning of the ambiguous sequence will be hampered in the dual-task condition. However, the data seem to indicate that learning of the unique and hybrid sequences is also hampered by the presence of the secondary task. One would therefore need to know more about the effects of parsing on learning of the unique and hybrid sequences. Presumably, parsing would also facilitate processing of these kinds of sequences, although to a lesser extent than for ambiguous sequences.

In the case of the SRN model, I found that specifically interfering with processing of the ambiguous sequence by adding noise to the connections from the context units to the hidden units would not produce the observed data. On the contrary, the simulations indicate that the interference produced by the secondary task seems to be best accounted for when noise is allowed to affect equally processing of information coming from the context units and information coming from the input units. Therefore, it appears that there is no a priori need to introduce a theoretical distinction between processing and representation of sequences that have a hierarchical structure, on the one hand, and processing and representation of sequences that do not, on the other. Naturally, I do not mean to suggest that sequence-learning never involves the use of explicit recoding strategies of the kind suggested by A. Cohen et al. (1990) and by Jennings and Keele (1990). As pointed out earlier, it is very likely that many sequence-learning situations do in fact involve both implicit and explicit learning, and that recoding strategies play a significant role in performance. Further research is needed to address this issue more thoroughly.

Elementary Sequence Learning and the Effects of Explicit Knowledge

As discussed in chapter 3, Lewicki et al. (1988) explored sequence-learning in a four-choice reaction time task. On any trial, the stimulus could appear in one of four quadrants of a computer screen. Unbeknownst to subjects, the sequential structure of the material was manipulated: Simple rules defined the relationship between successive elements, within sequences of five elements. Each rule defined where the next stimulus could appear as a function of the locations at which the two previous stimuli had appeared. Because the set of sequences was randomized, the first two elements of each sequence were unpredictable. By contrast, the last three elements of each sequence were determined by their predecessors. Lewicki et al. (1988) hypothesized that this difference would be reflected in response latencies to the extent that subjects are using the sequential structure to respond to successive stimuli. The results confirmed the hypothesis: A progressively widening difference in the number of fast and accurate responses elicited by predictable and unpredictable trials emerged with practice. Further, subjects were exposed to a different set of sequences in a later part of the experiment. These sequences were constructed using the same transition rules, but applied in a different order. Any knowledge about the sequential structure of the material acquired in the first part of the experiment thus became suddenly useless, and a sharp increase in response latency was expected. The results were consistent with this prediction. Yet, when asked after the task, subjects failed to report having noticed any pattern in the sequence of exposures, and none of them even suspected that the sequential structure of the material had been manipulated.

The experiment described above was seminal in initiating interest about sequence-learning as a paradigm for exploring the acquisition of implicit knowledge. This fact alone already makes it interesting to find out whether the SRN model is capable of accounting for the basic effect reported by Lewicki et al. (1988). But the model can also be used to explore questions that were not systematically addressed in the empirical study. One such question is: What exactly are the effects on learning performance of giving subjects explicit information about sequence structure? Lewicki et al. (1988) gave their subjects such information by associating serial positions within the five-element sequences with a particular note presented simultaneously with the stimulus. For instance, Note A was played when the first element of each sequence was presented, Note B was played for the second element, and so on. The authors claim that this information helped subjects to "parse" the material into logical blocks of five elements and thus to become sensitive to the sequential structure of the material. However, since the original study did not incorporate a control condition in which the sequences were presented *without* additional auditory information, it is impossible to reach definitive conclusions about the effects of this information. In the following, I present the results of simulations during which the SRN model was trained under both conditions.

Another important aspect of the original Lewicki et al. (1988) study is the authors' interpretation of the results. This interpretation has been recently contested by Perruchet, Gallego, and Savy (1990). Lewicki et al. (1988) argued that the difference between predictable and unpredictable trials emerged as the result of subjects' acquiring knowledge about the rules underlying the material. By contrast, Perruchet et al. (1990) argued that rather than acquiring knowledge about the generation rules, subjects simply become sensitive to the relative frequencies of transitions between successive events. They supported the latter interpretation by a number of fine-grained analyses of data from a replication of the original study. These new analyses indeed revealed that some aspects of the original data are incompatible with the notion that subjects are only becoming sensitive to the regularities entailed by the transition rules used to generate the material. In particular, Perruchet et al. (1990) showed that performance differences between specific trials that cannot be predicted based on the generation rules can instead be accounted for by assuming that subjects encode frequency information about specific movements of the target. In this framework, implicit knowledge thus boils down to mere sensitivity to elementary features of the material, leaving the impression that the phenomenon is uninteresting and simply reflects the operation of basic cognitive processes.

If Perruchet at al.'s (1990) data are indeed very convincing, there are two problems with the approach they propose to embrace. Their interpretation of the data rests on the assumption that subjects recode the material in terms of movements from one target to the next, along with information about their frequency of occurrence. But how is this information represented? As Perruchet et al. (1990) themselves discuss, it is not clear whether one should assume that all instances of, say, a horizontal movement of the target are represented together or separately. Further, how is this information acquired? Do subjects build lists of possible movements and update them with frequency information as training progresses? Are more complex movements involving two transitions represented separately from simpler ones? In short, it is not clear what kinds of mechanisms may account for the data based on processing of target movements. If the interpretation put forward by Perruchet et al. (1990) does indeed account very well for Lewicki et al.'s (1988) data, and effectively rules out abstract knowledge of the generation rules, it remains purely descriptive and does not help in advancing our knowledge of the mechanisms involved in implicit learning. As for other research described in this book, I think that a good strategy to start addressing hard questions such as those about knowledge representation consists of proposing plausible mechanisms that may account for performance, and of finding out what the properties of these mechanisms are and how they relate to human performance. In the following section, I examine whether the SRN model is capable of producing the patterns observed by Perruchet et al. (1990), and I discuss how the model provides a way of integrating the two interpretations. I propose a simpler (but functionally equivalent) alternative to Perruchet et al.'s (1990) movement frequency account, which consists of assuming that subjects become sensitive to the distribution of possible successors of each stimulus. In other words, what subjects acquire in the task is knowledge about which stimuli are likely to follow others in different contexts, that is, knowledge about the sequential constraints imposed by the generation rules on the stimulus material.

A Simulation of the Lewicki et al. (1988) Study

To simulate the Lewicki et al. (1988) study, an SRN with 15 hidden units (Figure 4.3) was presented with exactly the same material as subjects in the original study, and for the same number of exposures. The network used four input units and four output units to represent the four possible locations at which the stimulus could appear. Five additional input units were used to represent the notes that accompanied presentation of the stimuli. On each trial, the network was presented with the current stimulus and with the appropriate note by setting the activation of the corresponding units to 1. As in the other simulations reported in this book, the network was trained to produce the next element of the sequence on its output pool. The parameters used in this simulation were identical with those used for the simulation of the effects of attention and sequence structure. On each trial, the network's response was recorded, transformed into a Luce ratio, and subtracted from 1 to make it directly comparable with the human data.

The experiment was organized as follows: Subjects were exposed to 4,080 trials, divided into 17 experimental sessions of 240 trials each. The material in each session consisted of 12 different sequences of five elements, each presented four times, in random order (but with the constraint that no direct repetitions were allowed). The sequences were constructed from a set of transition rules defining the location of the next element of the sequence based on the two previous locations. The first two elements of each sequence were determined at random. The next three elements were determined according to the transition rules. These rules were based on the physical movement between one trial

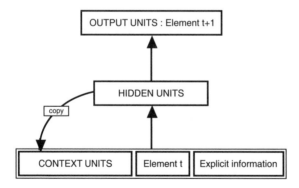

Figure 4.3
An expanded version of the simple recurrent network (SRN) model. The input layer incorporates an additional pool of units used to represent explicit information about sequence structure.

and the next. Since the four screen locations at which the stimulus could appear were organized in a square, and since the stimulus could never appear twice at the same location, there were only three different possible such movements: horizontal, vertical, or diagonal. For instance, one such rule was '1-H-2-V-3-D-4-V'. This rule says that if the transition between the first two (random) trials was a horizontal movement, then the movement from Trial 2 to Trial 3 was vertical, and so on. During the last two sessions of the experiment, the particular sequence of movements specified by each rule was reorganized. Thus, for instance, the contingency "horizontal transition between Trials 1 and 2 entails vertical movement between Trials 2 and 3" became "horizontal movement between Trials 3 and 4 entails vertical movement between Trials 4 and 5," and so on.

Figure 4.4 illustrates human and simulated performance over the 17 sessions of the experiment. Both the subjects and the model exhibit large savings up to the 15th session. At that point, the structure of the sequences was changed. In both the human and simulated data, this change results in worse performance. This clearly indicates that learning over the first 15 sessions was the result of an encoding of the sequential structure of the material.

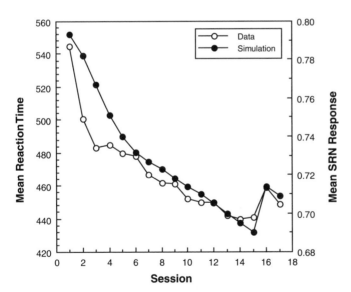

Figure 4.4
Mean human and simulated responses over 17 sessions of training on material from the Lewicki, Hill, and Bizot (1988) experiment. The simple recurrent network (SRN) model was provided with information about the sequence structure. The human data were adapted from Lewicki, Hill, and Bizot, 1988.

In a replication of the original study, Perruchet et al. (1990) analyzed these data in more detail. Their analysis consisted of decomposing performance by serial position within blocks of five successive trials. These data are illustrated in Figure 4.5. To allow for easier comparison with simulation results, all data points have been transformed into standard scores, with respect to the mean of the overall distribution. Based on the structure of the rule system used by Lewicki et al. (1988), one would expect to observe no learning for the first two (random) trials of each block (henceforth referred to as Trials A and B), and facilitation for the last three trials of each block (Trials C, D, and E). This is basically the pattern of results obtained by Perruchet et al. (1990), except for one crucial anomaly: C trials were not learned as well as D and E trials. Note that nothing in Lewicki et al.'s interpretation of the results could explain this difference: Since by construction, C trials are entirely determined by their two predecessors, as are D and E trials, they should be as learnable as the latter.

What does the SRN model's performance look like when broken down by serial position? Figure 4.6a illustrates the results of this analysis. As for the human data, the network's responses have been transformed into standard scores with respect to the mean of the entire

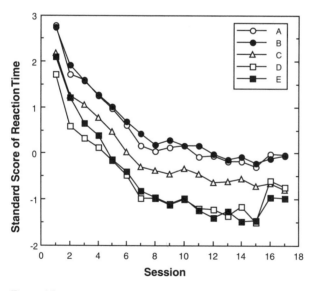

Figure 4.5
Mean reaction times (RTs) over 17 sessions of training on material from Perruchet, Gallego, and Savy, 1990, plotted separately for A, B, C, D, and E trials. Data points have been transformed into standard scores with respect to the mean of the entire distribution.

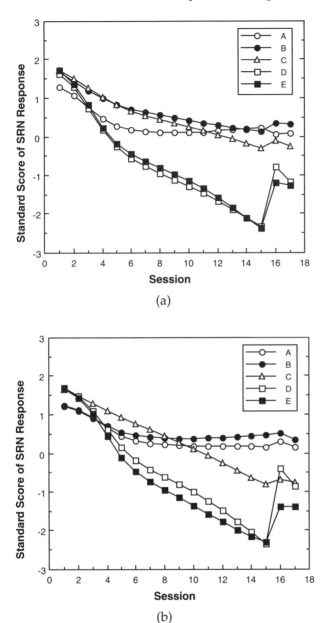

(a)

(b)

Figure 4.6
Mean simple recurrent network (SRN) responses over 17 sessions of training on
material from the Lewicki, Hill, and Bizot (1988) experiment, plotted separately for A, B,
C, D, and E trials. Responses have been transformed into standard scores with respect
to the mean of the entire distribution. The model was (a) or was not (b) provided with
information about the sequence structure.

distribution. Even though the correspondence with the human data is not perfect, one can see that, as predicted by Perruchet et al. (1990), if performance is indeed worse for A and B trials than for the others, C trials are nevertheless not learned nearly as well as D and E trials.

What explains this difference? The answer lies in a detailed examination of the structure of Lewicki et al.'s (1988) material, and in a reconsideration of their interpretation of the results. As Perruchet et al. (1990) point out, Lewicki et al.'s (1988) interpretation of their results is based on the notion that subjects parse the material in blocks of five elements and ignore transitions between blocks. Their reanalysis consisted of showing that when the frequency of transitions is considered over the entire sequence, C trials become less predictable than D and E trials. Indeed, as the experiments described in chapter 3 indicated, response speed in sequence-learning situations is proportional to the probability of occurrence of the stimuli given the temporal context. A detailed examination of the structure of the material used by Lewicki et al. (1988) revealed that a number of possible subsequences of two elements predict the elements that occur on C trials less often than the elements that occur on D and E trials. For instance, the subsequence '23' predicts '4' as its successor in C position, but '1' in both D and E positions. As a result, '4' is less likely than '1' as a successor of '23' and therefore elicits slower responses. In their analysis, Lewicki et al. (1988) simply overlooked this central determinant of response times. But shouldn't the explicit information provided to subjects allow them to parse the sequence completely? If this were the case, they would be able to distinguish between identical subsequences as a function of their serial position. For instance, in the above example, knowing that the subsequence '23' has occurred over Trials A and B unambiguously predicts '4' as the only possible successor. Similarly, a '23' subsequence occurring over Trials B and C unambiguously predicts '1' as its successor. One obvious explanation for the fact that subjects are not sensitive to the serial position at which specific subsequences occur may simply be that they fail to encode it. This is corroborated by anecdotal evidence from Perruchet (personal communication, December 1990), who reports that "subjects pay very little attention to the little music that accompanies the experiment." On the other hand, it is also possible that it is very hard to encode the extra information, even if it is attended to. To assess the impact of this explicit information in more detail, I trained an SRN to perform the task without the benefit of explicit knowledge about sequence structure. This network was trained in exactly the same conditions as the one described above, but no information was presented on the pool of input units representing the explicit information (i.e., the activation of these units was always equal to 0). Figure 4.6b illustrates the results of the serial position analysis conducted on the data from this simulation. Surprisingly, performance is barely different from that of the network trained with explicit information! Performance is even somewhat better on C trials (and actually closer to the human data; compare with Figure 4.5) in this version of the simulation. What explains this lack of impact of the explicit information on the model's performance?

A number of factors may be involved. First, the serial position information is useless in two-fifths of the cases because the first two events of each sequence are random. This may result in the network's learning to ignore the additional information, or at least in some slowdown in learning performance. Another factor may reside in the network's capacity to encode the extra information. To achieve perfect predictions whenever possible (i.e., for the last three trials), the network would need to encode 90 distinct conjunctions of events. Indeed, each of the 16 possible bigrams may start at each of the five possible serial positions. This complexity problem is further compounded by the fact that the same hidden units that receive the explicit information are also used to encode information about the temporal context. These different factors may all contribute to making the task of encoding and of using the explicit information quite a hard one. As a result, the network may in fact need much more training before the benefits of the extra information start being reflected in performance. This was confirmed by the results of a third simulation in which the network was trained on the same material for 10 times as many trials as in Lewicki et al.'s (1988) original experiment. The results of the last 17 sessions of training are illustrated in Figure 4.7a. It appears that performance is indeed considerably better after such extended training. C, D, and E trials now elicit very strong responses. Note that the network's responses are still not perfect, however. This is because responses are also affected by short-term priming effects. As a result of these effects, the strength of a particular response (i.e., the Luce ratio of its activation) tends to be somewhat weaker than would be predicted on the basis of its activation. Note also that C trials are still somewhat worse than D and E trials, even after such extensive training. Close examination of the figure reveals that the network is still learning about C trials, however: The corresponding curve is not entirely flat. By contrast, an SRN trained for the

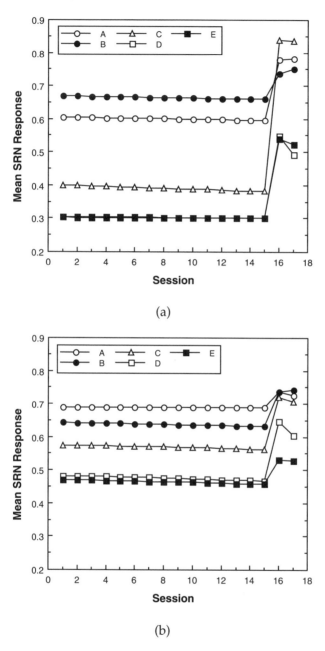

(a)

(b)

Figure 4.7
Mean simple recurrent network (SRN) responses over the last 17 sessions of training on
material from the Lewicki, Hill, and Bizot (1988) experiment, plotted separately for A, B,
C, D, and E trials. The model was trained for a total of 152 sessions, and was (a) or was
not (b) provided with information about the sequence structure.

same number of trials, but without the benefit of the serial position information, showed only much smaller improvements in performance (Figure 4.7b).

To summarize, it appears that the network is able to use—and actually does use—the explicit information when it is available, but doing so requires considerably more training than was given to the subjects in Lewicki et al.'s (1988) experiment.

Discussion

This set of simulations has demonstrated that the SRN model is capable of accounting in substantial detail for the data obtained by Lewicki et al. (1988). At first glance, this result is not very surprising. Indeed, the regularities embedded in Lewicki et al.'s material were relatively simple when compared with the kind of material used in the research described in chapter 3. Lewicki et al.'s material, however, is more complex than initially described. In particular, the analyses conducted by Perruchet et al. (1990) have revealed that the average predictability of some trials (i.e., C trials) is much lower than that of others (i.e., D and E trials), even though, by construction, all the structured trials should be equally predictable. This additional complexity is really the result of peculiarities in the material rather than the product of a design.

The simulations described in this section also suggested that providing subjects with information about the serial position of each trial, as Lewicki et al. (1988) did, is not likely to result in detectable improvements in performance, at least within the amount of training that subjects were exposed to. This somewhat surprising result is fully consistent with the position advocated by Perruchet et al. (1990): Subjects in this situation do not seem to use the extra knowledge, and their responses do not reflect the operation of parsing mechanisms. The fact that the SRN required considerably more training than in the original situation before it started encoding and using the serial position information also suggests that such encoding may be quite difficult. Of course, it is possible that modifications in the architecture of the network may facilitate this task. For instance, in the current version of the model, the same hidden units are used to represent the temporal context and the serial position information. A model with distinct pools of hidden units to encode these two sources of information may fare much better. But the fact remains that a model that can do the task (thereby demonstrating the sufficiency of its architecture) is also unable to use the extra information within the available amount of training (thereby demonstrating that encoding the extra information is a very complex task). In short, nothing in the data or in the simulations suggests that the additional explicit information has any kind of impact on performance.

Did subjects (and the SRN model) "learn the rules"? The question is important because it is at the core of many recent debates (e.g., Dulany, Carlson, & Dewey, 1984, 1985 vs. Reber, Allen, & Regan, 1985; or Perruchet & Pacteau, 1990, 1991 vs. Reber, 1990) in the implicit learning literature. Over the years, a number of investigators have attempted to demonstrate—through replications and reanalyses—that successful performance in implicit learning tasks does not require "knowledge of the rules" as defined by the original experimenters. Rather, as the argument goes, elementary knowledge of simple things, like the frequencies of events or a set of instances, is enough to account for human performance. This, of course, is also the approach illustrated in this book. But with a difference: I contend that the complex representations developed by information-processing models of the kind instantiated by the SRN model demonstrate that rich knowledge can emerge from elementary mechanisms. It appears unnecessary to pit sensitivity to elementary features of the stimulus material against acquisition of rich knowledge. This may not be so obvious without the benefit of a detailed information-processing model. So, in a sense (and ignoring the design peculiarities of the material), subjects in Lewicki et al.'s (1988) task do acquire "knowledge of the rules," since the distribution of their responses reflects the statistical organization of the material. Yet, when viewed from another perspective, this knowledge is little more than a sensitivity to the conditional probabilities of successive events. The SRN model shows how the former can emerge from the latter through elementary mechanisms.

General Discussion

The goal of the work described in this chapter was to demonstrate that the SRN model has the potential to provide a unified and parsimonious account of many different empirical phenomena related to sequence processing. As a first step toward that goal, the model was successfully applied to two different sequence-learning paradigms. Taken together, these simulations provide additional support for the SRN model: It appears that the processes underlying learning in the different situations I explored may all be based on the same elementary mechanisms instantiated by the model. Perhaps more importantly, this work also illustrates three important uses of simulation models.

First, the model accounted for the effects of a number of variables on sequence-learning performance. For instance, I described how the effects of attention may be captured within the SRN model by allowing random noise to influence processing. The model also accounted for the effects of sequence complexity on performance.

Second, the model was used as a tool for exploring the effects of variables that have not yet been explored empirically, or to generate new predictions that would have been hard to come by without the use of simulation models. An instance of this approach is provided by the simulation of Lewicki et al.'s (1988) experiment. Indeed, the simulations of the effects of explicit knowledge on performance suggest that this variable actually has very little impact on performance, at least within the available amount of training. Naturally, there may be other ways of improving the model's performance by providing it with additional information about the sequence structure. The lack of impact of explicit information that I observed in these simulations may very well be limited to this particular experimental situation and to this kind of explicit information. I will return to this point in chapter 7.

Finally, the use of simulation models also provides the means of integrating different interpretations of existing empirical data, and of starting to develop an understanding of the similarities and differences between various paradigms. In the case of sequence-learning, the work reported in this chapter is an encouraging first step in that direction.

Chapter 5
Encoding Remote Context

If the work described in the previous chapters has clearly demonstrated that the SRN model appears to be able to account for many aspects of human performance in sequence-learning situations, it failed to provide a definitive test of some of its more specific predictions. The SRN model's performance is essentially based on its ability to represent and use the temporal context to anticipate subsequent events. But this ability must be a necessary characteristic of any architecture that exhibits even elementary sensitivity to sequential structure, and therefore it does not distinguish the SRN model from other models of sequence processing. One difficulty in identifying contrasting predictions is that there is no competing architecture that has been elaborated to the point that it allows direct comparisons with the SRN model to be conducted. Nevertheless, there is a set of processing principles that characterize the SRN model and that distinguish it from other schemes for representing temporal information. In the following sections, I describe and discuss these principles. Next, I contrast these principles with those underlying two alternative mechanisms: table-lookup mechanisms and decay-based mechanisms (instantiated by two different architectures). Models implementing these different mechanisms entail different predictions insofar as maintaining long-term information is concerned. I describe an empirical situation that allows some of these different predictions to be tested, and report on the results.

Long-Distance Contingencies and Prediction-Based Learning

As described in chapter 2, a particularly crucial issue in sequence-learning is to identify whether the system is able to maintain information about long-distance contingencies over embedded material. This work revealed that an important limitation of the SRN model is that it tends *not* to encode information about sequence elements that are not locally relevant to the prediction task. For instance, in cases where the training material consists of sequences generated from the grammar illustrated in Figure 2.16, the network would need to maintain information about the head of the two long-distance contingencies ('T'→ 'T' and 'P' → 'P', on the outermost arcs) over a set of irrelevant elements (the elements of the subgrammars) to predict correctly the identity of the last element ('T' or 'P') when presented with the last element of the embedding (an 'S' or a 'V'). When the sequences generated from the two subgrammars are identical, this task is almost impossible for the SRN. The network has a hard time with such contingencies because information that is not locally relevant in predicting the next element (such as the head of the long-distance contingency above with respect to predicting the elements of the embedding) tends to be obliterated by the back-propagation learning procedure. Indeed, back-propagation tends to homogenize the internal representations corresponding to the embedded elements since they require identical predictions on each time step. As a result, these representations tend to become increasingly similar as more training on the embedded material is given to the network. Once these representations have become identical, they contain no trace whatsoever of the head that preceded the embedding, and the network is therefore unable to predict correctly which tail will occur. Interestingly, the failure of the SRN model to encode the long-distance contingencies in the symmetrical version of the grammar really results from training itself: It is *because* the network is trained on the irrelevant intermediate elements that it tends to develop internal representations that fail to represent information about the head.

However, Servan-Schreiber, Cleeremans, and McClelland (1991) also showed that when the embedded material depends (even only slightly) on the head (such as when one element of the embedding has a slightly higher probability of occurrence after a particular head has occurred, as illustrated in Figure 2.16), the network has a much easier time maintaining information about it, *even over those embedded elements that do not directly depend on the head.* This is because the network has now learned to develop different internal representations for each element of the embedding (since they entail slightly different successors as a function of the head), so that different predictions about the tail now become possible even when the input information is identical. Thus, it appears that the SRN model is able to maintain information about long-distance contingencies across identical embeddings as long as the *ensemble* of potential pathways through the embeddings is differentiated during training.

To summarize these points, the SRN model makes one main prediction about the learning of sequential material:

• Learning requires the material to be prediction-relevant at every step (even if in only very subtle ways). However, the network will perform well on particular sequences that *in themselves* are not prediction-relevant at every step, as long as the *ensemble* of elements is prediction-relevant. By contrast, if the embedded material is *not* globally prediction-relevant at every step, the network will fail to learn the long-distance contingencies that span this embedded material.

This prediction is unique to the SRN model and therefore contrasts with other network models as well as with other nonconnectionist schemes for representing temporal information. In the following section, I consider three such alternative models: decay-based models such as Jordan networks or buffer networks, and mechanisms based on table lookup.

Comparison with Other Architectures for Sequence Processing

Jordan Networks
An interesting alternative to the SRN model is instantiated by the sequential network proposed by Jordan (1986), briefly discussed in chapter 2. Figure 5.1 represents the architecture of a Jordan network.

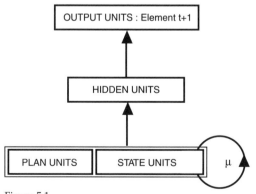

Figure 5.1
A Jordan network. This representation is somewhat different from, but equivalent to, the usual representation of a Jordan network. Plan units and state units constitute the input layer. State units feed back on themselves with a delay of one time step. The recurrent connections implement a simple form of time averaging controlled by the μ parameter and are not modifiable by the learning procedure. See the text for additional details.

(Note that this representation is different from, but equivalent to, the network illustrated in Figure 2.1, when the task is prediction. Jordan's original network also incorporates additional recurrent connections from the output units to the input units. These connections are unnecessary when the task is prediction because the previous output is identical with the next input.) The input layer of Jordan networks typically consists of two components: a set of "plan" units, and a set of "state" units. Jordan (1986) originally explored the ability of such networks to generate sequences of outputs given a specific "plan" representing an arbitrary code corresponding the sequence to be produced. For instance, a particular plan may represent a word, and the network's task would be to produce sequentially the phonemes corresponding to the spoken version of the word. The temporal context necessary to perform such tasks is maintained by having an explicit trace of the sequence of outputs represented over the state units. This temporal trace arises as the result of time-averaging the current activation of each state unit with its own previous value. How much averaging takes place is defined by a single parameter, μ, according to the following equation:

$$\text{activation}(t) = \text{activation}(t) + \mu * \text{activation}(t - 1)$$

How long the trace of a particular past event is maintained depends both on the magnitude of μ and on the structure of the material.

Training Jordan networks to predict successive elements proceeds in the same way as for the SRN model. On each time step, the network is presented with Element t of the sequence. The pattern of activation corresponding to Element t is time-averaged with the pattern of activation that already exists over the state units, and the resulting vector is then clamped back onto these units. The network is then trained to produce Element $t + 1$ on its output layer. The plan units are not used, because, unlike the original tasks explored by Jordan (1986), the prediction task does not require entire sequences of outputs to be generated on the sole basis of a single initial state (provided by the plan). It is interesting to note, however, that some investigators have explored how the plan units may be used to disambiguate subsequences in sequence-learning tasks similar to those described in this book. For instance, Jennings and Keele (1990) (whose work was described in chapter 4) have used a Jordan network to model the effects of attention. When several identical subsequences may be followed by different successors, the network's prediction performance may be improved by disambiguating each subsequence, by providing the network with different patterns of activation on the plan units.

Because Jordan networks do not have to elaborate their own representations of the sequence, the question of the prediction-relevance of successive elements is much less of an issue. Indeed, the time-averaged traces present on the input layer incorporate information about remote past events regardless of whether the more recent events are relevant for predicting the next one. More specifically, it would appear that the ability of Jordan networks to maintain information about the temporal context depends only on the "width" and on the "resolution" of the temporal window. As described earlier, the "width" of the temporal window depends on the magnitude of the μ parameter. The "resolution" depends on both the complexity of the sequence and the ability of the network to make fine discriminations between levels of activation in the input layer. As a result, Jordan networks, unlike the SRN model, predict that there would be little or no difference between performance on either version of the grammar illustrated in Figure 2.16.

Finally, it is interesting to note that Jordan networks may represent an entire class of more general models of sequence processing based on the use of a decaying trace of the temporal context. Although further evidence for this correspondence must await detailed mathematical analysis, it would appear that some earlier "statistical learning theory" models, such as Laming's, share many of their basic assumptions (e.g., decaying traces) with Jordan networks. This makes a comparison between the predictions of the SRN model and of the Jordan model all the more interesting. In the next section, I examine one such other class of decay-based network models: buffer networks.

Buffer Networks

A well-known and comparatively ancient way to represent time in connectionist networks is instantiated by architectures that use a spatial metaphor to represent successive events (see Cottrell, Munro, & Zipser, 1987; Elman & Zipser, 1988; Hanson & Kegl, 1987, for examples). Figure 5.2 illustrates one such model, in which four identical pools of input units are used to represent the possible sequence elements that may occur on each of four time steps. On each time step, the contents of each pool are copied (and possibly decayed) to the previous one (in time: e.g., $t - 4 = t - 3$)., and a new element is presented on the pool corresponding to Time t, the current time step. The contents of the pool corresponding to the most remote time step are lost. As Elman (1990)

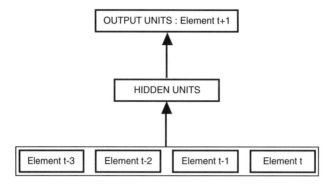

Figure 5.2
A buffer network with a temporal window of four time steps. The input layer contains isomorphic pools of units. The units of each pool represent the possible sequence elements in a localist way. Each pool corresponds to a different time step. Sequence elements are presented one at a time to the network, starting with the rightmost pool, which corresponds to the current time step, t. On each time step, the contents of each pool are copied (and possibly decayed) to the next one (in time: e.g., $t-1 = t$), and a new element is presented on the rightmost pool. The contents of the leftmost pool are lost.

suggested, buffer networks represent time by means of making the effects of events occurring at different time steps explicit, as opposed to models such as the SRN or the Jordan network, in which previous history modulates processing of subsequent events by virtue of the fact that these networks have a dynamic memory of their own past. In chapter 2, buffer networks were dismissed as interesting computational objects based on the fact that they have a number of important limitations. In addition to the wasteful duplication of input units that the buffer architecture entails, the most important limitation of these models is that events that fall outside of the "temporal window" available to the network are irretrievably lost for further processing. Thus, one is faced with two equally awkward possibilities: to determine the size of the window based on the longest (and potentially infinite!) interval between the time when relevant information is presented and the time when it is needed to make a prediction response, or to settle for a necessarily arbitrary size and forfeit the network's ability to process sequences longer than the chosen length. Either possibility is computationally undesirable, and both seem psychologically implausible (particularly in light of language-processing facts).

   Despite these important shortcomings, buffer networks are worth considering here as an instantiation of another elementary way to represent time. It is interesting to note that when the task is prediction, a buffer network can be thought of as equivalent to an "unfolded" Jordan network if events are decayed when they are shifted down the buffer at a rate identical with the value of μ used in the Jordan network. One crucial difference between the two models, however, is that traces in the Jordan network may be subject to interference by identical subsequent events because of the time averaging that takes place over the input units. By contrast, buffer networks are always guaranteed to hold separate traces of identical events occurring at different time steps. A further consequence of this fact is that buffer networks would fail to generalize to sequences that share the structure of the stimulus material, but have never actually been presented during training. In particular, these models would fail to generalize to sequences containing embeddings longer than those used during training, even if the architecture were such that enough buffers were available to represent these longer sequences. This is because different pools of input units are used to represent sequence elements occurring at different time steps. As a result, a buffer network does not have any basis for generalizing to identical contingencies separated by varying numbers of irrelevant elements. By contrast, both the SRN and the Jordan network develop representations that preserve similarity over absolute displacement of the elements of the contingencies in the sequence, because the same units are involved in representing the same events at different time steps.

This contrast between the SRN and the Jordan network on the one hand, and buffer networks on the other hand, provides the basis for distinguishing between models that use the same structures to represent events that occur at different time steps and models that use different structures to do so. The former make the following specific prediction:

• Models that use the same structures to represent identical events occurring at different time steps will tend to generalize to sequences that share the structure of the training material, but have never actually been presented during training. In particular, they will generalize to sequences containing embeddings longer than those they were actually trained on.

For reasons detailed below, the simulations and experiment described in the rest of this chapter could not be designed to test for this difference between the two classes of models (but see chapter 6 for relevant material). However, they were designed to test for differential predictions between all three network models and the even simpler table-lookup mechanisms described in the next section.

Table-Lookup Mechanisms
Finally, another broad class of models for sequence processing is based on the simple notion that the system continuously records "raw" instances of sequences and the probabilities of their successors. Obviously, there may be many possible models based on this assumption and on some auxiliary mechanisms (which specify, for instance, when and how much to update the records). It is easy to show that systems based on such mechanisms are necessarily very limited. In particular, such systems would tend not to exhibit sensitivity to the overall organization of the training material. In other words, this kind of model would fail to distinguish between the successors of specific sequences that *in themselves* do not contain information about the successor. Hence, either one assumes that such systems are recording statistics about *all* possible sequences of all lengths, which is clearly implausible, or one tolerates that they will fail in a number of cases (e.g., when the length of the embedding exceeds an arbitrary maximum beyond which information is no longer recorded) that the SRN and other models would be able to master successfully[1]. The key feature of the network models is that they are likely to generalize to new instances because of the rich similarity-based structure of their internal representations. I will not examine table-lookup models in much more detail. However, the simulations and experiment reported on below were designed to allow the predictions of these models to be tested.

An Empirical Test

How may the predictions entailed by these different models be tested empirically? In fact, part of the motivation behind the design of Experiment 2 described in chapter 3 was to address this point. Subjects were presented with sequences generated from the symmetrical version of the grammar illustrated in Figure 3.5. Naturally, as in Experiment 1, the material also incorporated random stimuli so as to allow relevant comparisons to be made between predictable and unpredictable stimuli. I hoped to be able to contrast human performance on the symmetrical and asymmetrical versions of this grammar, much as in the case of the simulation work described in chapter 2. However, it appeared that the added complexity resulting from both the noise and the random material inserted after Node #13 made this grammar too hard to learn; the network failed to learn it, even in the asymmetrical case. In the following paragraphs, I present a grammar that helps alleviate this complexity problem. Next, I introduce the design of an experiment that makes it possible to contrast the SRN model's predictions with those entailed by either decay-based networks or models based on table-lookup mechanisms.

Grammar and Stimulus Generation   The grammar illustrated in Figure 5.3 generates sequences that may contain three different long-distance contingencies, the elements of which (the *head* and the *tail*) may be separated by a varying number of embedded elements. Thus, all the possible sequences that start at even-numbered nodes (the *internal* nodes in Figure 5-3) have the following minimal structure:

$$H - E^* - T$$

where the tail T depends probabilistically on the head H, and H and T are separated by a varying number of embedded elements E. The tail

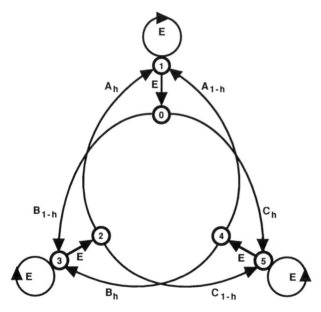

Figure 5.3
A finite-state grammar with three long-distance dependencies spanning random embedded material. Capital letters represent sequence elements or classes of sequence elements, subscripts represent probabilities, and digits represent nodes. See the text for additional details.

T of any such sequence serves as the head of the next one. Heads and tails (the set of which I will henceforth refer to as the *outer* elements) are instantiated by three different tokens: the letters 'A', 'B', and 'C'. To avoid short-term priming effects between the outer elements, the grammar was designed so that no head may be followed by itself as tail. As a result, each head has only two possible tails. For instance, 'A' as head may be followed only by 'B' or 'C' as tails. Each head is associated more strongly with one of the two possible tails than with the other one. The strength of this association is identical for all three heads and is thus controlled by a single probability h. For instance, if 'A' appears as the head of a particular sequence (going into Node #1), 'C' will tend to appear as its tail in h% of the cases, and 'B' will tend to appear as its tail in the remaining $1 - h$% of the cases (coming out of Node #0). Of course, it is this difference in the conditional probability of the tails that makes it possible to assess whether the system is encoding the regularity between heads and tails. Indeed, because tail elements have the same overall average probability of occurrence (when pooled over the heads), any difference in the response elicited by likely and unlikely tails would clearly indicate that the system has encoded information about the head.

Between heads and tails, a number of embedded elements (collectively represented by the label 'E' in Figure 5.3) may occur. At least one embedded element must occur between any head and tail. These mandatory embedded elements are represented by the label 'E' on the arcs going from odd-numbered nodes to even-numbered nodes in Figure 5-3. A random number of additional embedded elements may appear with probability l on the loops of Nodes #1, #3, and #5. The embedding is instantiated by five different tokens: the letters 'X', 'Y', 'Z', 'M', and 'N'. In the symmetrical version of the grammar, one of these tokens is simply chosen at random whenever an embedded element needs to be generated. The embedding therefore has no relevant structure, either internally or with respect to the regularities between the outer elements (i.e., its elements do not convey any information about which tail is more likely to occur after the embedding).

An interesting asymmetrical version of this grammar can be obtained by having the embedding depend slightly on the head. For instance, the internal structure of the loops at Nodes #1, #3, and #5 may be changed in such a way that the probability of selecting specific embedded elements now depends on the head. This was achieved in the following way: First, of the five possible elements of the embedding, two ('M' and 'N') were chosen to be entirely neutral. These two elements were always chosen with the same probability $n/2$ regardless of which head had occurred. Thus, these elements did not convey any information about which tail was most likely to occur after the embedding in either version of the grammar, and they serve a useful role in performance comparisons. Next, each of the three remaining possible elements of the embedding ('X', 'Y', or 'Z') was chosen with probability $(1-n) * b$ when one head had occurred, or with probability $(1-n) * ((1-b)/2)$ when either of the other heads had occurred. For instance, 'X' was more likely to occur as a token of the embedding on Node #1 than either 'Y' or 'Z'. Since 'A' is the head leading to Node #1, this implemented a simple contingency between 'A' and 'X'. Similarly, the selection of embedded elements was biased in favor of 'Y' at Node #2 and 'Z' at Node #3. Note that the average probability of 'X', 'Y', and 'Z' pooled over all three loops remains the same as in the symmetrical version, and that no element is excluded from occurring in the embedding. It is only the relative distribution of these elements that changes as a function of the head. Even so, because specific embedded elements tend to occur more often after specific heads, the embedding as a whole now has an internal structure that contains some information about which tail is more likely to occur. This contrasts with the symmetrical version of the grammar, in which the embedding never contains any information relevant to the outer contingencies. Table 5.1 shows the distribution of embedded elements after each head, in the symmetrical and asymmetrical cases. In this example, the grammar parameters n and b have been assigned the values of 0.4 and 0.333 (symmetrical case) or 0.4 and 0.666 (asymmetrical case) respectively. Note that the neutral elements 'M' and 'N' always have the same distribution.

The interesting point is that the SRN model predicts that learning of the outer contingencies will be considerably facilitated when the

Table 5.1
Distribution of embedded elements ('X', 'Y', 'Z', 'M', and 'N') after each head ('A', 'B', or 'C'), for the symmetrical or asymmetrical grammars.

	Symmetrical			Asymmetrical		
	A	B	C	A	B	C
X	.2	.2	.2	.4	.1	.1
Y	.2	.2	.2	.1	.4	.1
Z	.2	.2	.2	.1	.1	.4
M	.2	.2	.2	.2	.2	.2
N	.2	.2	.2	.2	.2	.2

embedded material has an asymmetrical structure. In particular, the network will learn to predict correctly which tail will occur even in the specific cases where the embedding contains only neutral elements. In other words, the network would learn to encode information about the head and would be able to use this information even in the cases where the embedding is irrelevant. By contrast, an SRN trained on material generated from the symmetrical version of the grammar would simply fail to encode the outer contingencies.

Test Material   To ensure that the comparison between the models' performance on either version of the grammar was not biased in any way, each network was tested on exactly the same material. Since I was interested in obtaining information about the networks' learning performance, testing was achieved by inserting a number of specific sequences at random points during training. All these sequences had the following form:

$$H - E^{\{1, 2, 3\}} - T$$

where the embedding was composed exclusively of the neutral elements 'M' and 'N'. This guaranteed that the test material only contained embeddings that in themselves do not provide any cue about the identity of the tail. (Of course, such neutral elements already occur in the grammar itself, but the very low frequency with which longer neutral embeddings occur made it necessary to insert additional ones.) There were 48 such sequences, each presented once during each session. Out of these 48, there were 16 sequences each for embedding lengths 1, 2, and 3. For each length, half of the sequences (i.e., 8) ended with a likely tail (given the head), and the other half ended with the corresponding unlikely tail. Head elements were counterbalanced over three training sessions. There were eight different embeddings of length 3, representing all the combinations of the two neutral elements in sequences of 3. Because there are only four possible different neutral embeddings of length 2 (i.e., 'MM', 'NN', 'MN', and 'NM'), each was represented twice within a group of 8 sequences. Similarly, each of the two possible embeddings of length 1 was represented four times in a group of 8 sequences.

To summarize, this design yields eight data points per embedding length and per tail, for each session of training. This number may seem very small, but inserting such strings with higher frequency may have adverse effects on learning, since their distribution and structure do not reflect the grammatical contingencies between heads and tails.

These strings were inserted in the material generated from the grammar in a totally seamless way: Whenever a head identical with the head of the next string to be presented was about to be generated from the grammar, there was a fixed probability *s* that the head of that particular string would be presented instead. Subsequent elements of the string were then presented on the next trials, until the end of the string was reached. At that point, stimulus generation resumed based on the grammar, starting from the node to which the last element of the string was pointing. The probability *s* was high enough to guarantee that all the strings would be presented in a session, but low enough to ensure that their distribution was approximately flat.

To allow the second prediction (shared by the Jordan and SRN networks) to be tested, the grammar itself needed to be slightly modified. Indeed, even though a simple way of testing the network models' prediction that they will generalize to embeddings longer than those presented during training consists of testing them on such sequences, this was impractical because I wanted to be able to use the same material in experiments with human subjects. The problem with very long embeddings composed of only two different elements is that they are much more noticeable than shorter ones, and that their frequency of presentation must necessarily be low, so as to not upset the structure of the grammar's material too much. To avoid these potential problems, the grammar was modified in such a way as to allow this prediction to be tested without requiring the use of new material. The modification consisted of forcing the tails of neutral embeddings of length 3 to have the same probability (i.e., 0.5), thereby eliminating the long-distance contingency between heads and tails *for those embeddings only*. Either decay-based networks or the SRN model should generalize[2] to these sequences because they develop representations that are sensitive to the entire distribution of sequence elements. (Note that buffer networks should also generalize in this case, because a contingency still exists between head and tails separated by three embedded elements other than neutrals.) By contrast, models based on table-lookup mechanisms would fail to encode this contingency for those specific embeddings, even if information about the head had been recorded (since even the head does not convey information about the tail in these particular cases).

Network Architecture and Parameters   Two different networks of each type were trained for 60,000 trials on both the symmetrical and asymmetrical versions of the grammar and were tested as described above. In the symmetrical condition, the grammar parameters were as follows: $h = 0.85$ (i.e., 'A' predicts 'B' in 85% of the cases and 'C' in 15% of the cases; 'B' predicts 'C' in 85% of the cases and 'A' in 15% of the cases, etc.), $l = 0.666$ (i.e., on each relevant trial, there was a 0.666 probability of staying in the loop on Nodes #1, #3, or #5), $b = 0.333$, and $n = 0.4$. These parameters generate embedded elements according to the distribution illustrated on the left-hand side of Table 5.1. The same parameters were used in the asymmetrical case, except for b, which was now set to 0.666. With b set at this value, the distribution of embedded elements corresponds to the right-hand side of Table 5.1.

The SRN network had an architecture identical with the one illustrated in Figure 3.1. Its parameters were identical with those used in the first and second experiments described in this book. The Jordan network had the architecture illustrated in Figure 5.1. Its parameters were identical with those used for the SRN network. The value of μ was set to 0.5, so that the half-life of an input trace was one time step. Finally, a buffer network with the architecture illustrated in Figure 5.2 was trained in the same conditions as the other two networks, and with an input decay rate of 0.5. The size of the buffer (four elements) was determined based on the stimulus material (the contingencies of interest are four elements long at most). All networks had 15 hidden units, and all used both fast weights and running average activations on the output units, as for the SRN simulations described in chapter 3.

Results   For each embedding length, I computed the average difference between the response of each network on the likely and unlikely tails of the set of fixed strings, pooled over the three possible heads, and over sets of four successive sessions. These data are illustrated in Figures 5.4a (symmetrical grammar) and 5.4b (asymmetrical grammar) for the SRN model, in Figures 5.4c and 5.4d for the Jordan network, and in Figures 5.4e and 5.4f for the buffer network.

It is clear that the SRN trained on material generated from the symmetrical grammar is totally unable to encode the long-distance contingencies, even for the shortest embeddings. Indeed, there is no difference in the average Luce ratio elicited by likely or unlikely tails. By contrast, the network trained on sequences generated from the asymmetrical version of the grammar is able to maintain sizable Luce ratio differences (i.e., about 10%) over all embedding lengths. This clearly demonstrates that learning in the SRN model depends on the fact that the distribution of successive elements is relevant with respect to the prediction task.

By contrast, a Jordan network trained in exactly the same conditions as the SRN model does not exhibit this sensitivity to the prediction-relevance of successive elements. Figures 5.4c and 5.4d clearly show that the performance of the Jordan network is barely different on the symmetrical and asymmetrical grammars. In both cases, the network simply relies on the decayed trace of the head to predict the tail. Note, however, that the difference is slightly larger in the case of the asymmetrical grammar. This is because, during training in the asymmetrical condition, the input information does indeed contain some additional information about the head (in the form of slightly more activated traces of the biased embedded element), which may help the network encode the contingency. I doubt that this slight difference would be detectable experimentally, however. Further, the Jordan network is clearly able to learn the symmetrical version of the grammar, whereas the SRN model fails completely on the same material.

The buffer networks also learn the contingencies in either version of the grammar (Figures 5.4e and 5.4f), although with this particular value of decay, they exhibit several interesting differences from the Jordan network.

First, there are larger differences between the successors of embeddings of different lengths, with shorter embeddings being better learned than longer ones. In the symmetrical version of the grammar, for instance, sequences with three embedded elements are barely learned at all. This is a direct consequence of the fact that buffer networks use different units to represent identical sequence elements occurring at different time steps. As a result, the connection weights from the pool of units corresponding to time step $t - 4$, for instance, change slowly relative to the weights of connections coming from pools of input units corresponding to more recent time steps, because input activations in that pool are always lower than in the other pools. This stands in contrast to either the SRN or the Jordan network, in which changes to the connection weights from a particular input unit will be effected whenever the corresponding sequence element is presented to the network, regardless of the time step at which it occurs. Note that using increasingly lower decay rates will asymptotically make these differences in the apparent learnability of sequences with different embedding lengths disappear.

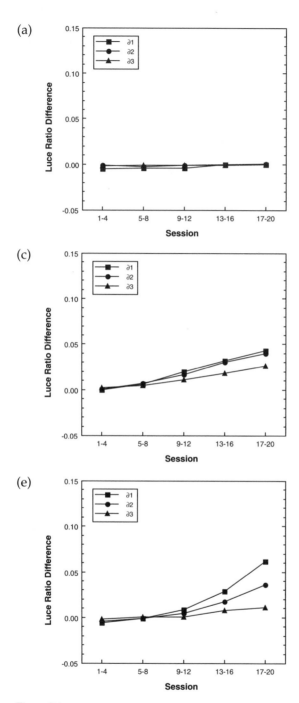

Figure 5.4
Luce ratio differences between likely and unlikely tails of sequences with one, two, or three neutral embedded elements. (a) and (b), simple recurrent network (SRN) model;

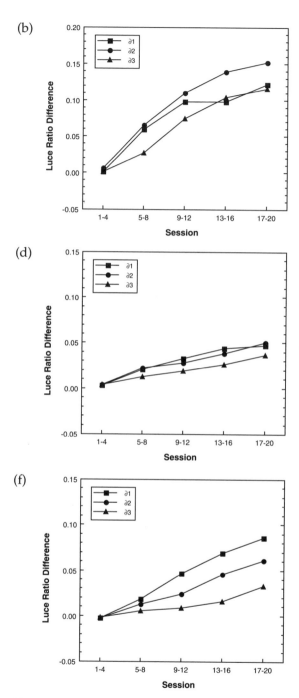

(c) and (d), Jordan model; (e) and (f), buffer network. Figures on the left side represent data resulting from training with the symmetrical grammar; figures on the right side represent data resulting from training with the asymmetrical grammar.

Second, buffer networks appear to be better able to learn the material from the asymmetrical grammar than the material from the symmetrical grammar. But this is again a consequence of the relatively high decay rate used in this simulation. To illustrate, Figure 5.5 shows the performance of buffer networks trained with a decay rate of 0.1 (i.e., 90% of the activation is preserved as traces are shifted down the buffer). Clearly, performance is now qualitatively similar to that of the Jordan network.

I conducted similar parametric explorations for the SRN and for the Jordan models. As a final test of the robustness of the SRN model's predictions, I ran two additional simulations exploring how its performance is affected by the number of hidden units. An SRN with only 3 hidden units was trained on the asymmetrical grammar, and another SRN with 60 hidden units was trained on the symmetrical grammar. Figure 5.6 shows the results. Even though there is some degradation in the asymmetrical case when the network had only 3 hidden units, it is clear that performance is only moderately affected by the representational resources available to the network (Figure 5.6b). Similar results were obtained in the symmetrical case (i.e., little improvement with more hidden units; see Figure 5.6a). The fact that an SRN with only 3 hidden units can nevertheless learn the task in the asymmetrical case indicates that this grammar is relatively simple compared to the ones used in Experiments 1 and 2. Indeed, in the limit, there are only three distinct states to be encoded: one for each head. It is important to note that the SRN with 60 hidden units does appear to be able to distinguish between likely and unlikely tails when trained on the symmetrical grammar, at least for the shorter embeddings. This is because with so much representational power to encode so little information (i.e., 60 units to represent three states), prediction-relevance again becomes less critical. In fact, with this particular architecture and on this particular problem, the SRN almost starts behaving like a Jordan network. Indeed, as discussed earlier, the recurrence already provides it with the means of representing sequential information, even prior to any training. When large numbers of hidden units are available, this natural ability of the network to maintain activation differences representing the temporal context will tend to be enhanced, and interference resulting from training on irrelevant elements will tend to have a weaker effect. Nevertheless, for a given number of hidden units, the SRN model still predicts large differences between the symmetrical and asymmetrical conditions. Further, based on the simulation work described in the rest

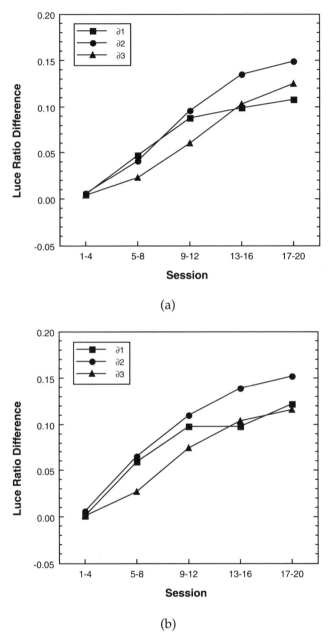

(a)

(b)

Figure 5.5
Luce ratio differences between likely and unlikely tails of sequences with one, two, or three neutral embedded elements produced by a buffer network with a decay rate of 0.1. (a): symmetrical grammar. (b): asymmetrical grammar.

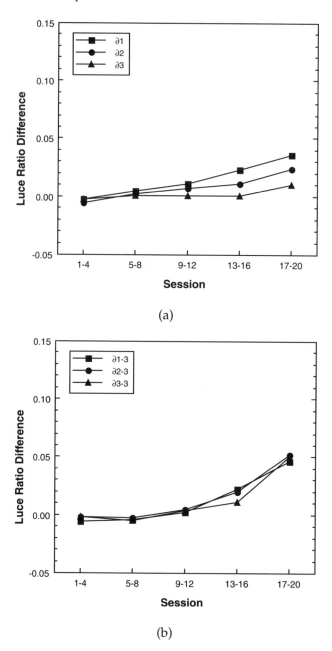

Figure 5.6
Luce ratio differences between likely and unlikely tails of sequences with one, two, or three neutral embedded elements. (a): simple recurrent network (SRN) with 60 hidden units, symmetrical grammar. (b): simple recurrent network (SRN) with 3 hidden units, asymmetrical grammar.

of this book, there is little reason to assume that large numbers of hidden units are needed to account adequately for human performance.

To explore how the performance of the Jordan network was affected by the value of μ, I conducted one additional simulation using the asymmetrical grammar and a μ of 0.7. This is already quite a high value for this parameter (i.e., 70% of the input activation at Time $t-1$ is carried over to the next time step), but even so, performance on the test material was not different from that illustrated in Figure 5.4d.

To summarize, the predictions entailed by the two classes of models (SRN vs. decay-based models) appear to be both robust and distinct from each other. How about predictions from table-lookup models? As discussed above, mechanisms based exclusively on table lookup would fail to produce different responses for the likely and unlikely tails of sequences containing three neutral elements, because in those specific cases, there was *no* contingency between heads and tails, even in the material generated from the grammar. By contrast, the network models appear to be able to encode these contingencies. This is because they actually learn which cues in the sequence are relevant for predicting the tail and because they can use that knowledge to generalize to similar instances.

How would human subjects perform on the same material? In the following section, I describe an experiment that was designed to answer this question.

Experiment 3

The purpose of this experiment was to test the SRN model's predictions, as outlined above, and to contrast them with those of decay-based models and of table-lookup models. This experiment was designed to yield detailed data about how well subjects are able to maintain information about remote context. Subjects were trained in exactly the same conditions as the simulation models.

Method

The design of Experiment 3 was almost identical with that of Experiments 1 and 2. Half of the subjects were exposed to material generated from the symmetrical version of the grammar illustrated in Figure 5.3; the other half were exposed to material generated from the asymmetrical version of the grammar. The following subsections detail the few methodological changes between this experiment and Experiments 1 and 2.

Subjects   Ten new subjects (Carnegie Mellon University undergradu-ates and graduates, aged 20–41) participated in Experiment 3. Half of the subjects were randomly assigned to the symmetrical condition; the other half were trained on the asymmetrical grammar.

Apparatus and Display   The experiment was run on several Macintosh II computers. The display consisted of eight dots arranged in a hori-zontal line on the computer's screen and separated by intervals of 2 cm. At a viewing distance of 57 cm, the distance between any two dots subtended a visual angle of 2°.

Stimulus Material   Stimulus generation proceeded in exactly the same way as for the simulations described above. To control for finger effects, a different mapping between keys and letters of the grammar was used for each subject within a condition. The same set of five mappings was used for both conditions. Thus, each of the five distinct mappings was assigned to 2 subjects, 1 in each condition.

Postexperimental Interviews   Subjects were fully debriefed after the experiment, as in Experiments 1 and 2. They were asked detailed questions about whether they had detected any patterns in the material.

Results

Overall Task Performance   Figure 5.7 shows the average RTs on correct responses for each of the 20 experimental sessions, plotted separately for each condition. As expected, response times improved dramatically with practice, and at about the same rate in both conditions. A two way ANOVA with one between factor and repeated measures on the second factor (condition [symmetrical vs. asymmetrical] by practice [20 levels]) revealed a significant main effect of practice, $F(19, 152) = 29.890$, $p < .001$, $MS_e = 700.651$; but no main effect of condition, $F(1, 8) = .083$, $p > .1$, $MS_e = 41584.990$, and no interaction, $F(19, 152) = 1.186$, $p > .1$, $MS_e = 700.651$. Although subjects appear to have been somewhat faster in the asymmetrical condition, this trend was not confirmed by the ANOVA. Overall, subjects were somewhat slower in this experiment than in the first two. There is little doubt that this is due to the larger number of choices used in this experiment (eight vs. six for Experiments 1 and 2).

Accuracy was very high throughout training, and similar in both conditions. Over the entire experiment, subjects averaged 96.4% correct responses in the asymmetrical condition and 96.1% correct responses in the symmetrical condition. A two-way ANOVA with one between factor and repeated measures on the second factor (condition [symmetrical vs. asymmetrical] by practice [20 levels]) again revealed a significant main effect of practice, $F(19, 152) = 1.922, p < .05, MS_e = .0002$; but no main effect of condition, $F(1, 8) = .041, p > .1, MS_e = .01$; and no interaction, $F(19, 152) = 1.186, p > .1, MS_e = .0002$. In contrast with Experiments 1 and 2, it appears that subjects in this experiment learned to be more accurate with practice. Figure 5.8 shows the average RTs elicited by likely and unlikely tails, pooled over five blocks of four successive sessions each, and for each condition. It is obvious that subjects in either condition appear to be able to successfully discriminate between the tails. It is interesting to note that subjects in the asymmetrical condition produce faster responses on the likely tails than subjects in the symmetrical condition, whereas performance on the unlikely tails appears to be comparable in both conditions. Note, however, that any difference between the two conditions could not be attributed solely to a better encoding of the head, since the embeddings of the asymmetrical condition contained information about the tail. Valid comparisons of this kind will be presented when I examine performance on the test material, which was designed to be neutral in either condition. A three-way ANOVA with one between factor (con-

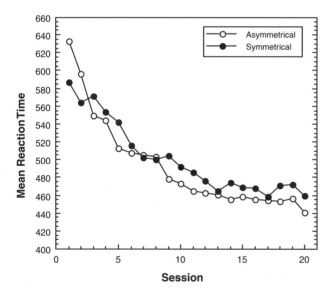

Figure 5.7
Mean reaction times in the asymmetrical and symmetrical conditions of Experiment 3, for each of the 20 sessions of training.

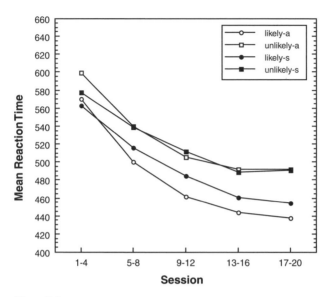

Figure 5.8
Mean reaction times elicited by likely and unlikely tails in the asymmetrical and symmetrical conditions of Experiment 3, for each of five blocks of four successive sessions of training.

dition [symmetrical vs. asymmetrical]) and repeated measures on the other factors (practice [5 levels] by successor type [likely vs. unlikely]) conducted on the data illustrated in Figure 5.6 revealed significant main effects of practice, $F(4, 32) = 54.764$, $p < .001$, $MS_e = 751.378$; and of successor type, $F(1, 8) = 53.917$, $p < .001$, $MS_e = 545.508$; but no main effect of condition, $F(1, 8) = .016$, $p > .1$, $MS_e = 32594.733$. There was a significant interaction between practice and successor type, $F(4, 32) = 391.958$, $p < .001$, $MS_e = 39.822$. The slight interaction trend between condition and successor type apparent in Figure 5.6 failed to reach significance.

Postexperimental Interviews   Nine subjects reported suspecting that the material was not fully random. However, it appears that this suspicion was in fact based on irrelevant cues. Indeed, 5 subjects (3 in the symmetrical condition and 2 in the asymmetrical condition) reported noticing "too many repetitions of the same key." Of course, repetitions tend to occur even in random material, and this observation cannot be taken as evidence that subjects were aware of the structure embedded in the material. Four subjects (3 in the asymmetrical condition and 1 in the symmetrical condition) reported noticing alternations between two or more screen positions. However, a careful examination of the correspondence between subjects' statements and the specific material each of them was exposed to failed to reveal any systematic pattern. When asked whether they had attempted to guess successive events, 8 subjects (4 in each condition) reported doing so at times. Of these 8, 5 also reported abandoning the strategy because of its inefficiency.

Based on these verbal reports, it appears safe to conclude that subjects had little or no knowledge of the overall organization of the material, or of the specific contingencies that were the object of the experiment.

Performance on the Test Material   Performance on the test material was averaged over blocks of four successive sessions, to yield 30 data points (2 tails × 3 embedding lengths × 5 blocks of sessions) per subject for the entire experiment. To simplify the presentation of these results, I computed the difference in reaction time between the unlikely and likely tails, for each embedding length and for each of five blocks of four consecutive sessions. These data are illustrated in Figures 5.9a and 5.9b. On first analysis, there are several important points worth remarking on.

First, although the data are quite noisy in places, there are obvious effects of practice and of embedding length in both conditions: The difference scores generally tend to increase with practice and to decrease with the length of the embedding. Note also that much of the learning seems to occur between Sessions 1–4 and Sessions 5–8. By contrast, the data from subsequent sessions appear to be relatively stable, at least insofar as learning is concerned. This is a further indication that the grammar used in this experiment is considerably simpler than the grammars used in Experiments 1 and 2.

Second, and more importantly, subjects in the symmetrical condition appear to distinguish clearly between likely and unlikely tails, for all embedding lengths. This result is at odds with the SRN model's predictions, but consistent with the predictions of decay-based models.

Third, although subjects in both conditions appear to become sensitive to the information conveyed by the head, the difference scores tend to be somewhat larger (about 20 msec) in the asymmetrical condition, particularly for the shorter embeddings. This result, by contrast, is inconsistent with the predictions of the decay-based models, but consistent with the predictions of the SRN model.

To confirm these observations, I conducted a four-way ANOVA with one between factor (condition [symmetrical vs. asymmetrical]) and

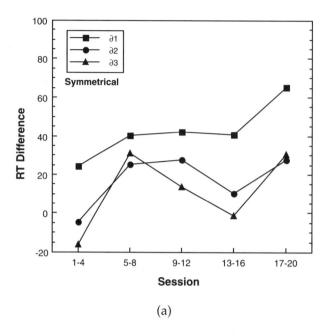

(a)

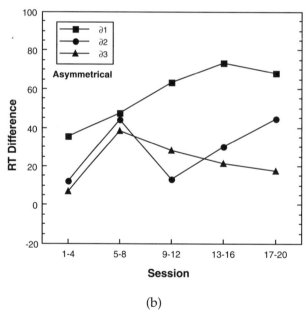

(b)

Figure 5.9
Reaction time (RT) differences between likely and unlikely tails of sequences with one, two, or three neutral embedded elements. (a): symmetrical condition, (b): asymmetrical condition.

repeated measures on three other factors (practice [5 levels] by embedding length [3 levels] by tail type [likely vs. unlikely]). This analysis revealed significant main effects of practice, $F(4, 32) = 37.313$, $p < .001$, $MS_e = 3504.179$; of embedding length, $F(2, 16) = 10.531$, $p < .005$, $MS_e = 399.314$; and of successor type, $F(1, 8) = 52.689$, $p < .001$, $MS_e = 1282.805$. There was no main effect of condition, $F(1, 8) = .001$, $p > .1$, $MS_e = 119921.392$. The following interactions were significant: practice by successor type, $F(4, 32) = 9.590$, $p < .001$, $MS_e = 244.722$; and embedding length by successor type, $F(2, 16) = 20.556$, $p < .001$, $MS_e = 377.413$.

Clearly, subjects in both conditions are able to discriminate between likely and unlikely tails. Their ability to do so improves with practice, and more so for the shorter embeddings. Not surprisingly, discriminating between the tails is harder for longer embeddings. The fact that subjects in the symmetrical condition appear to be able to encode information about the head of the test sequences constitutes clear evidence against the predictions of the SRN model. This failure to find a difference between the two conditions was very systematic, even in more restricted analyses (e.g., using only the data from the shortest embeddings, or limiting the analysis to specific points during training)[3].

Finally, subjects in either condition appear to become sensitive to the likelihood of the tail elements even when the embedding contains three neutral elements. Since there was no contingency between heads and tails either in the training material or in the test material, this result appears to rule out mechanisms based on table lookup. A three-way ANOVA with one between factor (condition [symmetrical vs. asymmetrical]) and repeated measures on the two other factors (practice [5 levels] by tail type [likely vs. unlikely]) confirmed this result: There were significant main effects of practice, $F(4, 32) = 29.607$, $p < .001$, $MS_e = 1436.531$; and of successor type, $F(1, 8) = 20.643$, $p < .002$, $MS_e = 205.305$; but no main effect of condition, $F(1, 8) = .004$, $p > .1$, $MS_e = 43530.375$. The interaction between practice and successor type reached significance, $F(1, 8) = 5.445$, $p < .002$, $MS_e = 339.899$. On the basis of these results, models based on table-lookup mechanisms may be ruled out. Indeed, this class of models cannot account for the fact that subjects discriminate between likely and unlikely tails after embeddings composed of three neutral elements. This result is also important for another reason: In this paradigm, it is the first demonstration of sensitivity to information occurring four time steps before the response is executed. Experiments 1 and 2 failed to reveal such sensitivity, but of course the material used in these experiments was more complex than the material used in Experiment 3.

Discussion

Subjects in Experiment 3 were exposed to an eight-choice serial reaction time task for 60,000 trials. In both conditions, the material incorporated long-distance contingencies (between "heads" and "tails") that spanned embeddings of up to three elements. In the symmetrical condition, the embedded material was irrelevant for predicting the tails of the long-distance contingencies. In the asymmetrical condition, by contrast, the distribution of embedded elements was such that the embedding as a whole conveyed some information about which tail was more likely to occur. Some "neutral" elements of the embeddings were independent of the head in either condition. Performance on long-distance contin-gencies that specifically spanned these neutral embeddings (the "test material") was used to assess the ability of subjects to maintain infor-mation about the temporal context. Further, to assess how well subjects were able to generalize to new material, the contingencies between heads and tails were suppressed when the long-distance contingency spanned neutral embeddings of length 3.

This design allowed the predictions of three distinct classes of models to be contrasted. The SRN model predicted that processing of the long-distance contingencies would tend to be facilitated in the asymmetrical condition, and that little or no learning of these contingencies would occur in the symmetrical condition. By contrast, decay-based models, such as the Jordan network and buffer networks, predicted no differ-ence between the two conditions. All network models predicted suc-cessful generalization to contingencies spanning neutral embeddings of length 3, in contrast with predictions from table-lookup models.

The experiment indicated that subjects were indeed able to generalize to contingencies spanning embeddings of length 3, thereby clearly ruling out table-lookup models. This result also documents sensitivity to the constraints set by a temporal context of four elements (the head + three embedded elements), for the first time in this paradigm.

The results were not as clear-cut insofar as distinguishing between the network models is concerned. On the one hand, subjects were clearly able to discriminate between likely and unlikely tails in the symmetrical condition, which appears to rule out the SRN model. On the other hand, there was some evidence for better performance in the asymmetrical condition, although this trend was not confirmed by statistical analysis. The fact that subjects in either condition exhibit a clear ability to discriminate between likely and unlikely tails even after neutral embeddings is in itself quite remarkable. The fact that there appears to be a trend toward better performance in the asymmetrical condition suggests that subjects learned the constraints of the grammar in a way that is affected by the distribution of embedded elements. This result is not fully consistent with the predictions of the Jordan network model, which failed to produce such a difference with two different values of μ. Buffer networks tended to be more sensitive to the specific value of decay used, but overall their performance matches that of Jordan networks in this particular case. Specifically, buffer networks are able, as is the Jordan network, to learn material from both the symmetrical and asymmetrical versions of the grammar. Clearly, then, the SRN's prediction is disconfirmed by the results of this experiment.

What are the implications of these findings? More precisely, do they mean that a complete reinterpretation of the work described in this book is at hand? Not necessarily so: It appears that there is a substantial overlap in the behavior of the SRN model and of the Jordan network. In fact, it may even be the case that the only significant difference between the two models lies in the distinct set of predictions that were tested in Experiment 3. To confirm this impression, I compared the responses produced by both models when trained on the material used in Experiment 1. The Jordan network used a μ of 0.5 and otherwise identical parameters as for the SRN simulations described in chapter 3. The responses of the two networks were pooled over the nodes of the grammar, as in the analysis illustrated in Figure 3.11. I then conducted a regression analysis on the data resulting from averaging the responses of both models over blocks of four successive sessions. The results are illustrated in Figure 5.10. The obtained r^2 coefficient is .901, indicating a high degree of correspondence between the responses of the SRN and of the Jordan network. The residual variance may probably be accounted for by differences in the distribution of initial weights, and by other factors such as the interaction between the effects of the short-term learning mechanisms and the different architectures of the two models. This high correspondence between the two models is a clear indication that there is indeed a large overlap in their behavior. Of course, another reason why there is such a high overlap is that the material of Experiment 1 was not designed to specifically reveal differences between the two models. In other words, much of the material used in Experiment 1 *was* prediction-relevant at every step and therefore not a potential problem for the SRN.

Thus, it appears that decay-based mechanisms may in fact be sufficient to explain human behavior. It is interesting that mechanisms even

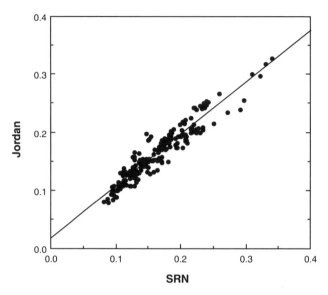

Figure 5.10
Correspondence between responses from the simple recurrent network (SRN) model and from the Jordan model on material from Experiment 1.

simpler than those implemented by the SRN model appear to be adequate to account for human performance. There may still be other conditions in which this may not be so, however. For instance, the fact that the shortest embeddings used in this experiment were only one element in length certainly contributed to the ability of the Jordan network to encode the long-distance contingency. Indeed, with only one time step between the head and the tail, the input trace corresponding to the head has only decayed by 50% when the embedded element is presented, and when the network is trained to predict the tail. It would be much harder for Jordan networks to encode this information if the shortest embeddings were allowed to be only of length 2 or 3. The SRN model would also fail to discriminate between likely and unlikely tails under these conditions, but again, only if the embedding had no relevant structure (i.e., it would be successful in the asymmetrical condition). An experiment addressing this contrast may be impossible to realize, however. It was already extremely difficult to design Experiment 3 in such a way as to ensure (1) that expected RT differences were high enough to be detectable, (2) that the test material was relatively unnoticeable, and (3) that the number of choices was within reasonable limits. One particular design difficulty with Experiment 3 was related to the number of neutral elements available to combine in the embeddings of the test material. With only two such elements, longer embeddings necessarily consist of highly noticeable—and therefore undesirable—alternation or repetition runs. A pilot experiment with 4 subjects in the asymmetrical condition indeed revealed that responses were strongly affected by the salience of the test material. As a result, the relevant RT differences between the successors of these salient embeddings tended to be obscured. An experiment with the design outlined above may therefore require more neutral elements, so that longer embeddings do not have such a salient structure. However, adding neutral elements would require increasing the overall number of choices, which is likely to result in even smaller differences between the relevant responses. There is no obvious way to solve this difficult chicken-and-egg problem. It is likely that future research will have to identify other means of revealing patterns of results that have the potential of contrasting possible remaining differences among the three models. One interesting possibility for distinguishing between the decay-based networks may consist of using the same material as in this experiment, but with the added constraint that heads followed by embeddings of length 3 would *never* be associated with a particular tail. Buffer networks would not generalize to such sequences, in contrast with the Jordan network. This is because different units and connections are used to represent events at different time steps in the case of buffer networks.

To summarize, the evidence obtained in Experiment 3 fully supports the notion that subjects are acquiring complex and structured knowledge about the stimulus environment. The fact that they generalize to contingencies that have not actually been presented during training suggests that sequential material is represented as a time-varying and distributed trace of successive events rather than as a collection of specific instances. Even though there is some evidence that subjects in the asymmetrical condition tended to become more sensitive to the head than subjects in the symmetrical condition, this result was not confirmed by statistical analysis. This, together with the fact that subjects in the symmetrical condition successfully discriminate between likely and unlikely tails, makes it clear that decay-based models such as the Jordan network and buffer networks are sufficient to account for this outcome. However, this does not necessarily means that the same pattern of results would be obtained in different conditions, for instance when the material is slightly harder to learn. Further research is needed to fully resolve this issue.

Chapter 6
Explicit Sequence Learning

All sequence-learning situations I have explored so far were choice reaction tasks. However, sequence-learning in general is not limited to choice reaction paradigms. For instance, another kind of situation that requires temporal context to be integrated consists of asking subjects to make explicit predictions about the successor of observed sequences. In this chapter, I explore one such situation, first described by Kushner, Cleeremans and Reber (1991), and extensions of it that address the important question of determining what kind of representations (abstract vs. exemplar-based) subjects acquire during training. At first sight, it may appear that these situations are not likely to involve implicit learning processes, but this need not be so. Indeed, as discussed in chapter 1, there is ample evidence that implicit learning processes play an important role even in situations where explicit decisions are required. The classic Reber task is a perfect example of such situations: Even though subjects are required to make overt decisions about the grammaticality of letter strings, the knowledge they use in doing so was acquired implicitly, through exposure to the training material. By the same token, it is also likely that these tasks involve additional, more explicit processes, because they place different demands on subjects (see chapter 1 for a discussion of task demands). Specifically, in both the Reber task and explicit sequence-learning situations such as the one described hereafter, subjects are undoubtedly aware of the fact that the only information available to them to perform successfully is contained in the stimulus material, and they are thus much more likely to engage in active hypothesis-testing strategies.

An Explicit Prediction Task

Recently, Kushner and Reber (personal communication, December 1990; see also Kushner et al., 1991) have started exploring a situation analogous to the original Reber task, but in the context of sequence-learning. Their subjects were exposed to series of five events presented successively on a computer screen and were asked to predict the location of the sixth stimulus. There were three possible locations at which the stimulus might appear, organized as the vertices of an inverted triangle. The first five stimuli appeared at random locations. The location of the sixth stimulus, by contrast, was determined based on the spatial relationship between the second and fourth stimuli. If they had appeared at the same screen location, then the sixth stimulus appeared at Location A. If they had been in a clockwise relationship, the sixth stimulus appeared at Location B. The sixth stimulus appeared at Location C if the second and fourth stimuli had been in a counter-clockwise relationship. The first, third, and fifth stimuli were thus always irrelevant.

What makes this design attractive is its complexity. First, there are more irrelevant events than useful ones. Second, the rule that defines the location of the sixth stimulus is complex because it involves a relationship between two events rather than the two particular events themselves (i.e., each crucial event is useless in and of itself). This results in each component of the rule being instantiated by different pairs of events, each of which may in turn be embedded in a large number of different irrelevant contexts.

Experimental Design and Results
The experiment conducted by Kushner and Reber was divided into three phases. In a first phase, subjects were asked to make 2,430 predictions, as described above. In a second phase, the rule was sur-reptitiously modified by shifting the location of the sixth stimulus by one position for each component of the rule. For instance, sixth events that had appeared at Location A in the first phase of the experiment now appeared at Location B, and so on. Finally, in a third phase, the rule was again modified. This time, the location of the sixth event was simply determined at random. Thus, the material of the second phase tested for transfer, whereas the material of the third phase may be used to assess how much performance improvement depends on knowledge of the rule. Subjects were asked to make 972 predictions in each of the second and third phases.

The results are illustrated in Figure 6.1. Subjects become increasingly better at making accurate predictions over the first 10 sessions of training and end up reaching about 45% correct responses in the 10th

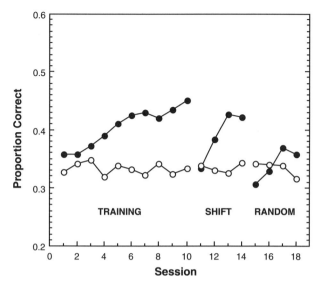

Figure 6.1
Mean proportion of correct predictions in the Kushner and Reber task, over the 18 sessions of training, and for the three phases of the experiment.

session. This is significantly above chance level (33%)[1] and indicates that subjects have acquired knowledge about the relevant regularities in the material. The second phase begins with a dramatic drop in performance (to chance level), but there is again evidence of learning over the next three sessions ($p < 0.1$). This suggests that subjects are able to transfer relatively easily from one stimulus-response set to another one. By contrast, performance in the third, random, phase is low and fails to be significantly over chance level.

Despite this clear sensitivity to the complex regularities embedded in the material, none of the subjects exhibited knowledge of the sequential structure when asked after the task. Post-experimental interviews revealed that subjects felt frustrated in their attempts to learn the rule that determined the location of the sixth stimulus. All subjects reported that they eventually abandoned the search for rules and started predicting according to their "hunches" or according to "what felt right." Subjects were unable to specify which covariations were crucial in the sequence of five stimuli, even in a general form such as "When the nth stimulus was in Location X, the correct answer was usually Y." No subject reported awareness of the rule shifts between the three phases of the experiment. Subjects' poor knowledge of the constraints embedded in the material was also confirmed by their performance on a ranking task, in which they were asked to rate each of the five stimuli in terms of their relevance in predicting the location of the sixth stimulus. The results failed to reveal sensitivity to the crucial events: On a scale of 1 (very important) to 5 (not important), the crucial events received average ranks of 3.5 (second event) and 2.67 (fourth event), whereas the first, third, and fifth events were ranked 3.33, 3.67, and 1.83 respectively. However, there was some evidence that particularly salient sequences that were reported by subjects also elicited very good predictions. For instance, sequences in which the first five stimuli had appeared at the same location always predicted A as the location of the sixth trial. (i.e., 'AAAAA → A', 'BBBBB → A', 'CCCCC → A'). Similarly, alternating sequences such as 'ABABA' always predicted Location A as well. Subjects could correctly predict the successor of repeating sequences in about 61% of the cases of the first phase (49% for the alternating sequences)—considerably better than average. Other data (Reber, personal communication, December 1990) from an experiment that was identical except for the fact that subjects received considerably more training also indicated that at least 1 subject did become fully aware of the contingencies and was able to report them to the experimenter. These results clearly indicate that, at least in some specific cases like this, subjects have become aware of some of the regularities embedded in the material and may rely on explicit knowledge to determine their responses. Subjects' successful prediction performance is far from being based only on these salient patterns, however: The average prediction score during the first phase only dropped by .0046 percentage points when the three possible repeating and six possible single-alternating sequences were eliminated from the analysis. Clearly, subjects have become sensitive to contingencies about which they are unable to report.

Simulations of Learning in the Kushner and Reber Experiment
How could the SRN model be applied to modeling this experimental situation? And is it appropriate to do so? The answer to the latter question resides in the mechanisms that underlie the SRN's performance. At a general level, the central processing features of the SRN model are (1) that it elaborates representations of sequential material, and (2) that its responses consist of predictions about subsequent events. In the case of the situation we explored, these predictions were assumed to result in preparation for the next event, but it seems perfectly reasonable to imagine that the same mechanisms may apply

in cases where overt predictions are required. That is, even though it is quite likely that other, more explicit mechanisms play a role in situations like Kushner and Reber's, the results also make it clear that most of subjects' predictions are based on implicit knowledge. How, then, may the SRN model be applied to this situation? I used the same architecture as described in chapter 3, but with the following three modifications.

First, it is obvious that short-term priming effects of the kind observed in Experiments 1 and 2 play no role whatsoever in this situation. The corresponding mechanisms in the SRN model (i.e., dual weights on the connections, and running average activations on the output units) were therefore prevented from operating by setting all the relevant parameters to 0.

Second, since no predictions are required from subjects during presentation of the first five trials of a series, learning was turned off for those trials. The network was therefore merely storing successive events during presentation of the first four trials. When the fifth trial was presented as input to the network, however, learning was turned on, and the network was trained to activate the unit corresponding to the location of the sixth event on its output layer.

Third, since trials (i.e., blocks of five events) were totally independent of each other, the context units were reset to 0 at the beginning of each trial. Thus, the temporal context could influence processing within a block of five events, but it was prevented from carrying over to the next block.

Ten SRNs with 15 hidden units each and a learning rate of 0.8 were trained on material identical to Kushner and Reber's, and for the same number of exposures. Each network used a different set of initial random weights. On each of the 18 sessions of training (10 during the first phase, and 4 each during the second and third phases), each network was exposed to 243 random sequences of five events[2]. A prediction response was considered correct if the activation of the unit corresponding to the actual sixth event was higher than the activation of the two other units. Figure 6.2 compares the human data with the average proportion of correct prediction responses produced by the networks during each of the 18 sessions of training. Perhaps surprisingly[3], the model fails completely to learn the regularity, its proportion of correct predictions hovering around chance (33%) during the entire simulation. One may wonder about the effects of using such a high value for the learning rate ($\eta = 0.8$), but additional simulations revealed

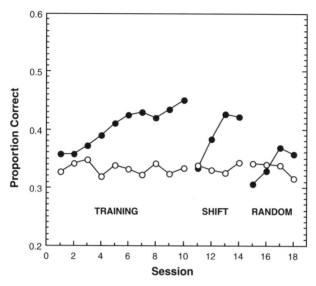

Figure 6.2
Mean proportion of correct predictions in the Kushner and Reber task, over the 18 sessions of training, and for the three phases of the experiment. Filled symbols represent human data; open symbols represent simulated data (simple recurrent network [SRN] model).

that the network also failed with considerably lower learning rates (e.g., $\eta = 0.01$). The reasons for this failure are in fact familiar: As pointed out in chapters 2 and 5, representing temporal context in the SRN model requires the material to be prediction-relevant at each step. However, none of the sequence elements of the material used in this experiment is prediction-relevant, since each sequence was generated randomly. As a result, no representation of the context can start to develop. Further training only tends to make this situation worse. On further analysis, the stimulus material used here is in fact rather similar to the material generated by the symmetrical version of the grammar used in Experiment 3 (see chapter 5), in that relevant information needs to be maintained for as many as four time steps before becoming useful.

What alternative model may be successful in mastering this task's material? An obvious candidate is the Jordan network, since it was able to learn the material from Experiment 3's symmetrical grammar and does not require sequence elements to be prediction-relevant at every step. Thus, 10 Jordan networks were trained in conditions identical with those used for the SRN simulations described above, and with the same parameters and performance criteria. All the networks used a μ

of 0.5. The average proportion of correct responses produced by the networks is illustrated along with the corresponding human data in Figure 6.3. Again, the model fails to learn the regularities: The average proportion of correct predictions remains at chance level in all three phases of the experiment. Additional simulations with different parameters yielded similar results: Neither changes in the learning rate nor changes in the value of μ resulted in the network mastering the material. A careful analysis of the network's performance revealed that its inability to learn the material stems from interference by the irrelevant elements that occur on Positions 1, 3, and 5 of each sequence. Recall that, in contrast with the sequences used in Experiment 3, the irrelevant elements are drawn from the same pool of possible elements as the relevant ones. Since the Jordan network's representation of the temporal context depends on a decaying trace of each element presented, a single unit in the input pool is used to represent the same event at different time steps. If repetitions are allowed, the time averaging will necessarily result in a loss of information, since the traces corresponding to the repeated elements are blended together to determine the activation of the corresponding input unit. With a μ of 1.0, for instance, the network would have no means of discriminating between identical

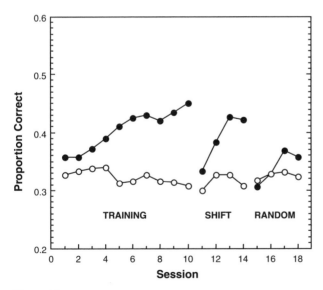

Figure 6.3
Mean proportion of correct predictions in the Kushner and Reber task, over the 18 sessions of training, and for the three phases of the experiment. Filled symbols represent human data; open symbols represent simulated data (Jordan model).

events that occurred at different time steps. In effect, μ determines the relative weight given to recent versus older events. In cases where events may be repeated, it is easy to see that the network will sometimes have to make very fine discriminations between input activations. To illustrate this, Figure 6.4 shows the entire training set as points in a three-dimensional space where each axis represents the activation of one of the three input units. Each point in the figure corresponds to the final pattern obtained after presenting all five events of a specific sequence to the network. The beautiful recursive object that emerges from this analysis may be described as follows: The outermost points at the vertices of the triangle correspond to sequences that consist of five repetitions of the same element. Each of the three large triangles groups 81 sequences that share the same final element. This organization is then repeated up to the point where each group is composed of only one unique sequence (and represented by a single point in the figure). Thus, each of the three smaller triangles that make up one of the largest ones corresponds to sequences that share both their last and penultimate elements, and so on. Consider now the case of one of the smaller groups that contain 9 sequences. All sequences in one such group share their last three elements. All sequences in one of the three

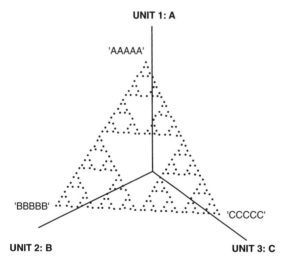

Figure 6.4
A three-dimensional representation of the input patterns presented to the Jordan network. Each axis corresponds to one of the three input units representing each of the three possible sequence elements. Each point in the figure represents a single sequence in the training set. The object has been enlarged for detail, so that the axis values are meaningless.

smaller triangles differ only in their first element, which is irrelevant for the prediction task. The problem comes from the fact that sequences that differ in either their second or their first element are often indistinguishable from each other. So for instance, the sequences 'AAAAA', 'ABAAA', and 'BAAAA' are represented by the input patterns in Table 6.1 after all five elements have been presented to the network. The first and third sequences predict the same successor ('A'), whereas the second predicts a different one ('B'). Yet its representation is almost identical to those of the other two sequences. This discriminability problem is repeated at many different places all over the space and makes it impossible for the network to learn the material. Using a different value of μ does not help solve this problem. This analysis is confirmed by the fact that if irrelevant events are not presented to the network (by setting the corresponding input pattern to 0.0), the network has no trouble learning the material.

This double failure prompted me to reevaluate the task in terms of the characteristics that differentiate it from the choice reaction time tasks explored so far. After analysis, there are two main relevant differences between choice reaction tasks and Kushner and Reber's explicit prediction task. First, it appears likely that subjects involved in the latter task will engage in an explicit effort to remember as much as they can from the sequence of five events that they observe during each trial. Indeed, subjects are certainly aware of the fact that the information they need to make correct predictions has to be present in the sequence for the task to make sense. A second difference is that the stimulus material used in Kushner and Reber's experiment is presented in chunks of five elements, and the instructions make it clear that sequences are independent of each other. Both aspects of this situation stand in sharp contrast with the characteristics of the choice reaction tasks described throughout this book, where encoding the temporal

Table 6.1
The representation of three sequences from Kushner and Reber's material over the input layer of a Jordan network.

	A	B	C
AAAAA	1.94	0.00	0.00
ABAAA	1.88	0.12	0.00
BAAAA	1.81	0.06	0.00

Note: Numbers represent the activation levels of the three input units, each corresponding to one of the three possible sequence elements ('A', 'B', or 'C').

context is not even necessary to comply with task instructions and to attain satisfactory performance levels. These differences would seem to make it plausible that subjects maintain detailed information about a fixed number of time steps.

Another way to think of this task is that the temporal dimension is not really relevant. In other words, this task is more akin to standard categorization tasks than to the choice reaction tasks explored in this book. Indeed, one may think of subjects as being asked to classify the sequences in three groups based on some features that are to be discovered. The fact that the elements are presented sequentially rather than simultaneously only makes it harder for subjects to encode the relevant regularities. It is likely that a simultaneous version of this task (using strings of letters, for instance) would be easier than the sequential version, because subjects would have more opportunity to detect common features among different sequences. Another interesting contrasting experiment would be to use this experiment's material in a choice reaction setting similar to that of the other experiments described in the book. Would subjects' reaction times reflect an encoding of the regularities? If so, it would be an indication that the same processes may underlie performance in both tasks. If not, it may constitute evidence that in fact the tasks place very different demands on subjects and that they elicit different mechanisms for maintaining information about the temporal context. Based on the other data reported in this book, I would expect subjects to fail in a continuous, choice reaction version of Kushner and Reber's task.

As discussed in chapter 5, one class of models that do not suffer either from interference from subsequent events (as the Jordan network does) or from the lack of trial-to-trial contingencies (as the SRN does) is instantiated by buffer networks (see Figure 5.2). Even though such networks are somewhat implausible in the context of choice reaction tasks and are computationally very limited, the features of this task make them good candidates here.

How well would a network of this kind learn Kushner and Reber's material? To find out, I trained 10 buffer networks with five pools of three input units each (i.e., a temporal window of five time steps) for the same number of trials as subjects in the experiment. As for human subjects, the network was only required to predict the next event when presented with the last event of each series of five. As a simplification, traces were not decayed; that is, the decay rate was 0.0. Note that this effectively eliminates any representation of the temporal dimension from the architecture: The network is identical with a simple three-layer back-propagation network. As before, a learning rate of 0.8 was used. The results are illustrated in Figure 6.5. The results indicate that the network is not only able to learn the contingency between Events 2 and 4 during training, but also able to transfer successfully to the shifted material. That these improvements depend specifically on learning of the contingency is demonstrated by the fact that performance on random material remains at chance level. Several interesting differences between the simulation data and the human data are also present.

First, the network tends to learn slowly at the beginning of training and faster at the end, whereas human subjects improve their performance at a more constant rate. This trend was present over a number of additional simulations with different learning rates and may indicate that subjects also rely on memory for specific instances during early training. As indicated above, there is evidence that subjects quickly learn to respond correctly to sequences that are particularly salient, such as sequences that consist of only one repeated element, or sequences that contain simple alternations between two elements. By construction, all sequences of this kind have the same successor, and it is therefore very likely that subjects rely on knowledge of these

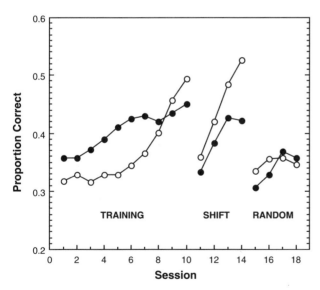

Figure 6.5
Mean proportion of correct predictions in the Kushner and Reber task, over the 18 sessions of training, and for the three phases of the experiment. Filled symbols represent human data; open symbols represent simulated data (buffer model).

sequences to respond during early training. The network model has no means of capturing this effect, since it is not sensitive to psychological salience and treats all sequences as equivalent.

Second, the network's performance on the shifted material presented during the second phase of the experiment is somewhat better than that of human subjects. Why is it so easy for the network to transfer to the shifted material? The answer lies in an examination of how the model stores and processes knowledge about sequences. Basically, in the case of this particular task, the connections between the input units and the hidden units implement a mapping between sets of sequences of events and distinct internal representations. Optimally, each set of sequences that results in the same prediction about Event 6 should be associated with a unique code on the hidden units. More likely, there are a number of distinct clusters of internal representations, with each cluster grouping those internal representations that result in the same response. (See chapter 2 for several detailed examples of this kind of organization.) The connections between the hidden units and the output units, in turn, map these clusters of internal representations onto the responses. The rule shift introduced in the experiment is in effect a change in the latter mapping. Indeed, it does not result in any change in which events are important, in the number of possible responses, and so on. As a result, all the network really needs to do to produce the shifted responses is to adjust the connections from the hidden units to the output units. Weight adjustments are typically much faster in the last layer of connections than in the others because the error signals are themselves much larger. The fact that the network is even somewhat better than subjects at transferring to the shifted material suggests that other factors may again influence human performance in this task. (Naturally, the final level of transfer performance is subject to parametric adjustment, but the network was systematically better than human subjects on the very first block of shifted trials.) In particular, it would seem that subjects confronted with a sudden and drastic drop in performance are likely to start adopting a more cautious strategy for tackling the new material, perhaps sticking to old responses for a while. This may account for the larger initial performance drop exhibited by human subjects. The network is of course incapable of representing such strategic adjustments. Note, however, that the slope of the curve corresponding to the shifted material is steeper than that corresponding to the training material for both the simulation and human subjects, which suggests that fast readjustments are taking place in both cases.

Finally, the very last point of the "shifted" curve for the human subjects may just be atypical.

Discussion

The simulation results described in this section highlighted interesting shortcomings of both the SRN and the Jordan network. Indeed, both models were unable to learn material from the explicit prediction task proposed by Reber and Kushner (see Kushner et al., 1991), but for different reasons. In the case of the SRN, the problem stems from the fact that representing temporal context requires sequence elements to be prediction-relevant at every step—a property that is not exhibited by Kushner and Reber's material. In the case of the Jordan network, the problem resulted from interference from repeated events and from the ensuing loss of discriminability among sequences requiring different prediction responses. I argued that buffer networks, which do not suffer from the above limitations, may well be an adequate model of this particular task, even if they lack generality as plausible models of temporal processing and suffer from other kinds of computational limitations. This analysis is based on the observation that Kushner and Reber's task places very different demands on subjects than do the choice reaction tasks explored in other parts of this book. In particular, I suggested that the task is more akin to a standard classification task made harder by the fact that the material has temporal extent. The observation that the network succeeds even without any representation of the fact that the material has temporal extent further reinforces the notion that the task is rather different from the choice reaction tasks described in the rest of this book. Using nonzero values for the decay rate results essentially in slower learning and has effects that are similar to changes in the learning rate.

Despite the fact that buffer networks appear to be good models of human performance in Kushner and Reber's task, other data suggest that other processes not implemented by the model may play an important role. Specifically, it would appear that subjects also rely on memory for particularly salient sequences, at least during the early parts of training, where it was found that human performance was quite systematically above that of the model. As pointed out earlier, the basic model has no way of representing the influence of such salient items and can only capture the emerging gradual sensitivity to the regularities present in the material. That the task involves both implicit, gradual processes, as well as more explicit processes such as memory for specific items, strategic readjustments, and active hypothesis testing, is not surprising. On the contrary, it appears likely that most experimental tasks used to explore implicit learning (or, for that matter, most real-life learning situations as well) involve both kinds of processes. This obviously contributes to the difficulty of assessing which processes are responsible for particular aspects of performance in any given situation. One strategy that appears useful in overcoming these essentially methodological difficulties consists of minimizing the role that either source of knowledge may play in performance. The choice reaction tasks described in the rest of this book are an attempt at doing so. Another approach consists of exploring what minimal mechanisms may be applied to model human performance and to search for plausible accounts of the unexplained variance. The buffer networks described in this section come close to implementing the minimal mechanisms needed to sustain performance in this task, although it is likely that even simpler architectures may be successful.

As a final comment on the data, it is interesting to elaborate on the fact that subjects in this task were found to be able to readjust their performance to the shifted material very quickly. Another, similarly intriguing transfer result has been repeatedly described in grammar-learning experiments. For instance, Reber (1969) reported that transfer performance was significantly above chance with material generated from a grammar that had the same structural properties as the grammar used during training, but a different set of letters. By contrast (but not surprisingly), transfer performance was much worse in a control condition in which the same set of letters was used, but a different grammar. There appears to be no simple way of accounting for these results in an otherwise successful architecture such as Servan-Schreiber and Anderson's (1990) competitive chunking framework. The basic problem is that successful models of implicit learning, including the SRN and the other models described in the book, base their performance on the processing of exemplars. If the representations that these models develop encode the relevant structural properties of the material, they are expressed in terms of the exemplars themselves, and not as more abstract characterizations of these structural properties. This problem is minimized in Kushner and Reber's task because the shift concerns responses rather than stimuli. The fact that subjects do transfer successfully to sets of isomorphic stimuli again suggests that some additional mechanisms not captured by current simulation models may play an important role in implicit learning performance. One such mechanism may be "abstract analogy" (Brooks & Vokey, 1991), through which corresponding elements of different stimuli are perceived as entering into similar relationships with other elements. There is no doubt that the current generation of simulation models of implicit learning phenomena will have to address this issue in the future. But there may be different ways in which the notion of "abstraction" may be understood. For instance, Perruchet (personal communication, January 1992) rightly points out that successful transfer to the shifted material in Kushner and Reber's experiment is more akin to "reversal" than a real indication of possession of abstract knowledge of the rules that underlie stimulus generation. In the next section, I examine experimental and simulation data that constitute more direct tests of transfer based on abstraction.

Transfer to New Material

The task proposed by Kushner and Reber is interesting because the simplicity of its design interacts usefully with the complexity of the material. These features make it possible to design straightforward transfer situations during which subjects are presented with material that was not presented during training, and to start addressing difficult questions related to knowledge representation. What kind of knowledge of the sequences do subjects end up with after training? As discussed in the previous section, it is likely that subjects develop both a knowledge base about specific salient sequences and more gradual knowledge about the regularities embedded in the material. The buffer network proposed as a model of performance captures the latter aspect of subjects' knowledge. What kind of internal representations does the network develop during training? An analysis of the pattern of connection weights between input units and hidden units revealed that the network progressively learns to ignore information presented on the pools corresponding to time steps 1, 3, and 5, on which only irrelevant sequence elements may occur: All the corresponding connection weights were very close to 0.0 after training. By contrast, the weights on connections between the pools corresponding to Elements 2 and 4 were large. In the network's layer of hidden units, specific units were used to encode the different possible combinations of Elements 2 and 4 that may occur. Thus, the network has clearly learned to distinguish between relevant and irrelevant sequence elements. Does this mean that the network has acquired abstract knowledge of the material? One strategy in answering this question consists of first asking another one:

What kind of data would constitute evidence for rule-like abstraction in this task, that is, abstraction that may not be accounted for by similarity to stored exemplars? An interesting suggestion (Perruchet, personal communication, January 1992, in press), is to test subjects on new components or new instances of the generation rules used during training. For instance, in the prediction task described above, abstraction would be demonstrated if subjects were able to predict successfully the location of the successor of the sequence for new transitions between the locations at which Events 2 and 4 appeared. As a reminder, the rule used to generate the material consisted of three components: (1) If Events 2 and 4 appeared at the same location, then the location of the sixth event was A; (2) if Events 2 and 4 were in a clockwise relationship, then Event 6 appeared at Location B, and (3) if Events 2 and 4 were in counterclockwise relationship, then Event 6 appeared at Location C. Each component of the rule was instantiated by three different contingencies between Events 2 and 4, and each of these three specific pairs of events was embedded in the irrelevant context set by the other elements of the sequences. There are numerous ways of testing for generalization with this material. For instance, one could train subjects on two instances of each component of the rule (say, 'A' & 'A' in Positions 2 and 4, and 'B' & 'B'), and find out whether they generalize to material generated based on the third instance ('C' & 'C'). Another similar, but perhaps less stringent, test would be to compare performance on test sequences that are equal in similarity to the training sequences, but that vary in the location of the changes. For instance, the sequences 'ABCBB' (which predicts 'A') and 'CAACB' (which predicts 'B') both differ equally from 'CBABB' (which predicts 'A'). Assume that subjects are trained on the latter sequences and are then presented with the other two, which were never presented during training. The new sequence 'ABCBB' predicts the same sixth event as the old 'CBABB' because they differ only in their irrelevant elements (i.e., the crucial second and fourth elements are the same in both sequences). By contrast, the new 'CAACB' differs from the old 'CBABB' in Elements 2 and 4 and therefore predicts a different Event 6. Different results would be expected in this situation depending on whether performance is based on abstract knowledge or on memory for exemplars. If performance is based on memory for exemplars, then subjects should predict the successor equally well in each case, since the new sequences of the example are equally similar to the old one. By contrast, if subjects induced that only Events 2 and 4 determine the successor (as well as which successor occurs in each case), then performance should be better on new sequences that share these events with the old ones than on those that do not. In the following sections, I examine two transfer situations designed to test these issues.

Transfer to Sequences with New Relevant Elements
Perruchet (in press) conducted an interesting and straightforward experiment that addresses these issues. His subjects were trained on only 162 sequences out of the possible 243 used in Kushner and Reber's original design. The sequences that were eliminated contained specific combinations of Elements 2 and 4 drawn from each component of the generation rule. Recall that each of the three components ("same," "clockwise," and "counterclockwise") was instantiated by three different pairs of Elements 2 and 4. Perruchet removed one instance of each component from the training material and presented them to subjects during a transfer phase. For instance, sequences containing the pairs 'A' & 'A', 'B' & 'B', and 'C' & 'C' as Events 2 and 4 respectively all instantiate the "same" component of the generation rules and predict the same sixth event. During training, subjects saw only sequences containing 'A' & 'A' and 'B' & 'B' as their second and fourth events, and they were subsequently tested on sequences containing 'C' & 'C'. If subjects acquire abstract representations that characterize the relationship between Elements 2 and 4 in terms of their spatial relationships (i.e., "same," etc.), then they should be able to transfer successfully to new instances of each component of the rule (i.e., respond to sequences containing 'C' & 'C' in the same way as to sequences containing 'A' & 'A' or 'B' & 'B'). By contrast, if performance is based on memory for stored instances, then a different response pattern is expected. For instance, when presented with sequences containing 'C' & 'C' as Events 2 and 4, subjects may respond based on memory for sequences containing 'A' & 'C', 'B' & 'C', 'C' & 'A', or 'C' & 'B' as Events 2 and 4. All these other sequences predict sixth events different from that predicted by sequences containing 'A' & 'A' or 'B' & 'B'.

Subjects were trained for nine sessions of 162 trials each and tested during a single session consisting of two presentations of the remaining 81 sequences. After training, subjects could predict the location of the sixth stimulus in about 41% of the cases—a performance level roughly similar to that observed by Kushner and Reber. By contrast, performance dropped to about 20% on the transfer material. An analysis of subjects' prediction preferences during transfer revealed that they responded based on similarity to the training material rather than based on abstract knowledge of the generation rules. Overall, the proportion of responses corresponding to an abstract encoding of the rules (e.g., choosing the same successor for sequences containing 'C' & 'C' as for sequences containing 'A' & 'A' or 'B' & 'B' as Events 2 and 4) averaged only .227.

To find out how buffer networks would perform on this task, I conducted several simulations of Perruchet's experiment using the buffer network architecture described above. For each simulation, 10 buffer networks were trained and their performance averaged for further analysis. I adjusted the learning rate until performance after training was roughly equivalent to that of subjects in Perruchet's experiment (i.e., 41% of correct predictions). A learning rate of 0.6 yielded good fits with the data[4], resulting in an average proportion of correct responses of 39%. Over transfer, the average proportion of correct responses dropped to 19%. Next, I computed the networks' response preferences as described above and found that the proportion of responses reflecting an encoding of the generation rules averaged .198—a value close to the .227 observed by Perruchet. Higher learning rates resulted in most networks' learning the task perfectly. For those networks, the proportion of prediction responses reflecting an encoding of the generation rules fell to 0.0. Buffer networks produce response patterns that reflect those of subjects. In both cases, there are clear indications that predictions are based on similarity to stored exemplars rather than on abstract knowledge of the generation rules.

Transfer to Sequences with New Irrelevant Elements
If the results described in the previous section appear to rule out performance based on abstract knowledge, there may be other conditions in which transfer would be successful. Consider for instance what would happen if the transfer material differs from the training material only in the irrelevant elements of the sequences. For instance, one could train subjects on sequences that contain all the possible combinations of Events 2 and 4, but embedded in only some of the possible random contexts. Transfer would consist of presenting subjects with sequences containing these new random contexts. A buffer network would (and does) exhibit perfect transfer to this kind of material, simply because during training it learns to ignore information coming from pools of input units representing irrelevant elements. If subjects were to perform as well as the model on this kind of transfer material, it would

be a good indication that they learned to differentiate relevant events from irrelevant ones. Whether one wants to take this ability as an indication of abstraction is a matter of language, but it certainly indicates that the model's performance is based on knowledge that is a step away from rote memory of specific exemplars, in that it was able to extract the relevant structural properties of the material and to respond based on this information. I return to this important point in chapter 7.

Chapter 7
General Discussion

Commenting on Reber's survey of the field (Reber, 1989), Lewicki and Hill (1989) discuss at some length why research on "implicit learning" is still necessary even though it is so obvious that so many of human mental activities occur outside of consciousness. Among other reasons, they propose that

> another, and probably the most important, reason why such research should be conducted is that we know hardly anything more about those processes (of nonconscious acquisition of knowledge) than that they exist and must play a ubiquitous role in human cognition. (p. 240)

Later, they continue by remarking that

> real progress in this area of cognitive psychology will be achieved only after we go beyond mere demonstration of the processes of nonconscious acquisition of knowledge, and manage to learn something about the nature and dynamics of these phenomena. (p. 240)

These statements document very clearly what the field of implicit learning is most in need of today. The work reported in this book is a first step in the twin directions of (1) obtaining new and detailed experimental data about implicit learning processes, and (2) contributing to knowledge of the mechanisms on which these processes are based. To be more specific, the main contributions of this book may be summarized as follows:

- I explored an experimental situation tapping into elementary implicit learning processes, using a new methodology that allowed very detailed data to be obtained. The empirical work described in chapter 3 demonstrated that subjects exposed to complex and noisy sequential material in a choice reaction situation progressively come to encode the temporal constraints expressed in the material, despite being unaware of these constraints.

• I proposed a detailed information-processing model of the task based on the simple recurrent network architecture described in chapter 2. The model was successful both in accounting for human performance and in instantiating the general principles of implicit learning delineated in chapter 1. It suggests that sequence learning is driven by local anticipation of successive elements of the sequence. The model also made it possible to clarify and account for the effects of short-term factors, which have generally been overlooked in the recent literature on sequence learning.

• I showed how the model could be extended to capture the effects of a number of variables on sequence learning, and how it could be applied to different paradigms (chapter 4).

• *Attention:* The model demonstrated that the effects of a secondary task (as simulated by the use of noise) on sequence learning exerts similar detrimental effects on different types of sequences thought to elicit distinct learning mechanisms (automatic association vs. controlled induction of hierarchical representations). This distinction therefore appears unnecessary to explain the interaction between sequence structure and attention reported by Cohen, Ivry, and Keele (1990).

• *Explicit knowledge:* The simulation of Lewicki, Hill, and Bizot's (1988) results suggested that explicit knowledge plays but a minimal role in their situation. The model becomes sensitive to the additional information, but only after extended training. The simulations therefore support the notion put forward by Perruchet, Gallego, and Savy (1990) that subjects in this situation do not use the explicit information presented along with the stimulus sequence. This work is also a first step in the direction of exploring how the effects of explicit information combine with implicit learning performance in simulation models such as the SRN.

• I demonstrated that a patient presenting with a severe amnesia was nevertheless able to learn the complex and noisy material used in the experiment, and at about the same rate as normal subjects. This result indirectly confirmed that awareness plays but a marginal role in this paradigm.

• I showed that mechanisms even simpler than those implemented by the SRN model may be sufficient to account for human performance in the Cleeremans and McClelland paradigm: A third experiment (described in chapter 5) revealed that decay-based models such as the Jordan network or even buffer networks appear to characterize human processing of long-distance contingencies better than the SRN model. All network models provide a better account of the data than table-lookup mechanisms, however; subjects learn the grammar in a way that allows them to generalize to new instances. It also appears that there is a large overlap between the behavior of the SRN and the behavior of the Jordan model, at least in cases where the material is prediction-relevant at every step.

• For different reasons, neither the SRN nor the Jordan network was able to learn non-prediction-relevant material in an explicit prediction task (Kushner, Cleeremans, & Reber, 1991; see chapter 6) that subjects can master successfully. I argued that this task places different demands on subjects; in particular, subjects are more likely to try to memorize sequences literally, and the task naturally structures the stimulus material in chunks of five elements. I showed how a simple buffer network with no decay was sufficient to account for the human learning data, as well as for transfer to reversed material. Further, this model was used to derive predictions about transfer to new material. I argued that if the model cannot be characterized as acquiring rule-like abstract representations, its representations nevertheless encode which features of the stimulus material are relevant and which are not. This places its representational system (as well as that of other connectionist models) somewhere between purely exemplar-based and abstract representations.

In the following sections, I discuss a number of general issues that are central to implicit learning research, and I examine how my own work with the SRN and other models sheds new light on some of these issues. In the process, I also outline directions in which further research may be pursued.

Prediction-Relevance and Context Representation

The third experiment reported in this book revealed that subjects appear to be able to discriminate between likely and unlikely tail elements of long-distance contingencies even when the embedded material is not prediction-relevant. The implication of this result is that human performance in sequence-learning situations is likely to be based, at least in part, on a decaying trace of the temporal context. Does it mean that the SRN model is wrong? As discussed in chapter 5, there is little reason to believe that such a conclusion is necessary. Indeed, the SRN model shares a number of basic assumptions with decay-based models, and with other connectionist systems in general. Each of these shared basic assumptions instantiates one of the principles of implicit learning delineated in chapter 1.

- *Distributed knowledge:* Both the SRN and decay-based networks implement the notion that knowledge acquired implicitly is fragmented, that is, composed of a large number of elementary "knowledge units." In these models, such knowledge units take the form of associations between specific temporal contexts and specific responses, and are implemented in the connection weights.
- *Graded constraint satisfaction:* Processing in all models is sensitive to the gradual constraints set by the entire distribution of knowledge units available, as well as by those set by the input information. Responses are also graded accordingly.
- *Knowledge tuning:* Learning in all models proceeds by strengthening relevant associations and by weakening others through the error minimization procedure implemented by back-propagation. This results in local optimization of responses according to task constraints. Human subjects attempt to improve their reaction times to comply with task demands. The models suggest that they do so by progressively reducing the uncertainty associated with each response, on the basis of the information contained in the temporal context.
- *Context sensitivity:* Both the SRN and decay-based models process sequential material in context, but in different ways. This is in fact the only assumption about which the three models differ significantly. In the case of the SRN model, the network has to elaborate its own representation of the temporal context. By contrast, Jordan networks and buffer networks are *presented* with input information that already incorporates the temporal context, in the form of a decaying trace of previous inputs. For the former, it is important that each element of the sequence be relevant for predicting future events, at least when the representational resources available to the network are only moderate with respect to the size of the problem. The empirical evidence obtained in Experiment 3 clearly suggests that prediction-relevant embedded material is not necessary for human learning of long-distance contingencies to occur. Thus, the representation of the sequence used by human subjects is likely to be based on a decaying trace of the successive events. But in both

the SRN and the Jordan models, these representations encode the current stimulus *together* with the temporal context, in one global representation of the sequence so far. This "holistic" character of the representations developed by both models may very well account for the fact that human subjects often have so little to report about the knowledge they acquired during training. Buffer networks, on the other hand, keep representations of successive events separate, by activating corresponding units in different isomorphic pools corresponding to different time steps. Even though the current data do not allow a distinction to be made between Jordan networks and buffer networks, it is likely that buffer networks will fail to account for generalization to material that human subjects or the other models would be able to master successfully. As outlined in chapter 5, the computational limitations of buffer networks also make them implausible as general models of temporal processing, particularly in light of language-processing facts.

To summarize this analysis, it appears that two dimensions are important insofar as representing temporal context is concerned. The first dimension distinguishes between models that use the same structures to represent individual sequence elements and context information. The second dimension differentiates models that have to learn how to represent context from models that do not. The SRN is an instance of models that have to learn how to represent context and that elaborate representations that encode both the context and the current event. Jordan networks share the latter property with the SRN, but differ in that the input already contains a (nonchangeable) representation of the temporal context. Buffer networks differ from the SRN on both dimensions, and from Jordan networks by the fact that different structures are used to represent context and sequence elements. Other architectures may not be as easy to classify. For instance, the FSRN architecture proposed by Maskara and Noetzel (1992), in which an SRN is forced to also produce the current event and the context on each trial, has the same properties as an SRN with respect to the two dimensions, but is able to overcome the prediction-relevance problem by keeping representations of sequence elements separate from each other even in cases where their successors are identical.

Thus, the competing models all share a number of basic assumptions that implement principles central to implicit learning, but further research is necessary to address some of the finer points about context representation. It may turn out that these differences between the various models are really crucial and that some model other than the SRN will be best able to capture a wide range of experimental data. But at this level of disussion, the principles that characerize processing in the different models are sufficiently similar that they may all be regarded as essentially equivalent. In a way, it would be reassuring to find out that mechanisms even simpler than those implemented by the SRN may be sufficient to account for human performance. Indeed, such a finding would make the metatheoretical arguments developed in this book even more compelling: Implicit learning is based on elementary mechanisms.

Attention, Awareness, and the Role of Explicit Knowledge

The simulation results I reported in the section dedicated to the role of attention in sequence learning clearly indicate that the detrimental effects of a secondary task on performance can be simulated in the SRN model by allowing processing to be "noisy." In turn, this result may be taken as suggesting that sequence learning under single-task conditions involves nothing else than implicit learning processes. This interpretation contrasts with the hypothesis advanced by A. Cohen et al. (1990), who contend that explicit recoding strategies play a major role in learning sequences for which simple associations between successive elements are not enough to represent all the structure present in the material. The effects of a dual task would then consist of preventing subjects from using these explicit recoding strategies to "parse" the sequences, thus resulting in a drop in performance under dual-task conditions.

When such a theoretical alternative presents itself without clear data to favor either of its branches, it is standard practice to use criteria such as simplicity to decide which branch is more plausible. In this case, the SRN model was a winner because it provided a very good account of the effects of attention on different types of sequences without the extra computational machinery entailed by assuming that different processes apply to each case. By the same token, it is also clearly not the case that explicit strategies are *never* involved in sequence learning. As I pointed out earlier, subjects are always very likely to attempt using explicit strategies—even to a limited extent—when exposed to salient material (as is often the case with the simple repeating sequences typically used in sequence acquisition research). Moreover, these explicit strategies are likely to be successful in enhancing performance precisely under the same conditions. The effectiveness of such strategies in the case of sequence learning was recently confirmed by new empirical evidence obtained by Curran and Keele (1992). Curran and Keele conducted an extensive series of experiments investigating the distinction between awareness and attention in sequence learning. Basically, they showed that explicit instructions to look for structure, or awareness of the sequence (as assessed by a questionnaire), lead to superior learning performance (over subjects who are assessed not to be aware of the sequence) when attention can be focused on the main sequence-learning task. This pattern disappears when the same subjects are subsequently asked to perform the same task under conditions of divided attention (by means of adding a secondary and concurrent tone-counting task). Both groups now exhibit the same learning of the sequence. Thus, in this situation, the effect of the secondary task is to suppress the expression of explicit knowledge acquired during the first part of the experiment. Further, Curran and Keele also showed that subjects who start the experiment under dual-task conditions do not improve their performance once they switch to a subsequent, single-task test phase (that is, they exhibit about the same amount of sequence learning). Thus, it appears that the secondary task also blocks the *acquisition* of explicit knowledge. Curran and Keele conclude from these and other experiments that three different mechanisms may be involved in sequence learning: nonattentional learning mechanisms, attentional mechanisms that require awareness of the sequence, and attentional mechanisms that do not require awareness of the sequence.

How could these results be accounted for by the SRN model? Presumably, subjects who are aware of the exact sequence of repeating elements may use this knowledge by rehearsing it concurrently with the task[1]. This rehearsing would provide the network with additional input about the identity of the next element, with the obvious learning facilitation this entails. There are several possibilities for implementing such a scheme in the SRN model. For instance, one could present the network with a representation of the *next* element of the sequence in addition to the current element, thus implementing a kind of self-teaching in which some other part of the system tells the network how to map the current input onto the next element. Further, this explicit information could be made to be more or less reliable by random variations in the input patterns. I explored a similar idea in the section of chapter 4 dedicated to the work of Lewicki, Hill, and Bizot (1988). The results indicated that it was actually quite hard for the network to become sensitive to the additional information, and that the effects of such additional information only started affecting performance late in training. However, the explicit information given to the network in the case of the simulation of Lewicki et al. (1988)'s experiment consisted only of information about the serial position of successive events. This is admittedly much less information than would be provided by rehearsing the sequence explicitly. Another way to implement the same function is to use the notion of indirect processing pathway developed by Cohen, Dunbar, and McClelland (1990) in the context of the Stroop model. In this extension to the model, additional intermediate processing units with fixed connections between the model's internal processing units and the output units allow it to achieve fast initial responses, whereas the direct pathway strengthens only gradually. Of course, implemented as such, this scheme is inadequate in the context of a learning situation because it would result in little or no learning in the connections underlying the direct pathway (since the error signal is already minimal). Thus, additional assumptions are needed to implement this kind of mechanism for modeling the use of explicit knowledge during learning. One possibility would be to assume that the fixed connections underlying the indirect pathway tend to decay over time, as a function of the magnitude of the connections underlying the direct pathway. Exploring the possibility of incorporating such mechanisms in the SRN architecture appears to be one of the next natural long-range goals after having developed a detailed model of the mechanisms underlying implicit learning itself. But, as Curran and Keele (1992) point out, it may not be easy to disentangle awareness, attention, and their interactions. At present, it seems clear that awareness of the sequence structure has facilitative effects on learning. Whether distinct mechanisms are required to implement these effects, and whether learning with awareness results in different representations than when awareness is not involved, are important issues for further empirical research and modeling.

Another kind of interaction between sequence learning and attention was recently reported by Goshke (1992). In a nutshell, Goshke presented his subjects with a choice reaction time task similar to that used by Curran and Keele (1992) and explored the effects of a secondary tone-counting task by varying the delay between presentation of a tone and presentation of the next stimulus. Goshke found that learning of the sequence was completely blocked when the secondary task interfered with the formation of new event-to-event associations, but that only learning of higher-order temporal contingencies was impaired when the secondary task interfered with memory for the temporal context. These results can readily be accommodated by the SRN model. Indeed, as described in chapter 2, the SRN model develops its representations of the temporal context based on the formation of event-to-event associations. If a secondary task prevents the formation of such associations, or if the material does not contain such associations (as in the experiment described in chapter 6), no context representation can develop. By contrast, interfering specifically with the network's ability to encode information about the temporal context will leave processing of event-to-event associations intact, as described briefly in chapter 4.

Conscious and Unconscious Knowledge

Perhaps the most enduring debate in the field of implicit learning concerns the status of knowledge acquired implicitly. Is it available to conscious access or not? Some authors argue that knowledge acquired in "implicit learning" situations is essentially unconscious (e.g., Reber, 1989; Lewicki & Hill, 1989). For others, however, "implicit knowledge" is little more than fragmentary explicit knowledge, which, for one reason or another (possibly related to the inadequacy of the methods used to assess subjects' knowledge), is hard to verbalize (e.g., Dulany, Carlson, & Dewey, 1984, 1985). Recently, other positions have started to emerge. For instance, Servan-Schreiber and Anderson (1990) contend that learning in the Reber task results from the operation of conscious recoding strategies (chunking), but admit that the end product of these learning processes (e.g., a large collection of chunks) may well be unconscious. In a way, this book is an attempt to dismiss this entire issue as irrelevant, or at best secondary. This contention is based on the idea that a more useful way to approach the empirical phenomena subsumed under the expression "implicit learning" consists of exploring what kinds of mechanism may account for them. Based on these initial explorations, it may then become possible to start addressing considerably more complex questions, such as the one above. One obvious problem with this question is that, as posed, it is too vague to elicit the kind of definitive answer that investigators have somehow come to expect. A further problem is that it is not yet entirely clear what is meant by "unconscious." Is it "unconscious" as in the Freudian sense of the word? Or simply "hard to express"? From my perspective, these questions are undecidable at this point, and not only so because of methodological issues about how to "correctly" elicit knowledge acquired implicitly, but because of the very nature of the questions. Perhaps the safest perspective is the one taken by Reber (1989).

> Knowledge acquired from implicit learning procedures is knowledge that, in some raw fashion, is always ahead of the capacity of its possessor to explicate it. Hence although it is misleading to argue that implicitly acquired knowledge is completely unconscious, it is not misleading to argue that the implicitly acquired epistemic contents of mind are always richer and more sophisticated than what can be explicated. (p. 229)

However, recent evidence by Perruchet and Amorim (1992) casts doubt even on this very cautious position. They showed that awareness of fragments of a sequence tends to develop in parallel with sequence-learning performance, even after very little training. However, the material used in their experiments consisted of a simple repeating sequence 10 elements long. Further, the first experiment was not controlled for spatial location, so that all subjects were exposed to some very salient subsequences, in which successive elements formed a left-to-right pattern, for instance. It is perhaps not surprising that subjects exposed to this kind of material develop awareness of some aspects of it.

Do current simulation models of implicit learning provide any insights into why the sort of knowledge that is produced by implicit learning processes may be hard to express? As discussed above, the form of the knowledge developed by some simulation models of implicit learning may in fact account for at least some aspects of why this knowledge is difficult to state explicitly. For instance, in the competitive chunking architecture developed by Servan-Schreiber and Anderson (1990), the relevant knowledge units are chunks that represent covariations in the task material. The empirical evidence collected by the authors makes it clear that subjects have conscious access to these chunks, since they elaborate them explicitly in the course of learning. However, there is no reason to assume that subjects have similar conscious access to the strength associated with these chunks, or to their relationship with other chunks. This, together with the fact that a very large number of chunks are elaborated during a typical training session, makes it compelling that such mechanisms may allow for successful performance despite the lack of conscious access to all the components of the acquired knowledge. Similarly, in the SRN model, the key feature is that the representations of the temporal context that are elaborated during training do not incorporate distinct components representing which elements of the sequence are crucial and which are irrelevant. Rather, as described earlier, the model develops representations that are distributed, time-varying, and "holistic." The crucial information is embedded in these complex representations and is not readily available for analysis. Again, if these kinds of representation allow successful performance, they are also very hard to analyze. Whether one wants to dub these representations "unconscious" or not is—and I suspect will remain—debatable. Note also that in some other cases, such as buffer networks, the internal representations developed by the network do not have the complex dynamics and global character of the representations developed by the SRN and related models. Incidentally, it is in the kind of task of which buffer networks were found to be good models of (here, explicit prediction tasks) that subjects also seem to be most likely to develop awareness of the relevant contingencies.

In the end, what comes out of these studies is as follows: It appears that implicit learning tasks do not *require* explicit or conscious access to the information on which performance is based, even though in many cases, subjects demonstrably acquire some explicit knowledge about the task material. There are two components to this claim. The first— and hardly debatable—component is that humans are endowed with powerful abilities to extract and manipulate structure in an explicit way (see Perruchet, in press, for further discussion of this point). That these abilities are used continuously, even in tasks dubbed as implicit learning situations, is not surprising. The second component is that humans are also endowed with elementary learning mechanisms that operate outside consciousness. This is supported by many sources of converging evidence. Indeed, in line with the evolutionary arguments put forward by Reber (in press), if implicit learning mechanisms are truly elementary, then the kind of material that is learnable implicitly by human subjects should also be learnable by animals, by human subjects who suffer from impaired learning and memory abilities, or by simulation models that use only elementary learning mechanisms. There is evidence of learning in all three of these cases. Thus, Capaldi (see Capaldi & Frantz, in press, for a review) repeatedly demonstrated that rats were able to process sequential material in a situation where the only information that would facilitate responses was contained in the order and nature of previous trials. Unless one is prepared to accept that rats possess the same kind of consciousness that human beings do, this is clear evidence that encoding sequential structure requires but minimal intervention from explicit strategies, if any at all. Knowlton, Ramus, and Squire (1992) showed that amnesics were able to perform about as well as normal controls in a grammar-learning situation, despite marked impairment in the ability to recognize similar strings. Other data (Nissen & Bullemer, 1987), as well as the experiment described in chapter 4, suggest that this is also the case with sequence learning. The robustness that characterizes implicit learning processes is also corroborated by the results of a study by Reber, Walkenfeld, and Hernstadt (1991), in which performance on an artificial-grammar-learning task was shown not to correlate with IQ. By contrast, an equally difficult but explicit task (series completion) correlated significantly with intelligence. Finally, there is abundant evidence, including the work reported in chapter 2, that connectionist models—which typically use only elementary learning mechanisms—are able to process sequential material to a surprising degree of complexity. I doubt that anybody would be willing to endow connectionist models with consciousness (at this point!). Thus, it would appear that there is substantial evidence that elementary learning processes may be sufficient to account for most implicit learning data. This issue is really different from another one: that some subjects indeed do become aware of the information on which performance is based, and that their knowledge can be revealed under appropriate test conditions. But this process is secondary in nature: It typically comes after successful performance (but see Perruchet & Amorim, 1992) and does not appear, in principle, to be necessary for it.

Transfer and Abstraction

Knowledge acquired implicitly is often characterized as abstract. What is meant by "abstract" here is that the knowledge is neither based on memory for specific exemplars, nor based on processes that operate on the common relevant features of these exemplars, but that it is rule-like. Thus, what I learn in an artificial-grammar-learning experiment is the grammar itself, or some other imperfectly correlated but equally abstract grammar, as if I had memorized the diagram representing the grammar and were using this knowledge to make grammaticality judgments—albeit unconsciously. This strong position is almost certainly wrong. There is abundant evidence that what subjects acquire is fragmentary knowledge about local constraints, and little evidence for the idea that the acquired knowledge is abstract *in the sense defined above*. Two kinds of arguments have been used to support the abstractness position: One is that subjects show evidence of possessing knowledge that is clearly more abstract than mere memory for exemplars, the other is that they transfer to material that does not share surface features with the material used during training. To address the second argument first, the main evidence that supports it consists of the artificial grammar studies in which subjects were trained on a grammar using one letter set and subsequently tested on material generated from the same grammar but using a different letter set (Reber, 1969; Mathews, Druhan, & Roussel, 1989). Transfer performance was very good, suggesting that subjects have acquired representations of the training strings that are independent of the surface features of these strings, that is, abstract representations. Evidence by Brooks and Vokey (1991), however, suggests that transfer performance may be based on a process that the authors call "abstract analogy," by which subjects perceive the abstract relationships between corresponding strings (e.g., the letters of 'MXVVVM' and 'BDCCCB' enter into similar relationships with each other). They provide evidence for this process through a clever design that manipulates grammatical status and similarity independently. That is, some new nongrammatical strings may be more similar to old grammatical strings than new grammatical strings.

The first argument, that subjects exhibit knowledge that goes beyond mere sensitivity to stored exemplars, is still the object of debate. In some cases, it appears that performance may be accounted for by assuming that subjects base classification performance on similarity to stored exemplars; in others, this explanation does not hold. For instance, subjects correctly classify new nongrammatical strings even though they may be very similar to old grammatical strings (McAndrews & Moscovitch, 1985). Thus, both similarity to old instances and reliance on higher-level abstract representations seem to play a role in discrimination performance, and the available empirical evidence does not make it easy to distinguish between the effects of either variable. Further, task instructions and the training environment may also contribute to induce subjects to adopt different strategies with regard to the processing of specific exemplars. For instance, McAndrews and Moscovitch (1985) suggest that Vokey and Brooks's (1992; see also Vokey, 1983) training procedure, in which relatively few strings were presented many times, may have induced subjects to rely more on memory for specific items than is typical in artificial-grammar-learning experiments.

As discussed in chapter 6, evidence for "real" abstraction would come from studies that indicate clearly that subjects generalize based on the abstract rules defining the structure of the material. At least one experiment (Perruchet, in press) indicates unambiguously that subjects tend to generalize based on similarity with old exemplars. However, one may argue with what is meant by "abstraction." According to the *Online American Heritage Dictionary*, to abstract is the "act or process of separating the inherent qualities or properties of something from the actual physical object or concept to which they belong." By that definition, the simple buffer networks that were found to account for performance in Kushner and Reber's task do acquire abstract representations of the stimulus material because they have isolated which features of the input are relevant and which are not. Subjects in the experiment conducted by Perruchet (in press) may similarly exhibit knowledge of which events are relevant for the prediction task. It remains to be seen how well human subjects transfer to material that incorporates new random contexts. But rather than speculate, I would like to examine whether connectionist models may be able to achieve successful transfer in these situations, and what it means for such models to develop abstract representations.

When one looks inside an SRN trained on material from a finite-state grammar, it becomes apparent that the representations of the network may, under some conditions, be very close to the abstract representation of the grammar: Each state is encoded by a different cluster of similar patterns of activity over the hidden units of the network (see Figure 2.7, for instance). Is this kind of representation abstract? In some ways, it is, because the network has clearly developed representations that encode relevant underlying dimensions of the training material (as opposed to, say, representations that are literal copies of specific training items). But in other ways, it is not abstract, because performance is still very much dependent on surface features of the material. That is, if one were to switch to a different letter set (represented by using new input units), for instance, the network would fail completely to predict the successor, even if this new material had been generated from the same grammar. This, of course, is not surprising, since there is no way for the network to induce that different letters play similar roles in each grammar. Thus, additional mechanisms that allow the network to evaluate and use the abstract similarity between the strings generated from the two grammars are necessary. In the case of the prediction task described in chapter 6, this could possibly be achieved by using input representations that capture the spatial relationships between successive events, rather than the local representations used so far. That is, the network needs to be able to represent in some way what "clockwise" and "counterclockwise" mean. In the case of artificial grammar learning with different letter sets, a similar problem needs to be solved (i.e., the input representations must make it explicit that strings from either letter set may be structurally similar to each other). At this point, it is not clear how this may be achieved. Abstract analogy is obviously not an easy problem for connectionist networks. This is not to say that connectionist networks cannot, in principle, exhibit sensitivity to the abstract dimensions of the stimulus material. On the contrary, there is abundant evidence that they do. For instance, Hinton (1986) showed that a back-propagation network trained to produce the patient of an agent-relationship pair given as input (for instance, Maria is the wife of Roberto) developed internal representations that captured relevant abstract dimensions of the domain (here, family trees), such as nationality or age. The crucial point is that the input representation contained no information whatsoever about these abstract dimensions: Each person or relationship was represented by activating a single input unit. Further, the model generalized to new instances of specific input-output pairings that had never been presented during training (albeit in only a limited number of test cases). Thus, in Hinton's words, "The structure that must be discovered in order to generalize correctly is not present in the pairwise correlations between input units and output units" (p. 9). Examples from the work reported in this book also support this notion. For instance, an SRN trained on only some of the strings that may possibly be generated from a finite-state grammar will generalize to the infinite set of all possible instances (chapter 2). Thus, connectionist networks of this kind are clearly more than simple associators that only encode input-output correspondences based on a set of stored training examples. Abstract knowledge can emerge from elementary and nonsymbolic mechanisms, even if only at the level of performance. Note also that whether a network will develop abstract representations depends in part on the relevance of doing so to satisfy task constraints, and in part on the resources available to the network. In Hinton's family tree example, the network is forced to develop shared representations of the training examples because resources (i.e., the number of hidden units available for processing) are scarce and therefore not sufficient to represent each instance separately. Similarly, in the simulations reported in chapter 2, SRNs with many hidden units tend not to develop internal representations that represent the grammar's structure in as isomorphic a way as when only few hidden units are available. Thus, there appears to be a representational continuum that extends from storage of exemplars (i.e., many micro-associations) to the development of representations that encode the shared properties of many instances. The training environment is also a crucial factor in determining whether a model will generalize. With only few training examples, for instance, there is little basis for generalization.

The observation that abstract knowledge may emerge from elementary, associationist learning contradicts the popular conception that abstract knowledge is necessarily acquired through the operation of symbolic mechanisms that produce rule-like representations. Thus, the opposition between abstract implicit knowledge and fragmentary explicit knowledge that is at the heart of so many debates about implicit learning performance begins to fade when one considers the way in which connectionist models represent and use information. Knowledge in connectionist and other models of learning (including exemplar-based models such as Hintzman's MINERVA 2) is fragmented, but the key to their successful performance is their ability to combine these fragments into bigger representational units that encode abstract relationships. These bigger units may take the form of chunks in the competitive chunking framework (Servan-Schreiber & Anderson, 1990), or the form of the time-varying, holistic representations that characterize the SRN. As Mathews (1990) puts it (in the context of artificial grammar learning), "Fragmentary knowledge of a grammar constitutes abstract rules that enable performance on complex tasks when integrated in a system for combining knowledge across rules" (p. 412). This is distinctly different from Perruchet and Pacteau's (1990) notion that subjects base their performance on unanalyzed fragments of explicit knowledge, such as bigrams when the material consists of strings, or sequence fragments when it is sequential (Perruchet & Amorim, 1992).

To summarize, there is no clear evidence that knowledge acquired in implicit learning situations is abstract in the strong sense of the word. But this does not necessarily entail that human performance is based only on knowledge about stored exemplars. By suggesting that abstract representations can emerge from elementary learning mechanisms based on the processing of exemplars, the work described in this book suggests a third possibility that borrows features from the two extreme positions described above. In more ways than one, architectures such as the SRN described in this book force us to reconsider traditional perspectives on cognition.

On Modeling

To close this discussion, I would like to reflect on what it means to elaborate information-processing models of human behavior. One of the lessons of this work is that there may be many ways to model the same phenomenon. For instance, as briefly described in the section dedicated to Kushner and Reber's work (chapter 6), increasing the decay rate in buffer networks tends to have the same effects as lowering the learning rate: Both manipulations tend to slow encoding of the sequential structure of the material. Similarly, adding random noise to the net input of each unit in the network or only to the hidden units results in comparable interference in the performance of an SRN trained on material from the study of A. Cohen et al. (1990). As an even more striking example of these kinds of equivalent manipulations of the network's parameters and architecture, it appears that the SRN, the Jordan network, and buffer networks may sometimes produce responses whose respective distributions exhibit a large overlap.

What do these observations entail for modeling? They certainly contribute to the widespread feeling that modeling in general, and connectionist architectures in particular, are too underconstrained to allow good theorizing. This kind of reaction to simulation work has been expressed repeatedly since computer technology made it possible to develop complex models of behavior, but it has perhaps gained increased visibility since the onset of connectionism, mostly because connectionist networks are notoriously hard to analyze. McCloskey (1991), for instance, claims that a theory instantiated in the form of a connectionist network is not really a theory if one does not also understand exactly how the network functions, and how variables that affect its performance relate to the psychological variables that affect human behavior. For the most part, the point is well taken. After all, if I can model so many aspects of sequence learning in so many different ways, how much of an insight does my simulation work yield about the underlying processes? The answer is of course that one needs to explore and analyze the kind of knowledge that develops in connectionist networks. A good fit between simulation and data is not reason enough to assume that my theory is right. In this book, I have tried to depart from this approach in several ways: (1) by providing a detailed account of the computational characteristics of the model (chapter 2), (2) by exploring whether alternative models may also account for the data (chapter 5), and (3) by trying to relate the model's behavior to theoretical principles. But simulation models offer more than just an alternative way of theory building. There are at least three additional different benefits to be gained by the use of simulation models.

First, without using simulation models, it would have been very hard to come to realize that the effects of some variables are in fact equivalent. Thus, models are beneficial because they are useful in exploring which parameters (relevant to the theory) are critical, and which have nondetectable or equivalent effects on performance. As a result, they allow theories to be refined and tested in ways that would be impossible through experimentation only. Note that this really is an essential part of simulation work: It is precisely through that kind of exploration that one discovers which classes of mechanisms are equivalent. But how do we decide which mechanism is actually used by the mind? This, it would appear, is simply an undecidable question without the benefit of other sources of constraints (such as constraints from the biological structures underlying behavior, or from optimality considerations and an assessment of the structure of the environment; see Anderson, 1990).

Second, simulation models allow both the underlying theory and the experimental data to be explored simultaneously, thereby speeding up the process of refining our understanding of the corresponding empirical phenomena.

Third, simulation models make it possible to cast theories in a way that is formal enough that their fit with the data can be evaluated in great detail. For instance, the SRN model generates responses on every trial, and the more complex analyses described in chapter 3 came close to being based on comparisons between trial-to-trial human and simulated responses. This is considerably better than could be achieved by means of more general theories about the underlying processes.

For all these reasons, and probably many more, I think that progress in understanding of mechanisms underlying behavior is made through the specification of theories in the form of simulation models. The unavoidable residual uncertainty is a problem that needs to be addressed by other means, but it cannot be cast as an argument against the use of simulation models.

Conclusion

To return to a question raised in chapter 1: What *does* a rat finding its way in a maze share with a college undergraduate attempting to solve the Tower of Hanoi? I cannot claim to have come even close to answering that question. However, if one is to believe evolutionary arguments of the kind put forward by Reber (1990, in press), it may be that what the rat and the undergraduate share is exactly the kind of processes that I have explored in this book: elementary learning processes, which must be an essential component of any cognitive system. The work reported in this book has begun to demonstrate how exploring elementary learning from an information-processing perspective may contribute to our understanding of the mechanisms that govern its operation, and of their relationship with the more complex functions of the cognitive system. Connectionist models appear to be particularly well suited to pursuing such explorations and provide natural primitives with which to characterize the form and function of implicit learning processes. In particular, they make explicit facts about learning and cognition in general that are also becoming increasingly clearer through empirical research: Processing is graded, random, interactive, and adaptive (see McClelland, 1991, for a discussion of these principles; and Movellan & McClelland, 1991, for their implementation as a new connectionist learning algorithm). Most importantly, connectionist models, as well as other kinds of adaptive information-processing models, demonstrate how complex knowledge may emerge from the operation of elementary learning mechanisms. I believe that this crucial property of the models I have explored in this book will help reconcile otherwise incompatible positions about both the nature of knowledge acquired implicitly and the nature of the mechanisms involved in implicit learning. In short, we can have our cake and eat it too!

Notes

Chapter 1

1. Billman discusses the concept of *stimulus salience*. I think the expression *regularity salience* is more appropriate in this context.
2. Or, if they are not, then they typically result in worse performance.
3. Lewicki (1986) proposes a very similar set of central features characterizing implicit learning processes.
4. I can hardly imagine how knowledge acquired implicitly may be structured otherwise, but the issue is not as simple as it might appear. For instance, one might think that subjects in the Reber task acquire some kind of abstract representation of the structure present in the material, in the form of an imperfect "correlated grammar" that specifies how legal strings are generated. However, this seems unlikely to be the case in the light of the other assumptions, particularly Principles 2 and 3, which address processing and learning issues. I will return to this point in chapter 6.

Chapter 2

1. Modified versions of the BP program devised by McClelland and Rumelhart (1988) were used for this and all subsequent simulations reported in this book. The weights in the network were initially set to random values between –0.5 and –0.5. Values of η and α were chosen sufficiently small to avoid large oscillations and were generally in the range of 0.01 to 0.02 for η and 0.5 to 0.9 for α.
2. This is a simple consequence of error minimization. For any single output unit, given that targets are binary, and assuming a fixed input pattern for all training exemplars, the error can be expressed as:

$$C = (1-y)^2 + (1-p)y^2$$

where p is the probability that the unit should be on, and y is the activation of the unit. The first term applies when the desired value is 1, the second when the desired value is 0. Back-propagation tends to minimize the derivative of this expression, which is simply $2y - 2p$. The minimum is attained when $y = p$, that is, when the activation of the unit is equal to its probability of being on in the training set (Rumelhart, personal communication, Spring 1989).
3. Cluster analysis is a method that finds the optimal partition of a set of vectors according to some measure of similarity (here, the Euclidean distance). On the graphical representation of the obtained clusters, the contrast between two groups is indicated by the length of the vertical links. The length of horizontal links is not meaningful.
4. This fact may seem surprising at first, since the learning algorithm does not apply pressure on the weights to generate different representations for different paths to the same node. Preserving that kind of information about the path does not contribute

in itself to reducing error in the prediction task. We must therefore conclude that this differentiation is a direct consequence of the recurrent nature of the architecture rather than a consequence of back-propagation. Indeed, in earlier work (Servan-Schreiber, Cleeremans, & McClelland, 1988), we showed that some amount of information about the path is encoded in the hidden layer patterns when a succession of letters is presented, even in the absence of any training.

5. In fact, length constraints are treated exactly like atypical cases since there is no representation of the length of the string as such.

6. For *each order*, the analysis consisted of three steps. First, we estimated the conditional probabilities of observing each letter after each possible path through the grammar (e.g., the probabilities of observing each of the seven letters given the sequence 'TSS'). Second, we computed the probabilities that each of the above paths leads to each node of the grammar (e.g., the probabilities that the path 'TSS' finishes at Node #1, Node #2, etc.). Third, we obtained the average conditional probabilities (ACPs) of observing each letter at each node of the grammar by summing the products of the terms obtained in the first and second steps over the set of possible paths. Finally, all the ACPs that corresponded to letters that could not appear at a particular node (e.g., a 'V' at Node #0) were eliminated from the analysis. Thus, for each statistical order, we obtained a set of 11 ACPs (one for each occurrence of the five letters, and one for 'E', which can only appear at Node #6. 'B' is never predicted).

7. For example, with 3 hidden units, the network converges to a stable state after an average of three iterations when presented with identical inputs (with a precision of two decimal points for each unit). A network with 15 hidden units converges after an average of eight iterations. These results were obtained with random weights in the range [−0.5, +0.5].

8. Generally, small values for h and a, as well as many hidden units, help to minimize this problem.

9. The Luce ratio is the ratio of the highest activation on the output layer to the sum of all activations on that layer. This measure is commonly applied in psychology to model the strength of a response tendency among a finite set of alternatives (Luce, 1963). In this simulation, a Luce ratio of 0.5 often corresponded to a situation where 'T' and 'P' were equally activated and all other alternatives were set to 0.

Chapter 3

1. This transformation amounts to dividing the activation of the unit corresponding to the response by the sum of the activations of all units in the output pool. Since the strength of a particular response is determined by its relative—rather than absolute— activation, the transformation implements a simple form of response competition.

2. As Soetens, Boer, and Hueting (1985) have demonstrated, however, short-term priming effects also tend to become weaker through practice even in situations that only involve random material. At this point, the SRN model is simply unable to capture this effect. Doing so would require the use of a training procedure that allows the time course of activation to be assessed (such as cascaded back-propagation; see Cohen, Dunbar, & McClelland, 1990), and is a matter for further research.

Chapter 4

1. I thank José Morais for giving me access both to the patient and to the facilities needed to test him.

2. In work done independently, J. K. Kruschke (personal communication, June 5, 1990) has also explored the possibility of simulating the effects of attention on sequence

learning in SRNs. In one of his simulations, the learning rate of the connections from the context units to the hidden units was set to a lower value than for the other connections of the network.

3. I thank Steven Keele for providing the details about the experimental data reported by Cohen, Ivry, and Keele (1990).

Chapter 5

1. At this point, it is not yet entirely clear what the exact predictions of Bayesian learning procedures and similar models entail. However, Richard and Lippman (1991) have shown that multilayer back-propagation networks trained on classification problems produce outputs that approximate a posteriori Bayesian probabilities, so long as outputs are 1 of M and a squared-error or cross-entropy error function is used. These conditions hold for the research described here. Thus, more traditional Bayesian learning procedures would, in all likelihood, produce results similar to the ones obtained with the standard SRN.

2. A more precise characterization of the network's behavior in this particular case may be that it would tend to "hallucinate" the contingency, since it does not exist, either in the grammar or in the test material.

3. A careful examination of the data revealed that the variance was particularly high in the symmetrical condition, and that a substantial proportion of this variance was accounted for by 1 subject, who produced unusually high differences between likely and unlikely tails. Upon enquiry, I learned that this subject was a professional composer. This is anecdotal evidence at best, but it is interesting to speculate that such subjects may have specific abilities to process sequential material. Removing this subject from the analyses did not change the result that subjects in the symmetrical condition are able to discriminate between likely and unlikely tails. It did produce a significant interaction between condition and successor type, however. Therefore, it cannot be excluded that a replication would fail to produce exactly the same pattern of results.

Chapter 6

1. All statistical tests reported in this chapter were conducted by using a normal approximation to the binomial distribution, at the .01 level.

2. In the original experiment, subjects were exposed once to the entire set of 243 possible sequences of five events (3^5), presented randomly. In the case of these simulations, the network was presented with the same number of exposures, but the material for each session was not exhaustive. I doubt that this procedural difference is significant, particularly given the large number of trials involved.

3. Previously published simulation results (Kushner, Cleeremans, & Reber, 1991) were in error. A bug in the program that generates sequences for presentation to the network caused the material to be learnable!

4. A lower learning rate than in the previous simulation is required here because Perruchet's material is easier to learn than the original material: there are fewer training sequences, and, more importantly, Events 2 and 4 considered separately now contain some information about the nature of Event 6 because of the elimination of selected combinations. Subjects also seem to learn somewhat faster in Perruchet's experiment than in Kushner and Reber's task, but the difference is far smaller than in the case of simulations using the same learning rate in both cases.

Chapter 7

1. Naturally, this would only be possible when the structure of the sequence is simple enough to be memorized. I would expect explicit strategies of this kind to fail when the material is complex and noisy, as in the Cleeremans and McClelland situation.

References

Abrams, M., & Reber, A. S. (1989). Implicit learning in special populations. *Journal of Psycholinguistic Research, 17*, 425–439.

Allen, R., & Reber, A. S. (1980). Very long-term memory for tacit knowledge. *Cognition, 8*, 175–185.

Allen, R. B. (1988). Sequential connectionist networks for answering simple questions about a microworld. In *Proceedings of the Tenth Annual Conference of the Cognitive Science Society*. Hillsdale, NJ: Lawrence Erlbaum Associates.

Allen, R. B. (1990). *Connectionist language users* (Tech. Rep. No. AR-90-402). Morristown, NJ: Bell Communications Research.

Allen, R. B., & Riecksen, M. E. (1989). Reference in connectionist language users. In R. Pfeifer, Z. Schreter, F. Fogelman-Soulié, & L. Steels (Eds.), *Connectionism in perspective*. Amsterdam: North Holland.

Anderson, J. R. (1983). *The architecture of cognition*. Cambridge, MA: Harvard University Press.

Anderson, J. R. (1990). *The adaptive character of thought*. Hillsdale, NJ: Lawrence Erlbaum Associates.

Anzai, Y., & Simon, H. A. (1979). The theory of learning by doing. *Psychological Review, 86*, 124–140.

Baddeley, A. D. (1987). *Working memory*. Oxford: Oxford University Press.

Bartlett, F. C. (1932). *Remembering*. Cambridge: Cambridge University Press.

Berry, D. C. (in press). Implicit learning: Twenty five years on. In C. Umiltà & M. Moscovitch (Eds.), *Attention and performance XV: Conscious and nonconscious information processing*. Cambridge, MA: MIT Press.

Berry, D. C., & Broadbent, D. E. (1984). On the relationship between task performance and associated verbalizable knowledge. *Quarterly Journal of Experimental Psychology, 36*, 209–231.

Berry, D. C., & Broadbent, D. E. (1987). The combination of explicit and implicit learning processes in task control. *Psychological Research, 49*, 7–15.

Berry, D. C., & Broadbent, D. E. (1988). Interactive tasks and the implicit-explicit distinction. *British Journal of Psychology, 79*, 251–272.

Bertelson, P. (1961). Sequential redundancy and speed in a serial two-choice responding task. *Quarterly Journal of Experimental Psychology, 13*, 90–102.

Billman, D. (1983). Inductive learning of syntactic categories. Unpublished doctoral dissertation, University of Michigan, Ann Arbor.

Bradshaw, G. F., Langley, P. W., & Simon, H. A. (1983). Studying scientific discovery by computer simulation. *Science, 222*, 971–975.

Broadbent, D. E. (1977). Levels, hierarchies, and the locus of control. *Quarterly Journal of Experimental Psychology, 29*, 181–201.

Broadbent, D. E., & Aston, B. (1978). Human control of a simulated economic system. *Ergonomics, 21*, 1035–1043.

Broadbent, D. E., FitzGerald, P., & Broadbent, M. H. P. (1986). Implicit and explicit knowledge in the control of complex systems. *British Journal of Psychology, 77,* 33–50.

Brooks, L. R. (1978). Nonanalytic concept formation and memory for instances. In E. Rosch & B. B. Lloyd (Eds.), *Cognition and categorization.* New York: Wiley.

Brooks, L. R., & Vokey, J. R. (1991). Abstract analogies and abstracted grammars: Comments on Reber (1989) and on Mathews et al. (1989). *Journal of Experimental Psychology: General, 120,* 316–323.

Capaldi, E. J. (1985). Anticipation and remote associations: A configural approach. *Journal of Experimental Psychology: Learning, Memory, and Cognition, 11,* 444–449.

Capaldi, E. J., & Frantz, E. A. (in press). Retrospective and prospective remote associations in sequence learning. *Journal of Experimental Psychology: General.*

Capaldi, E. J., & Miller, D. J. (1988). The rat's simultaneous anticipation of remote events and current events can be sustained by memories alone. *Animal Learning and Behavior, 16,* 1–7.

Carmines, E. G., & Zeller, R. A. (1987). *Reliability and validity assessment.* Newbery Park, CA: Sage.

Chomsky, N. (1980). *Rules and representations.* New York: Columbia University Press.

Cleeremans, A. (1986). *Connaissances explicites et implicites dans le contrôle d'un système: Une étude exploratoire.* Unpublished master's thesis, Université Libre de Bruxelles.

Cleeremans, A. (1988). Relations entre performance et connaissances verbalisables dans le contrôle de processus. *Le Travail Humain, 51,* 97–111.

Cleeremans, A., & McClelland, J. L. (1991). Learning the structure of event sequences. *Journal of Experimental Psychology: General, 120,* 235–253.

Cleeremans, A., Servan-Schreiber, D., & McClelland, J. L. (1989). Finite state automata and simple recurrent networks. *Neural Computation, 1,* 372–381.

Cleeremans, A., Servan-Schreiber, D., & McClelland, J. L. (in press). Graded state machines: The representation of temporal contingencies in feedback networks. In Y. Chauvin & D. E. Rumelhart (Eds.), *Backpropagation: Theory, architectures, and applications.* Hillsdale, NJ: Lawrence Erlbaum Associates.

Cohen, A., Ivry, R. I., & Keele, S. W. (1990). Attention and structure in sequence learning. *Journal of Experimental Psychology: Learning, Memory, and Cognition, 16,* 17–30.

Cohen, J. D., Dunbar, K., & McClelland, J. L. (1990). On the control of automatic processes: A parallel distributed account of the Stroop effect. *Psychological Review, 97,* 332–361.

Cohen, J. D., & Servan-Schreiber, D. (1989). *A parallel distributed processing approach to behavior and biology in schizophrenia* (Tech. Rep. No. AIP-100). Pittsburgh, PA: Carnegie Mellon University, Department of Psychology.

Cottrell, G. W. (1985). Connectionist parsing. In *Proceedings of the Seventh Annual Conference of the Cognitive Science Society.* Hillsdale, NJ: Lawrence Erlbaum Associates.

Cottrell, G. W., Munro, P. W., & Zipser, D. (1987). Image compression by back propagation: A demonstration of extensional programming. In N. E. Sharkey (Ed.), *Advances in cognitive science* (vol. 2). Chichester, England: Ellis Horwood.

Curran, T., & Keele, S. W. (1992). *Attentional and nonattentional forms of sequence learning* (Tech. Rep. No. 92-3). Eugene, OR: University of Oregon, Institute of Cognitive and Decision Sciences.

Dienes, Z. (1992). Connectionist and memory array models of artificial grammar learning. *Cognitive Science, 16,* 41–79.

Dienes, Z., Broadbent, D. E., & Berry, D. (1991). Implicit and explicit knowledge bases in artificial grammar learning. *Journal of Experimental Psychology: Learning, Memory, and Cognition, 17,* 875–887.

Dienes, Z., & Fahey, R. (1992). The role of implicit memory in controlling a dynamic system. Ms., University of Sussex.

Druhan, B. B., & Mathews, R. C. (1989). THYIOS: A classifier system model of implicit knowledge of artificial grammars. In *Proceedings of the Eleventh Annual Conference of the Cognitive Science Society*. Hillsdale, NJ: Lawrence Erlbaum Associates.

Dulany, D. E., Carlson, R. A., & Dewey, G. I. (1984). A case of syntactical learning and judgment: How conscious and how abstract? *Journal of Experimental Psychology: General, 113*, 541–555.

Dulany, D. E., Carlson, R. A., & Dewey, G. I. (1985). On consciousness in syntactical learning and judgment: A reply to Reber, Allen & Regan. *Journal of Experimental Psychology: General, 114*, 25–32.

Elman, J. L. (1988). *Finding structure in time* (Tech. Rep. No. 8801). San Diego, CA: University of California, Center for Research in Language.

Elman, J. L. (1990). Finding structure in time. *Cognitive Science, 14*, 179–211.

Elman, J. L. (in press). Representation and structure in connectionist models. In G. Altmann (Ed.), *Computational and psycholinguistic approaches to speech processing*. New York: Academic Press.

Elman, J. L., & Zipser, D. (1988). Discovering the hidden structure of speech. *Journal of the Acoustical Society of America, 83*, 1615–1626.

Ericsson, K. A., & Simon, H. A. (1980). Verbal reports as data. *Psychological Review, 87*, 215–251.

Estes, W. K. (1957). Toward a statistical theory of learning. *Psychological Review, 57*, 94–107.

Estes, W. K. (1976). The cognitive side of probability learning. *Psychological Review, 83*, 37–64.

Estes, W. K. (1986). Memory storage and retrieval processes in category learning. *Journal of Experimental Psychology: General, 115*, 155–174.

Falmagne, J. C. (1965). Stochastic models for choice reaction time with application to experimental results. *Journal of Mathematical Psychology, 2*, 77–124.

Fanty, M. (1985). *Context-free parsing in connectionist networks* (Tech. Rep. No. 174). Rochester, NY: University of Rochester, Computer Science Department.

Feigenbaum, E. A., & Simon, H. A. (1962). A theory of the serial position effect. *British Journal of Psychology, 53*, 307–320.

Feigenbaum, E. A., & Simon, H. A. (1984). EPAM-like models of recognition and learning. *Cognitive Science, 8*, 305–336.

Goshke, T. (1992). The role of attention in implicit learning of event sequences. *International Journal of Psychology, 27*, 110.

Hanson, S., & Kegl, J. (1987). PARSNIP: A connectionist network that learns natural language from exposure to natural language sentences. In *Proceedings of the Ninth Annual Conference of the Cognitive Science Society*. Hillsdale, NJ: Lawrence Erlbaum Associates.

Hasher, L., & Zacks, R. T. (1984). Automatic processing of fundamental information. *American Psychologist, 39*, 1372–1388.

Hayes, N. A. (1986). Consciousness and modes of learning. Communication presented at the symposium "*Aspects of Consciousness*," Dec. 1–3, Bielefeldt.

Hayes, N. A. (1987). [Title not available]. Doctoral dissertation, Oxford University.

Hayes, N. A., & Broadbent, D. A. (1988). Two modes of learning for interactive tasks. *Cognition, 8*, 1–30.

Hebb, D. O. (1961). Distinctive features of learning in the higher animal. In A. Fressard, R. W. Gerard, J. Konorsky, & J. F. Delafresnaye (Eds.), *Brain mechanisms and learning*. Oxford: Blackwell.

Hinton, G. E. (1986). Learning distributed representations of concepts. In *Proceedings of the Eighth Annual Conference of the Cognitive Science Society*. Hillsdale, NJ: Lawrence Erlbaum Associates.

Hinton, G. E., McClelland, J. L., & Rumelhart, D. E. (1986). Distributed representations. In D. E. Rumelhart & J. L. McClelland (Eds.), *Parallel Distributed Processing: Explorations in the microstructure of cognition. Vol. 1: Foundations*. Cambridge, MA: MIT Press.

Hinton, G. E., & Plaut, D. C. (1987). Using fast weights to deblur old memories. In *Proceedings of the Ninth Annual Conference of the Cognitive Science Society*. Hillsdale, NJ: Lawrence Erlbaum Associates.

Hintzman, D. L. (1986). "Schema Abstraction" in a multiple-trace memory model. *Psychological Review, 93*, 411–428.

Holland, J. H., Holyoak, K. J., Nisbett, R. E., & Thagard, P. R. (1986). *Induction: Processes of inference, learning, and discovery*. Cambridge, MA: MIT Press.

Hyman, R. (1953). Stimulus information as a determinant of reaction time. *Journal of Experimental Psychology, 45*, 188–196.

James, W. (1890). *The principles of psychology*. New York: Holt.

Jennings, P. J., & Keele, S. W. (1990). A computational model of attentional requirements in sequence learning. In *Proceedings of the Twelfth Annual Conference of the Cognitive Science Society*. Hillsdale, NJ: Lawrence Erlbaum Associates.

Jordan, M. I. (1986). Attractor dynamics and parallelism in a connectionist sequential machine. In *Proceedings of the Eighth Annual Conference of the Cognitive Science Society*. Hillsdale, NJ: Lawrence Erlbaum Associates.

Jordan, M. I., & Rumelhart, D. E. (in press). Forward models: Supervised learning with a distal teacher. In Y. Chauvin & D. E. Rumelhart (Eds.), *Backpropagation: Theory, architectures, and applications*. Hillsdale, NJ: Lawrence Erlbaum Associates.

Karnas, G., & Cleeremans, A. (1987). Implicit and explicit knowledge in the control of complex systems: Some simulation results. In *Proceedings of the First European Meeting on Cognitive Science Approaches to Process Control*, Oct. 19–20, Marcoussis, France.

Kellog, R. T., & Dowdy, J. C. (1986). Automatic learning of the frequencies of occurrence of stimulus features. *American Journal of Psychology, 99*, 111–126.

Kintsch, W. (1970). *Learning, memory, and conceptual processes*. New York: Wiley.

Knowlton, B., Ramus, S. J., & Squire, L. (1992). Intact artificial grammar learning in amnesia: Dissociation of classification learning and explicit memory for specific instances. *Psychological Science, 3*, 172–177.

Kushner, M., Cleeremans, A., & Reber, A. S. (1991). Implicit detection of event interdependencies and a PDP model of the process. In *Proceedings of the Thirteenth Annual Conference of the Cognitive Science Society*. Hillsdale, NJ: Lawrence Erlbaum Associates.

Laird, J. E., Rosenbloom, P. S., & Newell, A. (1985). *Towards chunking as a general learning mechanism* (Tech. Rep. No. CMU-CS-85-100). Pittsburgh, PA: Carnegie Mellon University, School of Computer Science.

Laming, D. R. J. (1969). Subjective probability in choice-reaction experiments. *Journal of Mathematical Psychology, 6*, 81–120.

Langley, P., & Simon, H. A. (1981). The central role of learning in cognition. In J. R. Anderson (Ed.), *Cognitive skills and their acquisition*. Hillsdale, NJ: Lawrence Erlbaum Associates.

Lewicki, P. (1986). *Nonconscious social information processing*. New York: Academic Press.

Lewicki, P., Czyzewska, M., & Hoffman, H. (1987). Unconscious acquisition of complex procedural knowledge. *Journal of Experimental Psychology: Learning, Memory, and Cognition, 13*, 523–530.

Lewicki, P., & Hill, T. (1989). On the status of nonconscious processes in human cognition: Comment on Reber. *Journal of Experimental Psychology: General, 118*, 239–241.

Lewicki, P., Hill, T., & Bizot, E. (1988). Acquisition of procedural knowledge about a pattern of stimuli that cannot be articulated. *Cognitive Psychology*, *20*, 24–37.

Logan, G. (1988). Towards an instance theory of automatisation. *Psychological Review*, *95*, 492–527.

Luce, R. D. (1963). Detection and recognition. In R. D. Luce, R. R. Bush, & E. Galanter (Eds.), *Handbook of mathematical psychology* (Vol. 1). New York: Wiley.

Marescaux, P.-J. (1991). *Contribution à l'étude de la distinction entre connaissances explicites et implicites: Une approche des difficultés méthodologiques de l'évaluation des connaissances du sujet dans des tâches de contrôle dynamique.* Unpublished doctoral dissertation, Université Libre de Bruxelles.

Marescaux, P.-J., & Karnas, G. (1991). *The implicit versus explicit knowledge distinction revisited: When finding associations between verbalizable knowledge and some performance criteria* (Rep. No. 4PR3GK of the Kaudyte project, Esprit BRA #3219). Brussels: Université Libre de Bruxelles, Laboratoire de Psychologie Industrielle et Commerciale.

Marescaux, P.-J., Luc, F., & Karnas, G. (1989). Modes d'apprentissage sélectif et non-sélectif et connaissances acquises au contrôle d'un processus: Evaluation d'un modèle simulé. *Cahiers de Psychologie Cognitive*, *9*, 239–264.

Maskara, A., & Noetzel, A. (1992). Forced simple recurrent neural network and grammatical inference. In *Proceedings of the Fourteenth Annual Conference of the Cognitive Science Society*. Hillsdale, NJ: Lawrence Erlbaum Associates.

Mathews, R. C. (1990). Abstractness of implicit grammar knowledge: Comments on Perruchet and Pacteau's analysis of synthetic grammar learning. *Journal of Experimental Psychology: General*, *119*, 412–416.

Mathews, R. C., Buss, R. R., Stanley, W. B., Blanchard-Fields, F., Cho, J.-R., & Druhan, B. (1989). The role of implicit and explicit processes in learning from examples: A synergistic effect. *Journal of Experimental Psychology: Learning, Memory, and Cognition*, *15*, 1083–1100.

Mathews, R. C., Druhan, B., & Roussel, L. (1989). *Forgetting is learning: Evaluation of three induction algorithms for learning artificial grammars.* Paper presented at the Annual Meeting of the Psychonomic Society, November 18, Atlanta.

McAndrews, M. P., & Moscovitch, M. (1985). Rule-based and exemplar-based classification in artificial grammar learning. *Memory and Cognition*, *13*, 469–475.

McClelland, J. L. (1991). *Toward a theory of information processing in graded, random, interactive networks* (Tech. Rep. No. PDP.CNS.91.1). Pittsburgh, PA: Carnegie Mellon University, Department of Psychology.

McClelland, J. L., Cleeremans, A., & Servan-Schreiber, D. (1990). Parallel distributed processing: Bridging the gap between human and machine intelligence. *Journal of the Japanese Society for Artificial Intelligence*, *5*, 2–14.

McClelland, J. L., & Rumelhart, D. E. (1981). An interactive activation model of context effects in letter perception: Part 1. An account of basic findings. *Psychological Review*, *88*, 375–407.

McClelland, J. L., & Rumelhart, D. E. (1985). Distributed memory and the representation of general and specific information. *Journal of Experimental Psychology: General*, *114*, 159–188.

McClelland, J. L., & Rumelhart, D. E. (1988). *Explorations in parallel distributed processing: A handbook of models, programs, and exercises.* Cambridge, MA: MIT Press.

McCloskey, M. (1991). Networks and theories: The place of connectionism in cognitive science. *Psychological Science*, *2*, 387–395.

Medin, D. L., & Schaffer, M. M. (1978). Context theory of classification learning. *Psychological Review*, *85*, 207–238.

Miller, G. A. (1956). The magical number seven, plus or minus two: Some limits on our capacity to process information. *Psychological Review*, *63*, 81–97.

Miller, G. A. (1958). Free recall of redundant strings of letters. *Journal of Experimental Psychology, 56,* 485–491.

Millward, R. B., & Reber, A. S. (1968). Event-recall in probability learning. *Journal of Verbal Learning and Verbal Behavior, 7,* 980–989.

Millward, R. B., & Reber, A. S. (1972). Probability learning: Contingent-event sequences with lags. *American Journal of Psychology, 85,* 81–98.

Minsky, M. (1967). *Computation: Finite and infinite machines.* Englewood Cliffs, NJ: Prentice-Hall.

Morgan, J. L., & Newport, E. L. (1981). The role of constituent structure in the induction of an artificial language. *Journal of Verbal Learning and Verbal Behavior, 11,* 759–769.

Movellan, J. R., & McClelland, J. L. (1991). *Learning continuous probability distributions with the contrastive Hebbian learning algorithm* (Tech. Rep. No. PDP.CNS.91.2). Pittsburgh, PA: Carnegie Mellon University, Department of Psychology.

Mozer, M. C., & Bachrach, J. (in press). SLUG: A connectionist architecture for inferring the structure of finite-state environments. In Y. Chauvin & D. E. Rumelhart (Eds.), *Backpropagation: Theory, architectures, and applications.* Hillsdale, NJ: Lawrence Erlbaum Associates.

Neisser, U. (1967). *Cognitive psychology.* Englewood Cliffs, NJ: Prentice-Hall.

Newell, A. (1990). *Unified theories of cognition.* Cambridge, MA: Harvard University Press.

Newell, A., & Simon, H. A. (1972). *Human problem solving.* Englewood Cliffs, NJ: Prentice-Hall.

Nisbett, R. E., & Wilson, T. D. (1977). Telling more than we can know: Verbal reports on mental processes. *Psychological Review, 84,* 231–259.

Nissen, M. J., & Bullemer, P. (1987). Attentional requirements of learning: Evidence from performance measures. *Cognitive Psychology, 19,* 1–32.

Perruchet, P. (in press). Learning from complex rule-governed environments: On the proper functions of conscious and nonconscious processes. In C. Umiltà & M. Moscovitch (Eds.), *Attention and performance XV: Conscious and nonconscious information processing.* Cambridge, MA: MIT Press.

Perruchet, P., & Amorim, M.-A. (1992). Conscious knowledge and changes in performance in sequence learning: Evidence against dissociation. *Journal of Experimental Psychology: Learning, Memory, and Cognition, 18,* 785–800.

Perruchet, P., Gallego, J., & Savy, I. (1990). A critical reappraisal of the evidence for unconscious abstraction of deterministic rules in complex experimental situations. *Cognitive Psychology, 22,* 493–516.

Perruchet, P., & Pacteau, C. (1990). Synthetic grammar learning: Implicit rule abstraction or explicit fragmentary knowledge? *Journal of Experimental Psychology: General, 119,* 264–275.

Perruchet, P., & Pacteau, C. (1991). Implicit acquisition of abstract knowledge about artificial grammars: Some methodological and conceptual issues. *Journal of Experimental Psychology: General, 120,* 264–275.

Pew, R. W. (1974). Levels of analysis in motor control. *Brain Research, 71,* 393–400.

Pollack, J. (1989). Implication of recursive distributed representations. (1989) In D. S. Touretzky (Ed.), *Advances in neural information processing systems 1.* San Mateo, CA: Morgan Kaufmann.

Pollack, J. (in press). Recursive distributed representations. *Artificial Intelligence.*

Reber, A. S. (1965). *Implicit learning of artificial grammars.* Unpublished master's thesis, Brown University, Providence, RI.

Reber, A. S. (1967). Implicit learning of artificial grammars. *Journal of Verbal Learning and Verbal Behavior, 6,* 855–863.

Reber, A. S. (1969). Transfer of syntactic structure in synthetic languages. *Journal of Experimental Psychology, 81,* 115–119.

Reber, A. S. (1976). Implicit learning of synthetic languages: The role of the instructional set. *Journal of Experimental Psychology: Human Learning and Memory, 2*, 88–94.

Reber, A. S. (1985). *The Penguin dictionary of psychology*. New York: Viking Penguin.

Reber, A. S. (1989). Implicit learning and tacit knowledge. *Journal of Experimental Psychology: General, 118*, 219–235.

Reber, A. S. (1990). On the primacy of the implicit: A comment on Perruchet and Pacteau. *Journal of Experimental Psychology: General, 119*, 340-342.

Reber, A. S. (in press). An evolutionary context for the cognitive unconscious. *Philosophical Psychology*.

Reber, A. S., & Allen, R. (1978). Analogy and abstraction strategies in synthetic grammar learning: A functionalist interpretation. *Cognition, 6*, 189–221.

Reber, A. S., Allen, R., & Regan, S. (1985). Syntactic learning and judgment: Still unconscious and still abstract. *Journal of Experimental Psychology: General, 114*, 17–24.

Reber, A. S., Kassin, S. M., Lewis, S., & Cantor, G. (1980). On the relationship between implicit and explicit modes in the learning of a complex rule structure. *Journal of Experimental Psychology: Human Learning and Memory, 6*, 492–502.

Reber, A. S., & Lewis, S. (1977). Implicit learning: An analysis of the form and structure of a body of tacit knowledge. *Cognition, 5*, 333–361.

Reber, A. S., Walkenfeld, F. F., & Hernstadt, R. (1991). Implicit and explicit learning: Individual differences and IQ. *Journal of Experimental Psychology: Learning, Memory, and Cognition, 17*, 888–896.

Remington, R. J. (1969). Analysis of sequential effects in choice reaction times. *Journal of Experimental Psychology, 82*, 250–257.

Restle, F. (1970). Theory of serial pattern learning: Structural trees. *Psychological Review, 77*, 481–495.

Richard, M. D., & Lippman, R. P. (1991). Neural network classifiers estimate Bayesian a posteriori probabilities. *Neural Computation, 3*, 461–483.

Richman, H. B., & Simon, H. A. (1989). Context effects in letter perception: Comparison of two theories. *Psychological Review, 96*, 417–432.

Roter, A. (1985). *Implicit processing: A developmental study*. Unpublished doctoral dissertation, City University of New York.

Rouanet, H. (1967). *Les modèles stochastiques d'apprentissage*. Paris: Gauthier-Villars.

Rumelhart, D. E., Hinton, G., & Williams, R. J. (1986). Learning internal representations by error propagation. In D.E. Rumelhart &J.L. McClelland (Eds.), *Parallel Distributed Processing, Explorations in the microstructure of cognition. Volume 1: Foundations*. Cambridge, MA: MIT Press.

Rumelhart, D. E., & McClelland, J. L. (1982). An interactive activation model of context effects in letter perception: Part 2. The contextual enhancement effect and some tests and extensions of the model. *Psychological Review, 89*, 60–94.

Rumelhart, D. E., McClelland, J. L., & the PDP Research Group. (1986). *Parallel Distributed Processing: Explorations in the microstructure of cognition. Vol. 1: Foundations*. Cambridge, MA: MIT Press.

Rumelhart, D. E., & Zipser, D. (1986). Feature discovery by competitive learning. In D. E. Rumelhart & J. L. McClelland (Eds.), *Parallel Distributed Processing: Explorations in the microstructure of cognition. Vol. 1: Foundations*. Cambridge, MA: MIT Press.

Schacter, D. L. (1987). Implicit memory: History and current status. *Journal of Experimental Psychology: Learning, Memory, and Cognition, 13*, 501–518.

Schacter, D. L., & Graf, P. (1986). Effects of elaborative processing on implicit and explicit memory for new associations. *Journal of Experimental Psychology: Learning, Memory, and Cognition, 9*, 544–555.

Seibel, R. (1963). Discrimination reaction time for a 1,023 alternative task. *Journal of Experimental Psychology, 66*, 215–226.

Sejnowski, T. J., & Rosenberg, C. (1987). Parallel networks that learn to pronounce English text. *Complex Systems, 1,* 145–168.

Servan-Schreiber, D., Cleeremans, A., & McClelland, J. L. (1988). *Encoding sequential structure in simple recurrent networks* (Tech. Rep. No. CMU-CS-88-183). Pittsburgh, PA: Carnegie Mellon University, School of Computer Science.

Servan-Schreiber, D., Cleeremans, A., & McClelland, J. L. (1989). Learning sequential structure in simple recurrent networks. In D. S. Touretzky (Ed.), *Advances in neural information processing systems 1.* San Mateo, CA: Morgan Kaufmann.

Servan-Schreiber, D., Cleeremans, A., & McClelland, J. L. (1991). Graded state machines: The representation of temporal contingencies in simple recurrent networks. *Machine Learning, 7,* 161–193.

Servan-Schreiber, E., & Anderson, J. R. (1990). Learning artificial grammars with competitive chunking. *Journal of Experimental Psychology: Learning, Memory, and Cognition, 16,* 592–608.

Sherry, D. F., & Schacter, D. L. (1987). The evolution of multiple memory systems. *Psychological Review, 94,* 439–454.

Soetens, E., Boer, L. C., & Hueting, J. E. (1985). Expectancy or automatic facilitation? Separating sequential effects in two-choice reaction time. *Journal of Experimental Psychology: Human Perception and Performance, 11,* 598–616.

Stadler, M. A. (1989). On learning complex procedural knowledge. *Journal of Experimental Psychology: Learning, Memory, and Cognition, 15,* 1061–1069.

Stanley, W. B., Mathews, R., Buss, R., & Kotler-Cope, S. (1989). Insight without awareness: On the interaction of verbalization, instruction and practice on a simulated process control task. *Quarterly Journal of Experimental Psychology, 41,* 553–577.

Vokey, J. R. (1983). *The implicit learning of structure: Analogic and abstractive strategies in artificial grammar learning.* Unpublished doctoral dissertation, McMasters University, Hamilton, Ontario, Canada.

Vokey, J. R., & Brooks, L. R. (1992). Salience of item knowledge in learning artificial grammars. *Journal of Experimental Psychology: Learning, Memory, and Cognition, 18,* 328–344.

Williams, R. J., & Zipser, D. (in press). Gradient-based learning algorithms for recurrent connectionist networks. In Y. Chauvin & D. E. Rumelhart (Eds.), *Backpropagation: Theory, architectures, and applications.* Hillsdale, NJ: Lawrence Erlbaum Associates.

Willingham, D. B., Nissen, M. J., & Bullemer, P. (1989). On the development of procedural knowledge. *Journal of Experimental Psychology: Learning, Memory, and Cognition, 15,* 1047–1060.

Zhu, X., & Simon, H. A. (1987). Learning mathematics by examples and by doing. *Cognition and Instruction, 4,* 137–166.

Index